W9-ATR-197

MYSTERION

an approach to mystical spirituality

MYSTERION

an approach to mystical spirituality

by
Richard Woods

THE THOMAS MORE PRESS
Chicago, Illinois

 The Thomas More Association, 225 W. Huron St., Chicago, Illinois 60610.

ISBN 0-88347-127-2

Contents

I wish to dedicate this volume to two persons whose lives have so long reflected the presence of God in facets of love, laughter and support: James Everett Woods and Margaret Corcoran Woods, my parents.

PREFACE

THESE essays in mystical spirituality represent a revised and slightly expanded version of a study program published by the Thomas More Association in 1979-80. They are intended to serve as an aid to involvement, not as a substitute for it—something of a map rather than a travelogue. There are no real guide books to spirituality; it is something to be done and undergone, not something merely to read about.

Further, as an invitation to cultivate a contemporary spiritual lifestyle, these essays are introductory rather than comprehensive, and certainly not definitive. The topics considered fall fairly naturally into two categories. The first section considers the foundation and scope of mysticism from a contemporary perspective. The second explores the concrete manifestations of mysticism in the world's major religions. The concluding three chapters constitute a provisional attempt to integrate the historical background with the current situation, while casting an eye toward future developments.

As explained later on (see Chapter 1), the title refers to a central tenet of the Jewish and Christian faith, in fact of all religious mysticism, that Ultimate Meaning and Love can be found within human experience under the symbolic guises of nature, word and work. And the proper name for God's self-disclosure is *mystery*. The first Christian writer to employ the word systematically was the great third century Greek theologian and scripture scholar of Alexandria, Origen. My usurpation of the title of his book is a tribute of homage, not a theft of glory.

I wish to express my gratitude to Michael McCauley, my tireless and patient editor, and particularly to Dr. Joseph Roccasalvo, S.J., for his corrections of chapters thirteen and fourteen. His assistance was invaluable in realms where I am considerably less at home. Any errors of fact or interpretation remain egregiously my own, however.

Richard Woods, O.P.

Chapter 1

MYSTICISM IN EVOLUTION

The mystic who knows himself is a mystic, not because he finds his world so bad that he must effect a spiritual retreat from it; but because he finds his world so good that he must perform a spiritual journey to the heart of it.

William Ernest Hocking

Mysticism is as ancient as humanity's quest for immediate and personal contact with an ultimate source of meaning and value in the universe. It is as fresh and contemporary as our faint tingle of recognition as Obi Wan Kenobe explained The Force to Luke Skywalker in *Star Wars*. But it is as real as the concrete love-in-action of Gandhi, Dorothy Day, Dag Hammarskjöld and Mother Teresa of Calcutta.

As in the turbulent 14th century, when Europe was racked by apocalyptic waves of war, famine, plague and strife, there seems to be a simultaneous flowering of concern today in a more direct experience of God than that promised through established institutional channels. Our own century presents a striking parallel to the "calamitous fourteenth," as Barbara Tuchman calls it in her book, *A Distant Mirror*. Then, giants arose to forge a new consciousness among the frightened, restless and suffering people of Europe. Never has such an eruption of the mystical spirit so galvanized a civilization. Until perhaps our own times. The coming century, the "Age of Aquarius," may well be the most spiritually exciting and vital period in the history of the human race. Or it may be the worst and the last, as people feared in the 14th century.

Much of the modern interest in mysticism can be traced back to William James' immortal *Varieties of Religious Experience*, published first in 1902 and never allowed to go out of print.

James realized then, as few psychologists did, that mysticism was not a form of mental aberration, but had an important contribution to make to human health and welfare. The writings of Evelyn Underhill, especially her monumental *Mysticism*, confirmed James' scientific approach from the religious and personal side. Besides being a mystic, Underhill was also a scholar. So great did her authority eventually become, that like James' work, hers has never gone out of print.

Rufus Jones and William Ernest Hocking were other leaders of the mystical "revolution" in the early 20th century. Both were theologically trained philosophers and both were mystics. Hocking's great work, *The Meaning of God in Human Experience*, is also still in print. It may be the most profound as well as beautiful study of mysticism and social action ever composed.

MYSTICISM AND SCIENCE

Parapsychology and psychical research, as well as psychology, physiology and sociology, have added greatly to our understanding of mysticism and mystical experience, contributing as well to its acceptability. Initially, psychology and psychiatry addressed themselves to the study of mysticism as a pathological mania caused by religious illusion and thwarted sexuality. Thanks to the pioneering work of Edwin Starbuck, R. M. Bucke and especially James, scientific opinion began slowly to change.

Today, psychologists and psychiatrists are turning to the great mystics not as specimens of disease, but as teachers, hoping to learn something about dimensions of the human psyche which can benefit those in real need of therapy. Here, the *healing*, integrative aspect of mysticism has come dramatically forward in our own time. These studies have, in turn, added greatly to our understanding of the physical and neurological correlates of mystical experiences, the psychological "mechanisms" of mystical states, and the mental and emotional aspects of mystical development. Studies of meditation have especially enriched the practice and theory of mysticism as well as that of psychotherapy.

Parapsychology and the wider field of psychical research have similarly broadened our understanding of the further reaches of human nature. In particular, these fields of study have explored the incidence and frequency of psychical experiences, enabling us not only to grasp something of the *normalcy* of these extraordinary states and events, but to distinguish them from the more characteristic elements of mystical experience which they sometimes accompany.

Students and practitioners of mysticism must thus be prepared to try on various hats as they explore this interesting and fascinating field. But the chief exponent, teacher and student of mysticism remains the mystic. Experience itself remains the ultimate source of authority in the exploration of mysticism, but experience that is tested by the ordinary canons of reason and responsibility in theology, philosophy and the scientific disciplines. The tests have in many cases been severe; so far, the mystics have withstood them all.

Today's concern with the mystical does not turn only on psychological, philosophical or theological investigations or their findings. It seems, rather, that millions of people have begun to recognize the mystical dimension in their own experience, apart from all the books and studies. Their involvement with the mystical element of religion may well have much to do with disenchantment over the unfulfilled expectations of the 60s and 70s, sometimes with results like those of Jonestown—a phenomenon mirroring suicidal tragedies in the 14th and other centuries. Mystical enthusiasm does arise in the wake of social and natural tribulation. But today, thousands of persons have begun to take up the mystical way not because of reaction or dissatisfaction at society's ills and disasters, but in the hopes of finding greater depth and meaning in their experience. In short, we are more aware today of the human potential released and developed by mysticism, a power which may stem the tide of disaster in the coming generations. The goal is not escape, but development.

WHAT IS MYSTICISM?

The term "mysticism" is not old. It first appeared in English only in the 18th century. During the Enlightenment, it became a byword for fuzzy thinking, dreamy states of idle and not quite balanced minds, occult practices and beliefs, irrationalism, the pursuit of sensationalism, extraordinary phenomena, effete and withdrawn social introversion, mad political schemes, religious mania and about anything else opposed to common sense and practical action. Unfortunately, it still conveys many of these connotations. Nothing could be less true, however, despite the fact that all these odd and even dangerous counterfeits existed and still exist today.

By contrast, the term "mystical" is very old. It appears, of course, in the religious writings of the ancient Greeks in connection with the secret rituals of the various Mystery Religions, that is, the unofficial cults. It was later used by the Jewish philosopher and scriptural scholar, Philo, who lived in Alexandria at the time of Christ. Philo, however, used the term differently from the Greeks, as we shall have occasion to recall. "Mystical" does not appear in the New Testament, but it was used by the Jewish Christians of Alexandria by the 2nd century and has been part of the Christian vocabulary ever since. But these early Christian writers changed the meaning of the word even further.

The absence of the word "mystical" does not mean that the Bible is either opposed to mysticism or in fact unmystical. Rather, it is mystical from cover to cover, as Philo and the early Christian writers realized.

The New Testament writers, and apparently Jesus himself, used the word "mystery" (*mysterion,* in Greek) to signify what later generations recognized as "mystical." As we shall see later on, the two words stem from the same root. *Mysterion* is the earliest Christian term for the hidden presence of God—in Christ, in the sacraments (which were originally called *mysteria*—"the mysteries"), in Scripture, and in the events of everyday life—prayer, the supreme witness of martyrdom, and especially the call for help of the poor and the oppressed, as Jesus taught clearly in the parable of the sheep and the goats (Mt. 25:31–46).

Mysticism is not unique to Judaism or Christianity, of course. It exists in some form in every religion in the world and always has, with the possible exception of Zoroastrianism, according to the English Catholic scholar, R. C. Zaehner.

Even within Christianity, there are Catholic, Orthodox and Protestant mystics. There are good mystics and bad ones, crazy mystics and sane ones, mystics of all ages, sexes, temperaments and conditions in life. There are even agnostic and atheistic mystics. Mysticism is no less a religious phenomenon for that, and Christian mystics are no less Christian because they are mystics, nor less mystics because they are Christian.

Each religious tradition modifies the expression of its mystical dimension according to its own beliefs and practices, and the differences among them are as important as their similarities. Beneath all the differences and similarities, however, there seems to be something not only common to all the mystical traditions and even mystical experiences, but in fact the same. Nevertheless, it is probably more accurate to refer to mysticisms and mystics rather than mysticism and "the" mystic, except in the instance of a particular type or person.

The terms "mystic" and "mystical" no less than "mysticism" refer then to three basic areas:

First, a certain capacity of the human person to be open to an immediate and direct experience of the Absolute, however It (He, She or They) may be interpreted. Such an experience is usually and properly called "a" mystical experience.

Second, they refer to the teachings and systems of behavior

developed by particular mystics and passed on to their followers as a recognizable tradition, distinct from other traditions.

Third, they refer in general, and most loosely, to the whole range of persons, experiences, teachings, ways of life, and traditions included in the first and second areas.

For most of us, I suppose, the word "mysticism" is a bit worn out, all things considered. In most instances, I shall use the term to refer to the field of study, and use "mystical" in its ancient, Christian sense to indicate the transcendent character of experience, a lifestyle, teachings and specific traditions.

NARROWING THE FIELD: SOME DESCRIPTIVE PARAMETERS

The mystical dimension of religion, then, is our primary concern—taking religion here as both the particular beliefs, practices and experiences of individual persons and also a collective phenomenon, that is, religion in the sense of religions, Christian, Buddhist, Hindu, etc.

Religion, literally and simply speaking, is the "bond" between human beings and God, or, as Paul Ricoeur has suggested, between persons and whatever they consider to be sacred. Mysticism may still be religious in that sense without reference to a definite or, for that matter, *any* concept of God. It is almost a commonplace among mystics of all faiths that there can be *no* adequate concept of God in the first place. For the mystic, to limit God by attempting to express the reality of his presence conceptually is not only equivalent to idolatry, it is impossible.

But is a mystical experience possible which is not simultaneously an experience of God, that is, a religious experience? Many people have reported having had transcendent experiences, but do not claim to have encountered God, and may deny it explicitly. In Zen Buddhism, for instance, and for Buddhism in general, enlightenment is claimed to be a total integration of the "self" *without* reliance on God. Nirvana is not the same as the Beatific Vision.

Nevertheless, most students of mysticism not only include Buddhism as a religion, but consider enlightenment experiences such as Satori to be truly mystical. Jacques Maritain, who initially denied the possibility of a "natural" mystical experience, eventually came to admit that these and similar experiences were factual, not only in Buddhism but in other traditions as well.

Whether someone *interprets* an experience as an encounter with God depends in large measure on whether one *believes* in God. But is it also possible for a non-believer to have an experience of God *without recognizing it as such*? The eminent American philosopher, William Ernest Hocking, argued that *all* experience is, in fact, an encounter with God. For him, mystical experience, as a development of ordinary religious experience, only raises to fuller awareness what all persons are dimly aware of in the depths of consciousness. Thus, it is just as likely that a professed atheist could have an experience of God which is not recognized as such, as it is that a religious enthusiast might claim as an experience of God what was, in fact, only the projection of a fantasy.

The great mystics have not been blind to the possibility of illusion and have supplied many criteria for discerning the authenticity of mystical experiences. Likewise, the great religions have their measures of genuineness regarding alleged experiences of God, generally based not only on past experiences proved to be authentic, but also on a normative theology itself founded upon a direct revelation from God. So it is worth noting that Hocking's thesis is just as likely as is the proposal that there can be a mystical experience completely devoid of God's presence. Atheists are no more immune from misinterpretations than are believers.

Thus, some transcendent experiences may well be unmystical, but the natural mystical experience remains a real possibility. However, the "atheistic" aspect may represent a difference of interpretation rather than a different *kind* of experience altogether. Hocking, who was something of a mystic himself, therefore described the work of religion as that of showing us how to recognize the divine presence in all experience worthy of the name human.

And thus many persons may have authentic mystical experiences, such as that of the "oneness of everything" which may well be a hidden encounter with God, unrecognized as such. This could be the case among people who have never seriously entertained the idea that God exists or who have rejected the idea for any number of reasons—including the failure of "God-fearing" believers to live up to the requirements of their faith.

From this perspective, then, it is perhaps wiser not to consider varieties of mystical experiences as different *kinds* of experience, but rather as manifesting different *degrees* of God-consciousness, from a vague sense of unity in nature, beauty, meaning, etc., to the ultimate awareness of union with God himself. Mystical *development* will therefore involve stages of personal integration in which our recognition of God is progressively purified and expanded, as was taught by St. John of the Cross and the whole Christian tradition.

Discovering the natural pattern of this process does not involve denying that the final, unitive stages of mystical development can be achieved only by the help of God's grace. It means, rather, that in Christian terms, the life of grace is naturally mystical, and that the ordinary course of mystical development tends toward union with God, the flowering of all grace. In the words of Georges Bernanos' country priest, "All is grace."

It should also be recalled that many orthodox Christian mystics, including saints such as Francis of Assisi and John of the Cross, have experienced God as a dark abyss, a void, emptiness and vast nothingness. Their quest for loving union with God has taken them into torturous "nights of the soul" in which all feeling of the Divine Presence has vanished. One of the lessons to be learned on the mystical journey is the insufficiency of all our concepts of God and the foolishness of relying on conceptual knowledge to draw near to him. Practically, this involves the discipline of stilling the conceptual mind in order to become more open to dimensions of experience closed off by reliance on conceptual representation and analytic reasoning ("left-brain" functions).

MISCONCEPTIONS OF MYSTICISM

The mystical way itself has been confused with all sorts of bizarre pursuits, as noted before. Eliminating some of the misconceptions of mysticism may help illuminate the simpler thing it is.

First of all, mysticism has little if anything to do with the occult—there are no secret doctrines and never were. The "secret" of mysticism is its simplicity. It can be practiced by anyone at any time with a minimum of training. Secondly, then, the mystical way is not *unusual* or *extraordinary* in the sense of "strange and mysterious"—full of weird and paranormal phenomena ("miracles") such as levitation, telepathy, stigmata, visions, or even raptures and trances. All these things exist, and some are more common than we think. Sometimes they appear in the lives of the mystics. But they are more usually resisted and avoided, and the wiser teachers caution their disciples against any interest in them at all.

Third, mystical states are not psychologically *abnormal.* Doctors and researchers such as William James, Abraham Maslow, Robert Ornstein, Walter H. Clark, R. D. Laing, Arthur Deikman and others insist that experiences which may seem unusual to us or to the mystics themselves in comparison to our ordinary waking consciousness are in fact not only fairly common but are healthy and health producing. Such "peak experiences" can enhance our lives. A life organized so as to utilize and enjoy the full range of human experience is a happier, fuller and holier one than that confined to the monotonous, greyed-over, nine-to-five daily grind.

But there is a vast difference between the mere pursuit of mind-expanding experiences and expanding the range of one's mind. Drugs may well explode the boundaries of ordinary consciousness, but without any beneficial results and probably with some rather harmful ones. On the other hand, it would be rash to deny that mind-altering drugs have in fact enriched our understanding of mystical states and may well have their place in the scheme of things.

Fourth, mysticism is not restricted to an "elite corps," some select body of spiritual Olympians who retire to remote cloisters or desert caves, disdaining the companionship of the dull lot of humankind not so extraordinarily graced. The mystical path has its solitary stretches, and necessarily so. Again, not everyone fully realizes their mystical capabilities and only a few do so to an extraordinary degree. There are, as well, extraordinary graces involved in the higher stages of mystical prayer. But anyone is capable of reaching these heights; we all start at the base of the mountain.

All human beings are, at bottom, mystics—whether they realize it or not, as Hocking would say. Mysticism is essentially a democratic phenomenon. It is found in the least likely as well as the most likely places, at all times, and among people of every race, creed, color, temperament, sexuality, age, constitution and state in life. The only qualification needed to excel is the will to do so, to become in fact what we are in principle. There are, of course, creative geniuses among the mystics as everywhere else—the Eckharts and the Teresas. But as with art and music, mathematics and literature, genius only sets the upper norms of the range of human possibility, limits that are as flexible as they are varied.

Fifth, mysticism is not passive—a withdrawn, introverted, ego-centric preoccupation of anti-social misfits. On the contrary, the greater mystics, including the creative geniuses, are, *as a result of their mystical development,* extraordinarily active and effective agents of social change, e.g., Francis of Assisi, Meister Eckhart, Joan of Arc, Ignatius of Loyola, Catherine of Siena, Teresa of Avila and, in our own time, Tom Dooley, Dag Hammarskjöld, Charles de Foucauld, Martin Luther King and Mohandas Gandhi. As Hocking insisted, mystical experience provides the foundation for prophetic action.

But mysticism is not a form of reliance on works as opposed to grace. If anything, mystical activity represents the epitome of the Christian ideal of grace-in-action, of works proceeding from an abundance of love and compassion.

In sum, authentic mysticism is available to all. Christian mysticism is founded upon a firm grasp of the common possession of God's presence, the Indwelling of the Trinity. It is based solidly on scripture and Christian tradition. It is a supernormal style of life in which the further reaches of human nature are approached and even surpassed. It is nonetheless a development of ordinary religious experience, a "raising to consciousness" of the fundamental relationship of the human spirit and God. It is socially active and productive. Furthermore, the mystical life is not obtrusive—it can flourish without attracting undue notice to itself, as in the case of Tom Dooley and Dag Hammarskjöld.

THE ESSENTIALS OF CHRISTIAN MYSTICISM

If it is possible to summarize the elements of Christian mysticism, I would include the following:

I. The "clear conviction of a living God as the primary interest of consciousness, and of a personal self capable of communion with Him." (Underhill, 1960, p. 3)

II. The Mystic Way: the "necessary acts and dispositions of the mystic himself, the development which takes place in him" (Underhill, 1960, p. 6). These include a developmental sequence of stages and a characteristic pattern of life:

1. The "Three Ages of the Interior Life." These phases of growth have been given two sets of titles in Christian tradition—the ways of Beginners, the Proficient and the Perfect, and the Purgative, Illuminative and Unitive ways. They are not the same, and both have their own validity.
2. The dialectic of contemplation and action, a pattern of withdrawal from and return to the social world.

III. Certain minimal but essential beliefs about human nature and its relationship to God:

1. The Ground: Every human person has the capacity to share consciously in the Divine Nature of God itself—an actualization of what medieval theologians called the "apex" or "scintilla animae"—the "point" or divine "spark" of the soul, what Eckhart and his followers called the Ground of the Soul.
2. The Way of "Unknowing": God cannot be comprehended by any form of conceptual knowledge, but apprehended only by "unknowing,"—*agnosia*—an inner sense of God's presence mediated by love.
3. Grace: Union with God cannot be achieved by any human effort but must be received as a pure gift of God's self-communication.
4. Mission: Authentic union with God always manifests itself in loving service, especially to the poor and oppressed.

PRACTICAL MYSTICISM

In terms of its fundamental practical element, Christian mysticism—perhaps all mysticism—amounts to what has traditionally been called "the practice of the presence of God," together, as Hocking would say, "with the theory of that practice." Psychologically it involves a shift of attention from the objects of daily preoccupation to the divine Field or Ground sustaining all things in creative existence. But it is a shift of attention accompanied by *love*, for the Field of Experience thus brought to awareness is perceived as somehow a living, personal agency of supreme beauty, goodness and especially *care*, as well as power.

Love alone is capable of relating us more closely to the Ground of our being than could the awareness of sheer dependence or even craven fear. Love is the ultimate "secret" of mysticism, the "blind, naked intent" of will described by the 14th century author of *The Cloud of Unknowing*. It was love that Christ ultimately revealed as the motive, end and means for his "bloody work" of redemption and so poignantly eulogized by the anonymous grand lady of English mysticism called "Julian of Norwich" for the church where she was immured:

> And I saw full surely that ere God made us He loved us; which love was never slacked, nor ever shall be. And in this love He hath done all his works; and in this love He hath made all things profitable to us; and in this love our life is everlasting. In our making we had beginning; but the love wherein He made us was in Him from without beginning: in which love we have our beginning. And all this we shall see in God, without end.

SUGGESTIONS FOR FURTHER READING:

The Cloud of Unknowing, tr. by Clifton Wolters, New York: Penguin, 1968 (paper).

Dag Hammarskjöld, *Markings*, New York: Alfred A. Knopf, 1964.

William Ernest Hocking, *The Meaning of God in Human Experience*, New Haven: Yale University Press, 1963.

Rufus Jones, *Studies in Mystical Religion*, New York: Russell and Russell (1909), 1970.

Julian of Norwich, *Shewings of God's Love*, Maryland: Christian Classics, 1974 (paper).

Jacques Maritain, *Redeeming the Time*, London: Geoffrey Bles, 1943.

Barbara Tuchman, *A Distant Mirror*, New York: Alfred A. Knopf, 1978.

Richard Woods

Evelyn Underhill, *The Essentials of Mysticism*, New York: E. P. Dutton, (1920) 1960.

Richard Woods, *Understanding Mysticism*, Garden City, N.Y. Doubleday Image Books, 1980.

Chapter 2

CHRISTIAN MYSTICISM AND BIBLICAL FAITH

Christian mysticism, with its long, rich and fascinating history, has been little understood outside the circle of mystics themselves. This may be because it differs in significant respects from that of the mystical dimension in other religious traditions. But even leading theologians such as Barth and Harnack considered mysticism to be an intrusion of Hellenistic philosophy into the original, simple faith of the early Church. A related belief, widely held in the 19th century, was that mysticism is an essentially otherworldly, withdrawn, passive absorption in which the individual is merged with the Absolute in timeless contemplation. Thus conceived (or misconceived), mysticism was pitted by many influential Protestant writers—Ritschl, Troeltsch, Heiler, Brunner, Nygren—against the prophetic Judeo-Christian ethic of this-worldly concern with social action. This view was embodied in early twentieth century America in the Social Gospel Movement of Walter Rauschenbusch.

This antagonism toward mysticism, while not universal among Protestants, and despite the existence of many Protestant mystics, is still widely held. It had its origins in the aftermath of the Reformation, especially at the hands of Calvinistic Reformers—later Lutherans and Methodists—eager to purify the Christian faith of all Roman and particularly "pagan" influences. Antagonism was no less engendered by the outbreak of self-proclaimed "mystical" movements which led to bizarre, bloody dictatorships and utopian nightmares in Geneva, Münster and elsewhere. By the end of the 17th century, the mystical spirit had been all but stifled in Protestant Germany, England and the Low Countries.

A similar Catholic bias against mysticism developed during the Counter-Reformation, despite the magnificent flowering of mystical spirituality in Spain and France among the Jesuits and Carmelites. Perhaps the principal factor was the emergence of an extreme form of mysticism later called "Quietism." Sprung from the teachings of a Spanish priest, Miguel de Molinos and a group of French aristocrats at Port Royale, a major center of Jansenism, Quietism held that since all human effort was futile in the quest for God, only complete and utter abandonment of all activity, all desire, even all moral effort, could be pleasing to God.

While it is bedrock Christian belief that salvation comes only through God's free and undeserved gift of grace, all "merit" being won once for all by Jesus, Quietism was overlaid with serious mistakes. Many of them reflected Jansenistic pessimism concerning the world of nature and human society. The most notable error was the belief that having abandoned themselves totally to God in pure faith, not only were the "mystics" free from the need for sacramental grace, but that they had become incapable of sin—even though they might behave in ways sinful for ordinary Christians.

Both Catholic and Protestant mystical extremists evolved this type of belief in personal impeccability. Eventually, along with other unacceptable teachings, it led to several condemnations of Quietism, even though individual Quietists, such as Madame Guyon and her able defender, Archbishop Fénelon, were good, even saintly persons.

The resulting wariness of Catholic theologians, first among them the Jesuit Giovanni Scaramelli, began to drive a wedge of dualism between the ordinary, "ascetical" and the mystical or "extraordinary" elements of the spiritual life. In the next two hundred years, especially among French, Italian and Spanish spiritual writers, the ordinary, normal Christian life was ever more sharply divided from the mystical life supposedly reserved to a few elite souls. Mysticism became almost synonymous with extraordinary phenomena—visions, raptures, levitation, the stigmata, ESP, etc.—a misconception still widely prevalent. Mystical Christianity was thus further and further removed from everyday concerns, while the unity of the spiritual life was fragmented.

A MYSTICAL REVOLUTION

Much of the Protestant and Catholic hostility toward mysticism had been rooted not only in opposition to exaggerated claims and even heretical counterfeits, but also in serious misconceptions about the nature of mystical experience and development as well as the character of the relationship between Christian and "Greek" influences in the 3rd and 4th centuries. But toward the end of the 19th century, just as theological anti-mystical feeling reached a climax, historical research began to clarify early Christian-pagan interaction, while psychologists and philosophers such as William James and William Ernest Hocking began to articulate the dynamic structure of mystical experience and development. Simultaneously, theologians and literary researchers—Denifle, Inge, Von Hügel, Underhill and others began to revive interest in long-forgotten mystical writings. A mystical revolution was underway.

The resulting antagonism between proponents and opponents of Christian mysticism led to a flurry of exchanges in theological journals and books. Rudolf Otto's pioneering work in Germany and that of Hocking and Rufus Jones in America began undercutting the Protestant bias. Similar research by the Dominicans Garrigou-Lagrange and Arintero and the Jesuits de Guibert and Maréchal succeeded in reversing the theological division of the spiritual life. The sympathetic attention given mysticism by the great Carl Jung added support directly as well as indirectly by challenging the psychoanalytic bias introduced by Freud.

The conclusions of these researchers and theologians—some of them mystics themselves—can be briefly summarized:

1) Mysticism was not a Greek intrusion into primitive Christian faith, but an integral part of the biblical tradition, arising out of the

encounter with Jesus and his Spirit.

2) Far from being a mere withdrawal into contemplative passivity, authentic mystical development results in a lifestyle of *increased* social activity, usually having long-lasting effects on both the Church and the civil order.

3) The mystical element in Christianity is not a different *kind* of religious experience, but the culmination of the Christian life itself. Christian spirituality is thus mystical *as a whole,* for its goal, ever-deepening union with God, determines its entire character.

4) The spiritual life is, therefore, a unified, integrating process to which all are called by their commitment to Christ. It is not reserved for an elite. Nor is it specially characterized by extraordinary phenomena. The elements of the mystical life, moreover, are those found in everyday concerns.

Full mystical development may be as rare as the appearance of genius and perfection in art, science or anything else. A Catherine of Siena does not appear in every generation any more than does a Michelangelo, a Marie Curie or an Elizabeth I. But everyman and everywoman possess the same, fundamental human characteristics that such giants had. It is of these that mystical development can forge a saint—that is, a fully human, *holistic* person.

THE ORIGINAL TRADITION OF CHRISTIAN MYSTICISM

Having glanced at the misconceptions of the Enlightenment view of mysticism and how they were attacked at the beginning of this century, perhaps the easiest way to grasp the essentials of Christian mysticism is to see how it developed from the beginning.

Far from being a pagan intrusion, Christian mysticism emerged out of *Jewish* mystical spirituality after centuries of Jewish resistance against Hellenistic influence culminating in the great Maccabean revolts from 175 to 135 B.C. That is to say, the origins of Christian mysticism are older and different from what the 19th century theologians supposed. Even the contacts in the 3rd and 4th centuries *after* Christ were different from the suppositions of 19th century scholarship regarding pagan-Christian interaction.

Furthermore, far from inducing passivity, the mystical element in Judaism and Christianity continued rather than interrupted the vital stream of prophetic activity intrinsic to biblical faith. Pagan mysticism may have practiced complete social withdrawal, but early Christian mysticism was not pagan.

EARLY DEVELOPMENT

We look first, then, to the Egyptian city of Alexandria as well as to Palestine for the birthplace of Christian mysticism. The development of Christian mysticism itself was not a sudden event, but a gradual elaboration of the mystical element of Judaism of the 1st century B.C., just as Christianity itself was only gradually disengaged from Judaism in terms of doctrine and practice. The central fact, of course, remains the mystery of Christ, the focus of all Christian spirituality. But it was the perception of Christ in terms of the *mystical* expectations of the Jews in the minds of the Evangelists and St. Paul that not only inaugurated the mystical tradition of Christian faith, but took one strand of Jewish mysticism into a new phase of evolution. (Other currents of Jewish mysticism continued their own development, as we shall see elsewhere.)

Alexandria at this time was the second city of the Roman Empire and its cultural capital, located on the Mediterranean coast some 350 miles west of Jerusalem and about 700 miles southeast of Athens across the sea. It was here that one great school of Jewish mysticism developed, and where, a century later, the first great mystical theologians of Christianity were to develop their teachings, modeled in part on the mysticism of the School of Wisdom.

In the first century B.C., there were over a million Jews living in Alexandria, according to the most influential Jewish writer of that time, Philo. Members of the Diaspora or "Dispersion," these Jews had lived for centuries outside of Palestine, although they kept close ties with the homeland, especially with regard to religion. It was for them that the Bible had been translated into Greek—the so-called Septuagint—which was the common Bible of the New Testament authors and early Christianity. The Wisdom literature of the Hebrew Bible, written in Greek, was composed mainly at Alexandria, and it is this tradition that gave rise to a distinctive mystical element in Judaism and eventually Christianity. St. Paul was especially influenced by the Wisdom tradition, with its emphasis on the vanity of conceptual knowledge and the priority of love and service. (Significantly, it is the Wisdom literature that was later excluded in large measure from the biblical canon by later Jewish and Protestant reformers.)

GREEK THOUGHT AND JEWISH BELIEF

Philo had closer connections with Palestine than did many of his fellow Jews in Alexandria. Yet it was Philo, a devout and orthodox Jew, probably a mystic himself, who is responsible for establishing definite connections between Greek *thought* (not religious practices) and Jewish belief, much as Clement of Alexandria would do as a Christian four generations later. Thus, Philo is far more worthy of attention as a "Father" of Christian mysticism than much later figures such as Plotinus, Porphyry and Proclus. It was Philo's thought, rather than that of the others, which so crucially influenced Clement, Origen, St. Gregory of Nyssa and even Ambrose.

Philo's lasting contribution to Jewish and Christian spirituality and biblical scholarship was his development of the allegorical or "mystical" interpretation of the Bible. That is, he (like St. Matthew and other Christian writers of this time) discerned a hidden or "secret" meaning in important, prophetic passages. He used the word "mystical" to refer to this deeper, spiritual significance, a practice taken over by the later Christian theologians of Alexandria.

Philo borrowed *mystikos* from the Greek mystery religions, but only in the superficial sense already noted. Based on the verb *muō,* which means to shut or close (i.e., one's mouth or eyes), *mystikos* referred only to the secret *rites* of the pagan cults, not to any secret doctrines. These rites were never to be revealed to outsiders, the "uninitiated." Those initiated into the rites were thus called *mystēs,* or "mystics," "those who keep 'mum'."

It was the notion of "hiddenness" that interested Philo, and he connected it with the Jewish concept of *mystery,* or in Hebrew, *mistar, sod* or *sether,* which refer to secret places, hidden counsels or plans—such as the "hidden things" of God. (Examples would be Gen. 49:6, Ps. 25:14, Prov. 3:32, Dan. 2:22.) Jesus and Paul used the Greek word *mysterion* in the same sense, as in Matt. 13:11, Mk. 4:11 and Lk. 8:10, as well as in Rom. 16:25, I Cor. 2:7 and over a dozen other places. *Mysterion* is not only derived from the same verb as *mystikos,* it is almost inevitably used in connection with *revelation,* that is, it refers to some kind of secret *now made known.*

THE MEANINGS OF "MYSTICAL"

It is important to see that not only Philo, but Jesus and Paul used *mysterion* or *mystikos* (which is not found in the Bible) to mean content, a fact or even a doctrine—thus departing completely from its ordinary usage in Greek religion and common talk. Philo used *mystikos* to refer to *meaning,* not ritual.

But later Christian writers went beyond Philo and St. Paul by including a ritual element in the meaning of *mysterion* and *mystikos.* For Clement, Origen and Gregory of Nyssa, as well as almost all the early Christian theologians, *mystikos* referred primarily to the "mysterious" meaning of scripture, the spiritual significance of certain passages, especially those which pointed to

Christ. But they also took over a practice that has an independent origin in Christianity—to refer to the Eucharist and Baptism as the Christian "mysteries." *Mysterion* was the first word to be used for what later, Latin writers would call *sacramentum,* "sacrament." A third use of *mystikos* in early Christian writings, the latest of the three, referred to the spiritual life itself, especially the prayer life of a Christian.

Importantly, each of the three major meanings of "mystical" in early Christianity referred to a hidden or "mysterious" presence of God in Christ—in Scripture, in the Sacraments and in the events of ordinary life, as in St. Martin of Tours' discovery that the beggar he had clothed was, in truth, Christ. "Mystical experience" would be, then, a "hidden" encounter with Christ and thus with God, one which only the eyes of faith could penetrate, but which was available to all who had been "initiated." For Christ was also present within each Christian by virtue of his Spirit, poured out in them by the effect of baptism and anointing with the laying on of hands. Further, because of persecution and the fear of profanation, the initiated were never to reveal to "outsiders" the practices of the rites, which were so easily misunderstood. (Many Christians were accused of cannibalism because they professed to eat the body of Christ and drink his blood!)

It is important to add here that none of the later Greek philosophers whose alleged influence on Christian mysticism was so detrimental used the word *mystikos* in this fashion. In fact, Plotinus never used it at all.

SOCIAL ACTION

The other serious misconception concerning Christian mysticism stems from the first meaning cited above. Insofar as it was considered to be a Hellenic intrusion into primitive Christianity, mysticism was assumed to be a kind of passive contemplation of eternal truths. In fact, the early Christian mystics were not only

Jewish by birth, or at least by religious affinity, they were very active prophetically. This is true not only of the Christians of the earliest generations, but of those who lived in the times of the great Cappadocian and Alexandrian Fathers. So characteristic is the active involvement of Christian mysticism, that any mystical tradition that divorces action from contemplation, such as in the Quietism of Madame Guyon, hardly deserves the name Christian.

Dag Hammarskjöld and Thomas Merton have insisted upon this point, as did Hocking, Underhill and even Henri Bergson early in this century. The social and political repercussions of an authentic experience of the presence of God are as unavoidable as they are usually difficult for the mystic. This has been the lot of the prophet since the beginning, and is no less true in our own day—as evident in the assassinations of Martin Luther King and Gandhi, and the great opposition Dag Hammarskjöld met as Secretary General of the United Nations.

Authentic Christian mysticism still bears the marks of its primitive heritage wherever it is found: it will be biblical, sacramental and rooted in the belief that in any event of daily life we can, in faith, encounter the living presence of God in Christ. It will be active and prophetically concerned with true liberation of the human person—spirit, mind and body—from all enslaving forces. Beyond that, it will be as varied and pluralistic as Christianity has been itself. It will be forever rooted, however, in the concrete particularities of past events as well as open to new possibilities, now and in the future. For Christian mysticism takes history seriously, but no less seriously than its mandate to shape history in the full freedom of God's friends.

MYSTICISM IN THE EARLY CHURCH

But what of Jesus and the early Christian community itself? Were they, in any sense in which we understand the term, "mystical"? Could not the Greek Christians of the 2nd and 3rd centuries have *interpreted* the Christian event and message in the light of their Alexandrian theology as being mystical when in fact they were not?

First of all, it is highly unlikely that the first Christian theologians could have so blatantly misinterpreted the life and teachings of Jesus without a severe struggle. But there is no testimony that such a struggle ever occurred, despite the evidence of plenty of conflict in the early Church. Secondly, pagan mystics, including Plotinus himself, were highly *critical* of Christian teachings and apparently even failed to recognize in them what they themselves considered mystical. Pagan mysticism was highly intellectualistic and tended away from a personal concept of God. The Christian "mysticism" of the early Church was, however, not only wary of "knowledge" (*gnosis*) which "puffeth up," preferring the path of love and service, but it was also vitally personalistic in respect to God and, of course, "Christic"—union with God *meant* union through Christ. Such union was not achieved by intellectual or corporal asceticism, but by faith alone, perfected by love. Authentic Christian mysticism at this state (and ever since) has been concrete and grace-oriented. That is, the encounter with God in Christ is made real in our experience by God's own self-communication, through the biblical Word, the sacramental symbol and the sense of Presence pervading the entire world. These were the Christian "mysteries" and still are—not abstract concepts, but real experiences, available to all, not just the wise and learned.

Thus the early mysticism of the Christian community centers about "mystery"—both in form and fact, the content and practice of God's presence.

GOSPEL MYSTICISM

Deciding whether the Christian "Way" was thus initially mystical in any radical respect or as a whole depends largely on what you mean by "mysticism" no less than what you mean by

Christianity. We have already noted the wide variety of concepts concerning "mysticism," and there are certainly no fewer ideas about what Christianity means. The gospels and other ancient Christian writings themselves testify to varied understandings of the meaning of Jesus' life and teachings. These emphases on the character of God and our relationship with God are also different. Matthew's and Mark's theologies, for instance, differ considerably from those of Luke, John and Paul.

However, if we narrow the inquiry, we might be able to fathom better the mystical aspect of early Christianity. For example, taking mysticism as the practice of the presence of God together with the theory of that practice (Hocking), we can find ample evidence for both in the New Testament. More exactly, both the message of Jesus and the teachings of the early Church clearly insist that it is possible to become more perfectly one with God by following the "right path," the Way of Christ. The Christian life-style is itself that path or "the Way." Jesus himself taught that he personally embodied that Way and that he was also the Gate, the Door, the Light and the Food which conveys Eternal Life, that is, participation in the life and nature of God.

In John's Gospel, Jesus is hyperbolically clear: "no one comes to the Father, but by me" (14:6). All, then, who come to the Father, come first to Christ, and those who come to Christ come to the Father. He is *the* mediator, the bridge between God and Humanity.

Christian mysticism is thus radically Christological. It is also holistic and ecclesial: the "mystical body of Christ" is more than the historical Church. It is the "whole gathering"—the *ekklesia "kata-holikos"*—of those who have found their way to God through Christ, wittingly or not. Or rather, of those God has directed to himself through Christ, known or unknown.

Other elements of mystical spirituality are clearly present in the New Testament. The term "mystical", as we have seen, does not appear in Scripture, perhaps because of the anti-Hellenic attitude of the early Christians. Paul uses a form of the verb *muō,* however, in the same commonplace sense found in Philo and in later writings: "I have learned the secret," he wrote—*memuēmai*—of being filled and going hungry" (Phil. 4:12). That is, he has been initiated into a kind of secret, in this case, simply how to be content with what he has been given.

Even if we take the characteristic elements of Christian mysticism as traditionally interpreted, they are evident throughout the New Testament, if they are not precisely identified with the terms later given them, much less systematically organized.

Union with God, especially through identification with Christ, runs like a great river through the intricate, thematic tributaries of John's theology, for instance. It is also present in the Synoptic Gospels and more evidently so in Paul's writings. (See John 6:56; Mt. 10:40, 25:40; Mark 9:37, 41; Lk. 10:16; Acts 17: 28, Rom. 11:36, Eph. 4:6, Gal. 2:20 etc.) The Ways of attaining to this union, classically known as "purgative" and "illuminative" find clear echoes in similar places. (See Mt. 10:39, 16:24; Mk. 8:34; Luke 14:26, Jn. 12:25, etc.) The necessity of action is manifest, especially in the Gospels (Mt. 5:14, and especially 25:31-46, for instance.) The pre-eminence of love over knowledge is a theme running again through the New Testament as a whole. (Cf. Mt. 22: 37, 5: 43-48; Lk. 6:27-28, 32-36.)

JESUS A MYSTIC?

Since he left us no written record himself, and his disciples recorded no direct claim, it can be argued—and has—that Jesus did not see himself as a mystic. But the undeniable mystical character of the earliest Christian writings, and the no less mystical tradition springing from them, strongly indicate that in the sense we have described it, Jesus' life and teaching were truly mystical. Further, from St. Paul to the present, all authentic Christian mysticism has been essentially Christological, rising to incredible heights in saints such as Francis of Assisi, Catherine of

Siena and Teresa of Avila, all of whom certainly perceived Jesus as their mystical Lover.

I am convinced that, as the fruit of the prophetic and Wisdom traditions constituting the fountainhead of Jewish and Christian mysticism, Jesus was not only the mystic *par excellence,* but saw himself as such and taught us to follow him. Even more: to join him in total union with the One he lovingly called "Abba." He may have had contact with the Essenes or other Jewish mystical sects—we have little way of telling. But as described by the Evangelists and St. Paul, he was, in his life and message, not only a mystic, but *the* mystic.

His union with God was complete and apparently consciously so, at least from the time of his baptism in the Jordan. Jesus, too, not only counseled, but practiced the way of renunciation, leaving home, family and possessions to preach the good news of salvation and to meet his mysterious destiny in Jerusalem.

Meditation, the contemplative prayer-life leading to increasing enlightenment, figured no less prominently in his life. Often Jesus withdrew into solitude to pray alone, sometimes all night. His last night on earth before his execution was so spent.

Significantly, Jesus never strove to communicate conceptual knowledge about God. He simply did not enter the theological fray, insisting, like the coming generations of Christian mystics, that the way to union with God was not paved with concepts, but with faith—often blind faith—love and service. Such a life of course entails knowing—but a kind of practical, existential knowing. A true Jew, Jesus always used "knowing" in that sense of immediate, first-hand *experience* of the Father and the Holy Spirit, as well as of himself—the ancient Hebrew *yadha.* But love was his commandment and the content of all his teaching. Without love, nothing can be of any avail with God. But love for Jesus, too, was always concrete love, love in action.

The pattern of his life clearly showed an alternation between strenuous activity—teaching, preaching, healing, exorcisms, traveling vast distances on foot—and prayer and relaxation among his friends. Most interesting, perhaps most conclusive, of the facts arguing for Jesus' being a mystic, is the settled fact, despite recurrent opinions to the contrary, that Jesus had no secret doctrines.

Jesus often stressed the mystical identity between himself and all men and women as a living reality (cf. Mt. 25: 40, John 17: 20-24), as well as a promise. It is this mystical identification that lay at the heart of his redemptive death. He is not only one of us, he is all of us! For the mystic, there are no essential differences between the part and the whole, the head and the body, the vine and the branches.

Scripture played a central part in Jesus' dramatic revelation of himself as the flesh-and-blood medium between God and humanity. His interpretative skills did not stop short of challenging the Scribes and Pharisees, but always brought his hearers closer to the mystery of God contained there. And, as noted in the gospels and epistles, Jesus affirmed that the "hidden meaning" of prophetic passages was in fact himself—a claim that nearly resulted in his death at the hands of angry crowds, long before his execution as a blasphemer and idolater.

Jesus no less clearly emphasized the mysterious presence of God and his own active presence in the bread and wine of Eucharist and the great Christian mysteries of reconciliation and initiation by water and the Spirit. And Jesus promised to be present in prayer, as his followers gather in his name, but no less as they meet the needs of the poor, the oppressed, the sick and straying. He would meet them again and again "on the road," in the garden, on the rooftop, in the upper room, on the sea shore, and, most particularly, in the midst of the calamitous events of the last days. The *logion* of Jesus preserved in the Oxyrhynchus Papyrus, probably an authentic saying, poetically captures the reality of this mysterious and pervasive Presence:

> *Wherever there are two, they are not without God: and where there is one alone, I say I am with him. Lift up the stone and there thou shalt find me: Cleave the wood, and I am there.*

SUGGESTIONS FOR FURTHER READING

Henri Bergson, *The Two Sources of Morality and Religion,* Garden City, N.Y.: Doubleday and Co., 1935.

Reginald Garrigou-Lagrange, *Christian Perfection and Contemplation,* St. Louis: B. Herder, 1942.

Joseph Maréchal, *Studies in the Psychology of the Mystics,* New York: Benziger Brothers, 1927.

Philo of Alexandria, *On the Contemplative Life,* trans by F. H. Colson, Cambridge: Harvard University Press, (Loeb Classical Library), vol. IX, 1967.

Chapter 3

THE ELEMENTS OF MYSTICISM

The characteristic assertion of mysticism in all its forms is that there is a vitally important and non-conceptual experience of God available to men who meet its conditions. The simplest and most usual expression of this thesis is that all men at all times are directly dealing with God, whether they know it or not.

William Ernest Hocking

Recently, the mystical aspects of human religious experience have attracted the interest of scientific researchers in a more positive way than formerly. After centuries of theological analysis, interpretation and debate, this newfound concern not only reflects the persistence of mysticism in human life, but has also shed some important new light on the structure and process of mystical development not always perceived by the theologians. Reciprocally, advances in our understanding of mysticism and mystical development are shedding new light on less pronounced manifestations of transcendent elements in human experience as a whole.

Therefore, in order to survey the various elements and relations of the mystical life at this point, we will be able to draw not only upon psychological studies, but also on the profound reflections of the mystics themselves and their students regarding the *meaning* of their experience. Among this latter group, I am particularly indebted to the great American thinker, William Ernest Hocking.

William Ernest Hocking (1873-1966), the gifted American philosopher and religious figure, was a life long student of mysticism, and himself a mystic. Born in Cleveland, he grew to manhood in Illinois and Iowa, becoming a student of Josiah

Royce and William James at Harvard. A life long Protestant, Hocking nevertheless considered himself a member of the "Catholic Church of the Future." He was extraordinarily active in promoting ecumenism among Christians and between Christian and non-Christian groups. His contribution to the study of mysticism included both psychological investigations and philosophical and theological appraisals. In attempting to establish the meaning and place of mysticism in human experience, Hocking was able to crack the spell which Cartesianism had cast over Western Thought for over two centuries.

For Hocking, the structure of human experience consisted of three irreducible elements—"I," "It," and "Thou." The "field" supporting and making possible all experience of the self, other selves and the world, was God, of whom all human beings have at least a rudimentary awareness in the depths of consciousness. Religion makes this divine presence salient in human experience, and mystical experience is but the extension of ordinary religious experience.

Thus for Hocking, mysticism was "the practice of the presence of God, together with the theory of that practice." His major works on mysticism include the books *The Meaning of God in Human Experience* (1912), *Living Religions and A World Faith* (1940), *The Coming World Civilization* (1956) and *The Meaning of Immortality in Human Experience* (1957). His major essays include "The Meaning of God and Human Experience" (1935) and "The Mystical Spirit" (1944).

Hocking, following the insight of his immortal teacher and predecessor at Harvard, William James, considered mysticism to be a variety of ordinary religious experience. Although this may seem obvious to us today, in the early part of this century, to view the range of religious experience as an extensive continuum of related forms, each distinct from its neighbor only by subtle degrees that ultimately encompassed widely different extremes, was a revolutionary approach. Theologically, however, it was matched by the efforts of Fr. Reginald Garrigou-Lagrange and his disciples in France who were attempting to restore the primitive Christian notion of the structural integrity, the *unity* of the spiritual life.

Despite important differences, both approaches considered it a mistake, psychologically and religiously, to regard mystical experience as an entirely different *kind* of experience from normal religious experience. They insisted that mystical development and its characteristic function, contemplative meditation, were part of ordinary religious or spiritual growth. That is to say, mystical experience, as we have seen, must be a dimension of *all* religion, a common rather than an elite phenomenon, and an ordinary rather than extraordinary manifestation of the religious spirit. Consequently, it would be wrong to maintain that there are two independent "ways" to the "perfection" of Christian life, the "ascetical" or prophetic and the "mystical."

But as a further dimension of ordinary religious experience, mystical experience has to be grasped both as a form of *experience* and as a manifestation of *religion*.

Religion, as we have seen before, can be considered to be the relation between human persons and what they consider to be sacred. It is the "bond" between men, women and God. Religious experience, then, refers to *any* felt awareness in which our relatedness to God becomes especially manifest or conscious.

THE ELEMENTS OF EXPERIENCE

But what is experience? Experience is as hard to pin down as any primordial fact of human existence. Originally, it meant to put something "to the test." In English usage, it has been largely associated with direct observation of anything—as long as it is first-hand and subject to some kind of personal or public scrutiny. Sometimes, we use experience to mean the events which have taken place within the knowledge of a person or even a group of people, possibly the human race as a whole: "universal" experience.

Philosophically, the problem of dealing with experience has been that, following the "turn to subjectivity" in the wake of René Descartes (1596–1650), it was generally conceived of as a dualistic, subject-object relationship, basically a form of knowledge. This view colored scientific and theological thought for centuries. But human experience is far richer than that.

The turn of this century brought Freud, Spencer, Marx and James to the point of a reconception of experience. But again, it was Hocking, even more than John Dewey, who overcame the radical dualism of Descartes. Experience, Hocking realized, is not limited to a "subject's" knowledge of or even transaction with an "object."

In his bid to recover something of the richness of human experience, Hocking argued that *three* elements were involved in the structure of all experience: a "self," and much more than a knowing self; an objective "fact-world" existing independently of the human mind; and a network of social interactions of a direct and immediate kind. These elements were linked in a common "field of reference" making interaction and especially communication possible. Later, Hocking identified this field of reference as God.

Here, following Hocking's analysis, we can say that human experience is an ongoing interrelationship of persons who share a common world of nature and society, grounded in the creative presence of God as the field of that experience. In every experience, there is an "I" (or "We"), an "It" and a "Thou" related in terms of common factors ranging from existence to actual engagement.

The "It," the shared fact-world of nature and society, may be either the background or the foreground of our attention. Similarly, our direct and unique experience of other selves as "thou" may recede into the background of consciousness as we deal with facts, but such "intersubjectivity" is *always* part of our experience. Particularly in love, but in many other direct encounters with other persons, the world in turn becomes the *context* of experience, but it, too, is *always there.* God, as the field of reference of experience, rarely becomes directly manifest in our concrete experiences, if only because we take that grounding presence so easily for granted. For it, too, is always there, but never as an object. Nor is it a "thou" like other "thou's." But any of the three elements of experience can mediate that presence to our awareness when, by a shift of attention, we advert to the *universal* context, ground or field of *all* the "objects" of consciousness, even our own self. And as that Field becomes more manifest in our consciousness, our awareness of self, of the world, and of other selves fades into the fringes of awareness, but they, too, *always* remain "there."

Religion, obviously, is a way of describing the relationship between God and selves in the context of living in a natural and social world. Religious experience is our direct consciousness of this relationship, usually rather impersonal and objective. Mystical experience and mysticism represent a further development of ordinary religious experience in which we become more acutely and *subjectively* aware of this grounding Field, not as an It nor even as a Him (or Her!), but as a *You,* a "Thou," or, as Hocking would say "the Thou of the world." So perceiving God is both the reason and the effect of the most distinctively *personal* relationship possible to a human being, *love.* And with this real, personal love comes the possibility of *union*—the goal and quest of all mysticism.

The elements of mysticism are therefore not merely related statically in a kind of tri-polar structure, but exist in a dynamic, unfolding process of interactions. There is *development* entailed in all experience, a dialectical interchange or dialogue in which each human self acquires a growing sense of individual identity by dealing more or less successfully with the world and with the field grounding both it and that world.

Before we look at the pattern of this process, however, we are faced with an initial mystical dilemma: the problem itself.

THE VANISHING SELF

What is this "self," the "I" which we discern in our experience as the original background behind every event, thing, memory and idea of which we are aware? We have seen that the dualistic idea of the self as a "soul" in a body is no longer considered valid. Rather, the self is taken as the integral identity of the body-mind-spirit of a person operating as a whole. Is there something else behind or within this three-fold structure of the person? The mystics say "no."

This is one of the most challenging and even unsettling notions in all mystical teaching, but in some form or another, the ultimate unreality of the self is a keystone of both practice and theory. In the doctrine of *anatta,* for instance, Buddhist teaching flatly states that there is no transcendental ego, some "self behind the self" which is the Observer, existing independently of the body, naturally immortal and unable of being known or even approached directly. In short, for orthodox Buddhism, in contrast to popular views everywhere, there is no *soul,* and the "self" is only a felt unity of connected experiences dependent on bodily and mental integrity. In modern language, this is to say that the only ego is the empirical ego. Behind that there is nothing—but a very special kind of nothing.

Here we also touch on a strand of *Western* mysticism which could have been influenced very early by Buddhist teachings. At any rate, in medieval mysticism, much emphasis is placed on "naughting" the self—reducing it to "nothing." In the teachings of Meister Eckhart, Catherine of Siena and *The Cloud of Unknowing,* as well as of St. Teresa and St. John of the Cross, we are told again and again that, in comparison to God as well as in terms of our own existence, the self is Nothing. Its existence is wholly gratuitous and rather precarious: arising out of nothing by a creative act of God, tending toward nothing, and preserved in being only by God's supporting power and love.

For the mystics, such a nothingness of the self is not an idea but an experience. They *feel* their radical insufficiency, their total dependency on the One who, in comparison to their nothingness, is their All. And to increase their awareness of total dependence on God, recognizing the truth of the human situation, they are driven to reduce self-awareness to *nothing,* even though in this life at least (as *The Cloud of Unknowing* teaches) we shall never wholly escape self-consciousness. This is a radical "self-naughting" not unlike that of the Zen monk who is asked to describe what his face looked like before his parents met!

Thus, the mystics are saying that to regard the "self" as some kind of *fundamental* reality on which our experience of everything else depends, is to fall under the spell of the greatest of all delusions. "Enlightenment" occurs when we perceive the radical contingency of our being, finding it to be in *fact,* nothing at all but the unity of our experience, a unity itself dependent on powers far beyond our ordinary awareness. Everything we are is given.

The *coherence* of our experience is an achievement, to be sure, and it results from our attunement to Reality. To mistake that coherence for ultimate reality is truly a delusion, however. To think of it as some imperceptible Super Self is to compound the error if not to lapse into self-idolatry. The way to true enlightenment, on the other hand, is to "deny the self," assume the burden of self-conscious existence, and "go out" of oneself, that is, to follow Christ in the *ek-stasis* of transcendent love.

The Self, then, is a field of experience constituting the unity of every person, the integrated body-mind-spirit concretely existing in space and time. But like all fields, this one is of itself empty; it is *that within which* things happen. The reality of the self is a function of the dynamic interactions between selves, the world and God, as the most fundamental field of all experience, the Ground of Being. As a field, God, too, is in a sense "empty"—for whatever is, is *in* God, but it *is* not God. God has no "contents." Yet, he is the "all"—another paradox.

A self, then, is an awareness, an awareness determined by our bodily existence, organized by our mental processes, and given value and purpose in terms of our spiritual sensitivity. Around the sharp focus of this awareness, moreover, there is a fringe or area of consciousness that is not normally available to our attention. It becomes imperceptibly, and even temporally, dimmer and dimmer as the focus of consciousness shifts. The "contents" of this fringe area are various: memories, all the forgotten, repressed or buried elements of our past experience, objects in the natural world, instincts, fears and drives. Some of these may be called to mind but some cannot. This is the unconscious self; not a *different* self, but evidence of a *larger* self, one which extends beyond the conscious unity of our empirically conscious ego. Perhaps, as Carl Jung believed, at the furthermost edges of this unconscious fringe, there is a permeable boundary where all human selves interact across all barriers of time and space, the "collective unconscious," a field of fields. If so, this would accord well with the almost universal mystical insight that all human beings are profoundly and ultimately one. And the infinite field necessary to ground the possibility of such a universal unity of finite fields can only be the One we call God. Perhaps it follows from this that the reason we are ordinarily so unattentive to the presence of the field in everyday consciousness is that it is most directly supportive in the nethermost reaches of the unconscious self. We may be able to find God more clearly then, as we expand the conscious field of our experience to include further areas of the unconscious, the work of meditation.

THE UNITY OF THE SELF

The identity or continuing unity of the self, then, is the product of the integrity of the body, mind and spirit—all of which *should* interact harmoniously on many levels of awareness. But they often do not. Thus, every disruption of bodily, mental and spiritual wholeness (health) is a diminishment of true selfhood. Our quest for integrity requires re-integration and healing.

Death is the end of the self as we know it, but not absolutely. For aspects of the whole self transcend the operation of the body and mind. Existence is a gift that is not taken away, but can be changed. Thus, death, the final renunciation, can and should be a liberation of the self—one that can begin at any time in this life with the realization of our nothingness. But the full integrity of the human person requires some kind of bodily-mental-spiritual dimension, and here we enter a truly mysterious zone, one symbolically, even sacramentally described in the fundamental Christian belief in the resurrection of the body, the hope of ultimate human integrity. Perhaps the Oriental notion of reincarnation is a different kind of tribute to this same human hope.

For the mystic, the self is not an isolated monad, although it can be deceived into such an illusion. Rather, each human self is a bright focus of awareness, concretely localized but not limited by time, shading gradually into a universal field of consciousness. And this consciousness is itself a *thought*—one incredible, eternal, limitless, unfathomable thought in the mind of an all-loving Personal Self beyond all selves.

A self, as we experience it—our own or others'—is a transaction between partial awarenesses and the world as a whole, a transaction sometimes experienced as grounded in a still deeper transaction with the sustaining field of both awareness and world. To attain to this experience, which is the essential art of mysticism, is to obtain true wisdom and eternal happiness. It is a process, moreover, which begins in this life. The necessary condition for human achievement in this life is the absence of the illusions and delusions which can distract us from developing that experience. *This* is to "naught" the self, to displace our egos from the altars of consciousness. The rest, we are told, is Grace.

Paradoxically then, typical mystical spirituality entails both the denial and the affirmation of the reality of the self. There *is* a self, the empirical ego, which is not the absolute center of value and being, much less the underlying foundation of all experience, although it can be mistaken as such—the error of subjective idealism. This *illusory* self must be denied, "naughted," reduced to zero, displaced from the center of concern. In its stead, consciousness must be shifted to the *real* ground of existence, the creative Source of *all* being and value.

The "self" as the particular field of experience of each person, exists not in its own right, but in total dependence upon the true Self of the Universe, in comparison to Whom it is nothing at all. This is both the mystics' insight and joy, for the less we succumb to the illusions of self-aggrandizement, the more we grow in authentic individuality, possessed of the certainty of being held and borne up forever by Infinite Care. ("He who loses his soul for my sake, shall find it unto life everlasting.")

Even more mysteriously, God, as the ground of our being, the field of all experience, is also, but in a remarkably more profound sense, empty, "no *thing*." God is not an object found among other objects which can be known individually. Into this "Nothing"—as Meister Eckhart and all great mystics tell us—we must sink all our security, for only "There" can we find the sure reality we seek. *This* Nothing is no illusion, but the true artist behind the fabric of being, the *only* Transcendental Ego.

As the great Jewish scholar and mystic, Abraham Heschel, insisted, *only* God can truly say "I"—and we can only say "Thou." How close this is to the insight of St. Catherine of Siena, who was told in ecstasy by God, "I am he who is, you are she who is not." Our whole being, then, consists in our response, the vocative expression of our entire life summed up in a word: *You*. Here, too, is the true meaning of the mystics' cries, "My 'me' is God!" and "It is no longer I who live, but Christ lives in me!"

MYSTERION

MYSTICAL DEVELOPMENT AND GROWTH

No religious tradition has ignored the fact that the spiritual life, like all life, shows a progression of stages which are fairly discernible and are set off from one another by transitional periods or series of experiences. Mystical spirituality is no exception. Generally, this process of development has been compared to that of the maturing process of the human person as a bio-social organism.

Three major phases of growth are characteristic of most Western schemes of development, based on the major thirds of life: childhood, young adulthood, and maturity. Thus in the earliest Christian traditions, we find reference to the "newborn," to the "young," and to the "mature." (Cf. I Cor. 3:1, I Cor. 2:6, II Cor. 10:15, Eph. 4:13-15, etc.)

The "youths" John speaks of in his First Epistle are elsewhere called *pneumatikoi,* "spirituals." The goal of development is *teleiosis* or "perfection," that is, complete maturity. This scheme has come down to us as "beginners, practitioners and completers"—or, beginners, the proficient and the perfect.

Other schemes were used from the earliest times, however, to refer to the gradual growth to full spiritual maturity. The early Alexandrian Fathers, influenced by Philo, spoke of climbing a mountain. Others spoke of running a race, as did St. Paul, or of a ship's journey. In the fourth century, Evagrius of Pontus wrote of the *praktiki,* the *physiki* and the *theologi,* referring to those who were especially involved in practical life, acquiring virtues and avoiding sin, those who had become attentive to the presence of God in their contemplation of creation, and, finally, those who devoted attention to God alone. Here we have a clear reference to action and contemplation. Not merely stages of growth, these three represented to Evagrius ever deepening levels of God-consciousness.

Richard Woods

Perhaps the most ancient and popular characterization of stages of spiritual development was organized around three kinds of mystical experience which are progressively related. Present in Jewish mysticism before the time of Christ in Alexandria and elsewhere, these were known as *katharsis, erlampsis* and *henosis* in Greek: that is, purgation, illumination and unification. Later, these were described in terms of the famed "three ways." Eventually, these "ways" or stages were linked by transitional experiences called the "dark nights" of the senses and the soul.

Despite the aptness of the analogy between spiritual and physical life—one more fitting than many early writers probably realized—and the perceived connections between kinds and sequences of mystical experience, there are important differences to be aware of.

First, growth in the spiritual life (assuming that we're speaking here of mystical spirituality in the most inclusive sense) is not simply a uniform linear process of development. The would-be mystic cannot follow a simple set of rules as if building a model railroad or baking a cake.

Rather, spiritual development consists of phases, three or more—it makes little difference how you count them—in which a person may be engaged more or less throughout a lifetime. Development is more cyclical and dialectical than linear. We often go over the same route many times, but with a different depth of comprehension. Purgative, illuminative and unitive experiences can happen at any time. The dark night of the soul may last 10 minutes or 10 years, or it may never happen at all. The spirit is not constrained by our categories.

Secondly, as there are very different types of personality and, as a result, personality development, so also there are different styles of spirituality and spiritual development. Early Christian mystics saw two fundamental *classes* of spiritualities, "solar" and "nocturnal." That is, spiritualities that differed with regard to the presence of purgative elements such as the famous "dark nights" so richly described by St. John of the Cross or the cloud theme found in *The Cloud of Unknowing.* Some mystics—William James' "once-born" souls—simply do not experience these "nocturnal" episodes, but travel, as Gregory of Nyssa was fond of saying, "from glory to glory."

The most important fact in all these schemes is that they witness that mystical development is a *growth process,* a gradual and progressive integration of the elements of all human experience. Important, too, is the realization that there *are* distinctive and characteristic experiences such as conversion, purgation, enlightenment, and unification, and that the focus of awareness *does* shift from self to others, to Nature and to God alone. Mystics *can* be described in terms of infants, youths and adults, as people can be in terms of almost anything else—art, politics, business, music, sports, etc. Even a life of crime has its "masters," beginners, and small-time crooks. All such schemes probably make sense to *someone,* if not to everyone. Behind them all is the fact that mystical spirituality has systematic phases of development. Knowing about them in advance can help a person avoid mistakes, misinterpretations, discouragement and disillusionment.

Is there an overall scheme that applies to everyone?

Recently, Dr. Kenneth Wapnick has argued that, on the basis of :omparative studies in psychiatry and mysticism, there are distinctive stages in all such inner growth to full spiritual integrity, just as Dr. Arthur Deikman found that some element of both renunciation and meditation figures in all forms of mysticism. Wapnick's categories harmonize remarkably well with those of Hocking, developed decades before. In the following section, I will present a rough compilation of both in terms of the classic model of the three "ways." Not everyone's experience will fit such a pattern, however, no matter how generalized.

Richard Woods

THE STAGES OF SPIRITUAL DEVELOPMENT

1. *Conversion.* Most spiritual writers agree that a spiritual "awakening" of some kind usually precedes the beginning of earnest mystical development. This conversion experience is often a form of moral enlightenment—often very striking—in which a man or woman perceives that there has to be a better way of living than the one they are pursuing. Their search for it usually requires a separation from their friends and family, severing social ties and suspension of ordinary activities in order to undertake a complete reorganization of life. This "withdrawal" may be a real geographical one or only a psychological break with accustomed modes of thought, feeling and action which can be described as "renunciation."

2. *Purgation.* Having withdrawn from ordinary involvement in the world, the apprentice mystic begins an often solitary and demanding re-evaluation of all values, beliefs, and traditions as "ways" to union with God. Many aspects of experience are voluntarily suspended in this negative phase of development, which, whether it is called "deautomatization" or the "active purification of the senses," produces the same result: acutely increased sensitivity to almost every aspect of human experience. This effort may go on for years, or it may be short, but it seems to give way to a more passive or receptive form of purification, in which many areas of the personality normally inaccessible to voluntary consciousness are systematically purified and strengthened. If so, this stage would correspond to the first "dark night," that of the senses.

3. *Illumination.* The discipline, renunciation and re-evaluation of the mystics' "negative path" of unlearning concerns mental processes as well as physical behavior. Meditation is the traditional method by which the ordinary, undisciplined activity of the mind is brought under voluntary control at this time. Various forms of "enlightenment" may and probably will occur,

in and out of meditation, from actual experiences of light to wholly new ways of perceiving reality, a transformation of consciousness. The active purgation of the mind gradually becomes more passive, as the "field" underlying meditative prayer, the presence of God, begins to dominate attention. Such a process is the initial form of contemplation. The personality becomes more and more receptive, but as the field of awareness expands, it becomes increasingly "empty." This begins the second "night," the dark night of the soul. For those who experience it (and not all do), it is a profoundly painful sense of self-awareness together with a lack of God-awareness. The inner longing for integration with God becomes acute.

4. *Union.* Integration occurs on conscious and unconscious levels of personality over a long period of time, probably long before the mystic is aware of it. Deep healing precedes the felt awareness of unity, but increasingly, a sense of oneness with God—as well as oneness with other selves and, indeed, the whole of creation—begins to emerge out of the unconscious depths of the spirit. Periods of ecstasy may alternate with despondency, but these alternations of mood gradually level out, if they occur at all. In the fullest experience of God's presence, the "advanced" mystic normally has the full use of all mental, emotional and physical faculties. Full integration occurs in the "everyday mind." Further, full integrity concerns not only relationships with God, the world, and other selves, but perhaps most basically, within oneself. This is the first and greatest healing.

5. *Return to the World.* Although many accounts of mystical development end with the unifying experience of God, this is not the final stage of spiritual growth. *Typically,* the "completed" mystic, having finished the solitary path of negative and positive integration, returns to the social world. Here, she or he becomes characteristically a whirling wind of prophetic action, initiating programs of reform and renewal, reaching out to meet the needs of the poor and the oppressed, teaching as well as offering concrete help and consolation, sometimes forming bands of

disciples, or at least preaching or writing the message. It is during this time that the dual aspect of all spiritual life becomes manifest: the reciprocal dialectic of action and contemplation. Like the beat of a great heart, the mystic-prophet is "excursive" and "reflective" in turns, but never fully leaving the felt presence of God. These two forms of experience have, of course, been present all along, in large measure determining the dialectical pattern of mystical development itself by their necessary interplay.

CONCLUSION

If we conceive of human growth and development in terms of certain patterns of behavior following upon each other in a kind of dialectical rhythm, often marked by severe transitional crises such as puberty, mid-life crisis, menopause, etc., then the elemental processes of mystical development can be seen to differ from that of ordinary experience only in intensity, not in kind. This is not naturalism, but a recognition of the way in which the life of the spirit, the mind and the body is all one. Mystical development is an extension of the religious dimension of all experience to the highest levels of conscious awareness. In this way, mystical experience is the manifestation in human consciousness of the divine field underlying all human experience, mediated by the mystic's encounters with self, other selves and the manifold world of nature and society.

Mysticism itself refers to the dynamic pattern of development deliberately undertaken by the mystic. It is the conscious and systematic cultivation of mystical experience, the practice of the presence of God. We can see, consequently, that mysticism as such has little or nothing to do with abnormal phenomena, strange behavior, unusual or extraordinary powers, or even raptures and ecstasies for the most part. Rather, mysticism is the art of being fully human in the most ordinary ways. It is a simplification of experience, a radical effort to uncover the essential elements of human existence, and to develop these elements fully through various stages of gradual improvement, aiming at spiritual, as well as bodily and mental maturity. As Hocking once said,

"The function of unusual experiences is, as a rule, not so much to answer questions as to open them. They stir us out of our habitual assumptions. They may illuminate; but the final answers must be in the common experiences of mankind—this has become my firm conviction. If there is any truth in 'mystic experience,' it is what every man subconsciously knows, and what thought can eventually validate."

Chapter 4

MYSTICISM: THE SPIRITUALITY OF HUMAN DEVELOPMENT

The 'mystical experience.' Always here and now—in that freedom which is one with distance, in that stillness which is born of silence. But—this is a freedom in the midst of other human beings.

Dag Hammarskjöld

Mystical spirituality as a contemporary lifestyle differs from the mysticism of the past in being more inclusive, more positive and more active than before.

Contemporary mystical spirituality is more inclusive in the holistic sense of that word. Today, it is possible to look back on roughly 6,000 years of mystical history and chart a general outline of the pattern of development followed by the human encounter with God in the immediacy of lived experience. In this regard, the history of mysticism is a history of the development of the human spirit itself.

It is not a history of political regimes, wars, revolution, agriculture, industry, economic expansion, the arts, sciences, literature or even of ideas or religion itself. It is a story of the evolution of the human spirit in quest of its highest ideals, aspirations and goals, precisely in view of the awareness of God's presence in individual experience as well as that of the race.

We should thus not be too surprised to find that the development of the individual person and that of humanity itself reflect each other in significant respects. And that they not only reflect each other, but that they influence each other reciprocally. The underlying evolution of the human spirit in dialogue with God is accomplished by a manifest dialectic between individuals and their societies. It is axiomatic in this series that those individuals "chosen," and in fact found to be the chief participants in this dialectic, are *by definition* the world's mystics.

Mysticism is thus not some rare and inbred form of pious wool-gathering on Mt. Carmel; it is the bedrock foundation of our common existence and experience, the total integration of the human person in terms of the maximum possibilities of development.

Accordingly, contemporary mystical spirituality will also become increasingly inclusive in the sense of "catholic"—all-embracing. Having overcome the two hundred year temptation to elitism, which would have doomed it to the moribund periphery of human affairs had it succumbed, mysticism has resumed its vital place in the midst of the world—in the life of a Dag Hammarskjöld, a Dorothy Day, a Tom Dooley, a Mother Teresa of Calcutta, a Pope John Paul I.

This is *everyday* mysticism, the common sense of God's presence in the world of ordinary human concerns and his passionate involvement with its people. It revels in ecumenism and the rich panoply of human differences, for it rests secure on the conviction that fundamentally and ultimately, all are One. It is the domain of no special class or caste, particularly of those who are "professionally" religious.

AFFIRMATION

Contemporary mystical spirituality is also more positive in its stance toward the world and the human situation in general than was the case in former centuries, especially from the end of the Middle Ages to the Enlightenment. The change is not merely a matter of optimism and affirmation versus pessimism and rejection. The mystics are, now as always, realistic and stern critics of the status quo. Prophets in the end, they cajole, harangue and reform—pulling down and rooting up where necessary, capable of heroic anger and destructiveness, as we find in the lives of Joan of Arc and Savonarola.

But there is a stronger sense today of hope in the world-process as a divine-human ("theandric") enterprise aimed at a transcendent goal of unity, harmony and peace among all people. The only future alternative, it could be suggested, would be a regression to total chaos, given the powerful forces loose in the world.

This more positive attitude is reflected, I believe, in the evaluation of the body as well as of society itself. The body is no longer seen as an enemy to be subdued, sequestered, kept under constant duress and finally and happily quit. Nor is the body to be ignored or pampered. Rather, the body is viewed as the spirit made manifest, not merely its vehicle. The body is the distinctively human way of being in the world. As such, it must be cared for, nurtured, strengthened and preserved *as* the way spirit is realized, "incarnate" in the world.

Similarly, the mind can no longer be considered as inimical to the life of the spirit. But an intellectual approach to religion cannot be allowed to determine the course of spirituality, as has sometimes been the case. Mysticism has characteristically denied the priority of cognitive stances concerning God, affirming, rather, the supremacy of love. We can never understand God, the mystics tell us; our concepts are illusions spun by our conceit, nets with which we hope to snare Freedom itself.

The way out of the cognitive blind alley of merely conceptual religion is not to become anti-intellectual, but to train the mind, to yoke the naturally inquisitive seeking of the brain to the equally impatient desire of the heart, quieting both so as to allow the divine presence to become manifest. Meditation, thus, is the art of *mastering,* not conquering, both body and mind, so as to release the spirit from its servitude to undisciplined ambition and zeal. And meditation is a *positive* skill, even though it utilizes negation as its tool to restrain the intellect and steel the will, just as it requires inactivity to calm the body. As a positive discipline, moreover, it leads to human *wholeness*—to mental balance, physical health and eventually to appropriate social action.

One area in which mysticism has developed most maturely is in the attitude toward the *self,* as we have seen. In all mystical traditions, great emphasis has been placed on self-denial, from the radical doctrine of "no self" *(anatta)* in Buddhism, to the "self-naughting" of the 14th century mystics, and the selflessness of Thérèse of Lisieux and Maximilian Kolbe. Again, however, selflessness or self-denial is not mere nihilism, a mad desire to "un-be", as the author of the *Cloud of Unknowing* calls it. It is the paradoxical condition for achieving true self-hood, as Jesus clearly taught. To be a "real" self, an individual, it is necessary to overcome self-consciousness, the reflexive stab of worry and anxiety that kills joy, freedom and action. Mystical spirituality has provided an invaluable resource in our insecure world by revealing the best, perhaps the only, way ultimately to get out of ourselves. And that is by the simple ecstasy of aiming for God.

Finally, the character of the social world has also been recast in contemporary mystical spirituality. No longer seen as the City of Death, the world is now even more than the scene for social reform and service, the stage on which the character of the saint is proved only to be struck at the end of the drama. The social world is, rather, the process of collective human development itself, concretely realized at this moment in time. It is the place of encounter between the God of history and the human race as a whole. God is present in the social world even more graciously and personally than he is in the world of nature.

Human society, like the human personality, is a process in motion. Without direction, discipline, ample scope and constant reintegration, it will inevitably and almost instantly turn to self-centeredness, dissolution and decay. Societies, too, can have spiritual and mental as well as physical breakdowns. But the mastery required to keep the social process en route to its goal can be no more coercive than that needed for individual health and integration. Control cannot be imposed from without in a truly adult society, and it will not be. It will arise from within by a process of judgment and decision based upon co-operation and collaboration. To this end, the work of the mystic, as William Hocking showed, is to renew and preserve *morale*—the willingness of women and men to work in harmony to bring about a better world.

ACTION

A third characteristic of contemporary mystical spirituality flows from the positive recasting of the social world as well as from the natural impetus of personal integration. Mysticism, as Hocking was finally able to demonstrate, must, *as* a social as well as an individual process, eventuate in positive social action. True mysticism has always so tended, despite occasional and largely verbal temptations to Quietism.

The contemporary situation is different mainly in the *recognition* offered to the importance of action and in the impetus given to it by a renewed commitment to social justice. It may well be that the rediscovery of mystical spirituality will prevent renewed social activism from burning out in a flurry of energetic but short-lived missions. Such has been the dialectical value of contemplation in the classic Christian traditions and in others as well.

EXEMPLARITY

As the product of a real history and, in effect, the cumulative result of past lessons in human development, a contemporary mystical spirituality will manifest its multiple heritage. But it will also be future-oriented. Because of its rootedness in actual experience, moreover, mystical spirituality bears with it the living memory of spiritual masters and mistresses who were true pioneers of the race—not, to repeat, as relics, but as models of a new humanity.

Abraham Maslow was acutely aware of the paradigmatic character of mystics as exemplars and heralds of a developing humanity. Like all true saints and heroes, they did not set limits to what human nature can become. They established *norms,* but norms which as *goals* can be and are superseded: "If we want to know the possibilities for spiritual growth, value growth, or moral development in human beings," he wrote, "then I maintain that we can learn most by studying our most moral, ethical or saintly people" (*The Farther Reaches of Human Nature,* p. 7).

It may be objected that Maslow was not speaking specifically of mystics, but in fact, I am proposing that the very qualities he mentions *define* what a mystic is—a person committed to the fullest development of human potential *as a whole,* including preeminently the human groundedness in God. This, too, is apparently how Maslow understood mysticism (See *ibid.,* p. 333). He continues: "It has been my experience through a long line of exploratory investigations going back to the thirties that the healthiest people (or the most creative, or the strongest, or the wisest, or the saintliest) can be used as biological assays, or perhaps I could say, as advanced scouts, or more sensitive perceivers, to tell us less sensitive ones what it is that we value" (*Ibid.,* p. 9).

Along these lines of inquiry, increased attention has recently been given to the pattern of human development, rather than merely to the product. This has included several connected areas of growth—cognitive, emotional, moral, sexual and social development among them. Child and adolescent development have become important areas of current psychological research and practice, and adult development, especially during the mid-years and senescence, has attracted growing attention.

Maslow's insight into the paradigmatic function of the mystics as a model for human aspiration and emulation suggests that some mutual light may be shed on mystical development and human development as a whole by means of a comparative study. This is obviously too vast an undertaking for this book. But it is possible, I believe, to sketch some of the outline of a "theology of human development."

DEVELOPMENTAL SEQUENCES

Technically, "development" can be taken to refer basically to the actualization of specific human capacities in the life of an individual, or even a group, by means of interpersonal transactions in a social environment conducive to full and harmonious integration. Less awkwardly, we are talking about the *life patterns* typically seen in the experience of ordinary men and women as they grow, mature and become aged.

From a holistic perspective, it is important to note at the outset that although we can speak of various areas of human development as if they were different, in fact they are not isolated from each other. The human person develops *as a whole,* and as part of a greater whole, or even a series of wholes: the family, the community, the state, the nation, eventually the human race itself. Such development can, of course, be incomplete or lopsided. But the process of human development is or at least tends to be a unitary one, aiming toward individual and social integration and harmony.

Thus, the various "areas" are in fact different *aspects* of a life in process, interrelated psychological, physiological and spiritual systems within a larger, encompassing system that makes up a human personality or a society: muscles, ideas, feelings, glands, values, relationships etc., on one hand, and, on the other, their collective extensions—social "muscle," "tissue," "bone," etc., that is, the various economic, educational, religious, defensive, and other systems. Needless to say in this day, in neither case do all these systems always work in harmony, whatever the ideal may be—and the ideal is what we mean by *health*. Thus, as we have seen in other respects, there is always need for reintegration and improvement, that is, healing or therapy.

INDIVIDUAL GROWTH

Two main processes can be discerned in terms of the gradual

development of the human spirit, one individual, the other social. The two are, however, necessarily interconnected.

The first process is a dialectical transition from a stage of initial integration, beginning perhaps with prenatal experience. An infant functions normally as a well-integrated whole, but in almost complete dependence upon its social environment. The process of development takes her or him through various challenges of socialization and accomplishment, with their real disintegrating potential, by means of phases of re-integration. Eventually, a young person achieves relatively permanent physical, mental, emotional, religious and social stability—balance and harmony. This is what we mean by maturity or adulthood.

The difficult years of adolescence involve a psychological disengagement of the individual-in-process from the social environment so that true adulthood, with all its demands for interdependence and agency, can become a quality of behavior. This process of "individuation" begins, of course, in infancy, when the child begins to undergo various forms of anxiety-producing separation from mother and father first, then the family as a unit, followed by the community, in order to acquire an increasing sense of independence required for a full life in the world.

In these increasingly major separations, the process of disengagement from society itself has been inaugurated, which is the prime element in the achievement of true individuality. It proceeds, however, largely unconsciously, at least at first. Moreover, individuation results not in the independence so ardently sought by the rebellious teenager, but in the capacity for interdependence, the willingness to curtail one's own freedom in order to co-create a new kind of social unity with another or other whole persons. A mature relationship requires the cooperation of mature individuals, not the merging of partial people. Adult men and women are not half-persons looking for the missing piece.

Thus, social disengagement provides a transition stage

between different levels of social engagement as a person matures. As these concrete partings and meetings continue, a deeper process is at work, as I mentioned, one of disengagement and re-engagement in which a person becomes distinct in fact and feeling from society itself without experiencing the disruption of severe alienation.

This process does not occur in isolation from spiritual development. Rather, the overall integrity of human experience argues for the interconnection of personality development and spiritual growth, if not their virtual *identity.* That is, if interpreted in terms of religious values, beliefs and behavior, the process described above is spiritual development.

SPIRITUAL PASSAGES

The titles given stages of spiritual growth and change are, as we have seen before, taken from the general pattern of human development—childhood, youth and adulthood—or alternatively from the processes at work during these stages in terms of spiritual maturation—awakening and discipline, enlightenment, and ultimate integration, both divine and human. The transition periods classically and poetically described by St. John of the Cross as the "Dark Nights" of the senses and the soul have their psychological and physiological correlatives in periods of change such as latency, puberty and menopause. They are not only correlative, however; in many respects they are interrelated and even simultaneous. Religious "conversions" (a term which Fr. Garrigou-Lagrange preferred to the more poetic language) *typically* occur at these and similar crisis periods of life. "Conversion" *(metanoia)* does *not* mean repentance in this regard, but a change to a new and higher form of personal integration.

Thus, it is important to realize that the process of mystical development is not divorced from the common world of everyday life; it is another and very valuable way of describing the whole process of human development. Even more, it is a helpful way of understanding and *directing* the process toward a goal implicit in the incarnational reality of Christian experience. Grace perfects nature, it does not destroy it.

SOCIAL DEVELOPMENT

The second major process discernible in spiritual development concerns the manner in which a person acquires a more or less explicit spirituality during the process of individuation. Here it is necessary to distinguish three meanings of the word "spirituality."

Most fundamentally, *spirituality* refers to the radical capacity of the human person to experience Life in the full openness and ecstasy of love and service. Spirituality is the character of the human person *as spirit.*

Secondly, spirituality refers to the constellation of beliefs, values, ideas and patterns of behavior which have been identified as structuring the collective experience of a people or a tradition, such as Jewish or Franciscan spirituality.

Thirdly, and most specifically, spirituality refers to the actual style of life adopted by an individual in explicit fulfillment of the human capacity channeled through a collective tradition. A person does not acquire a spirituality in isolation from the social world, but through it, as made concrete in the lived tradition of a people.

The process by which both the latent human capacity and the implicit spirituality of the group—the actual but never fully articulated system of beliefs, values, etc., that constitute the community's spiritual inheritance—is brought to explicit manifestation or "realized" in a concrete way is none other than that of human individuation itself. Here, we are viewing the process from a social rather than from an individual perspective. It is nevertheless true that the spiritual capacity of the human person and the group's spiritual character can only be brought forward in *someone's* experience; no society is conscious in the same sense that a single person is.

For the process of human development to be complete in the sense of being spiritually explicit, it is necessary for the spiritual component to be made consciously evident—although the process may never be *fully* complete in any given instance. This function of *recognition* and *interpretation* is the work of religion in the world. As Hocking would say, it is the function of religion to interpret the Whole as Divine. This it does by providing social structures, supports, interpretative categories and expert assistance when needed, by which the deeply underlying spiritual factors in human experience can be identified and cultivated.

Mystical spirituality is thus realized, made *real* in human development, by a dialogue between the individual and a society, mediated by a specific tradition of interpretation. If that is the ideal, in actual fact the dialogue sometimes becomes a shouting match or a mutual silence, and the deep values and primordial beliefs surface only by dint of an often excruciating detachment and clarification. Consequently the task of the mystic is sometimes to revitalize the very tradition from which she had hoped to draw sustenance during her lonely and precarious journey from wholeness to Wholeness.

SPIRITUALITY AS DEVELOPMENTAL WHOLENESS

Mystical spirituality as a contemporary lifestyle can thus be described as a pattern of life in which the development of body, mind and spirit is integrated in terms of ultimate values and concerns in order to attain eventual union with God. In this sense, spirituality is *total human health,* insofar as that can be achieved at any moment in a person's development. The possibility of achieving this kind of wholeness depends in large measure on the opportunities of the social environment, of course, which is certainly one reason why the great mystics have typically attempted to alter their society, to leave behind a devoted band of disciples, or at least leave a record of their solitary experience in the wasteland of spiritual pioneering.

From a strictly theological point of view, and also that of experience, the process of development, this dialogue between individuals and society, is permeated by God's grace, his concrete will shaping and healing, directing and attracting, working to bring this dialogue to its optimum conclusion. The dialogue is thus a "trilogue"—an on-going drama between human individuals, societies and the Field of Experience that sustains them both.

ANTI-SPIRITUALITIES

Many areas of human experience have been incorporated in attitudes and patterns of behavior that, from a mystical, developmental viewpoint, represent detrimental elements, in fact, "anti-spiritualities" when systematically present in social attitudes and individual lifestyles. Such anti-spiritualities are not deliberately adopted, but are acquired gradually, by incorporating the dominant style of life present in a culture or a group, much the way a language is acquired. These negative life patterns, which embody interrelated elements just as healthy spiritualities do, contain forces of disintegration, often more or less supported by social bias itself.

An example of such an anti-spirituality is brilliantly articulated by Drs. Meyer Friedmann and Ray Rosenmann in their important book *Type A Behavior and Your Heart.* Type "A" behavior, which is a way of living "designed," as it were, to create heart disease, and leading toward death, can be described as follows: "It is a particular complex of personality traits, including excessive competitive drive, aggressiveness, impatience, and a harrying sense of time urgency. Individuals displaying this pattern seem to be engaged in a chronic, ceaseless, and often fruitless struggle—with themselves, with others, with circumstances, with time, sometimes with life itself. They also frequently exhibit a free-floating but well-rationalized form of hostility, and almost always a deep-seated insecurity." (*Type A Behavior and Your Heart,* p. 14).

Type "B" behavior, the antithesis of Type "A" behavior, is described in terms of the same basic areas of life: The Type B person "is rarely harried by desires to obtain a wildly increasing number of things or participate in an endlessly growing series of events in an ever decreasing amount of time. His intelligence may be as good as or even better than that of the Type A subject. *Similarly, his ambition may be as great or even greater than that of his Type A counterpart.* He may also have a considerable amount of 'drive,' but its character is such that it seems to steady him, rather than to goad, irritate, and infuriate, as with the Type A man" (*Ibid.,* p. 84-85).

Significantly, *both* types of behavior are derived from one's social environment through a sequence of developmental stages. Type B behavior, however, is usually the result of a deliberate effort to overcome the Type A pattern as it is perpetrated by Western civilization itself. As such, it can be a reintegrative, therapeutic form of life, and as such is a concrete spirituality. Seeing Type B characteristics in terms of the *religious* values present in them brings it closer to the customary notion of spirituality, and it is not difficult to do.

CONCLUDING PROPOSITIONS

Contemporary mystical spirituality concerns the journey from one set of behavioral attitudes to another within the context of God's active presence in our experience. It is a passage negotiated through developmental stages from a "left"-brained, analytic approach to a "right"-brained synthetic one; from sexism to "androgyny," from authoritarianism (heteronomy) to freedom (autonomy), from Type "A" Behavior to Type "B" Behavior, from what Eckhart called the "merchant mentality" to a "noble" attitude toward life, from monarchical to democratic sensitivities, from adolescent acquiescence to adult agency, from anxiety to ecstasy, from fear and defensiveness to openness and respect, from egocentricity to "otherness," from passive aggression to active service. This is what it means to be a human person in the contemporary world, to grow toward further maturity.

We can anticipate our further investigations with several summary statements. These will become more concretely exemplified as we proceed.

First, the condition for the possibility of mystical spirituality is the character of the human person as spirit, as open to receiving and transmitting Life. This radical capacity for outgoing openness structures human consciousness and constitutes the foundation of human sexuality. It is the human reflection of God's creative, loving nature.

Second, the ground or Field of mystical experience exists and supports us as a personal Presence anterior to our own consciousness. But we can and do become aware of this Presence as we recover the ability to attend to the wholeness of experience in our transactions with the World of nature and society and other human persons.

Third, thus making explicit the implicit Field of our own spiritual awareness is the essential function of mysticism. It is a further development of ordinary religious consciousness in which the "object" or focus of worship shifts from an "It" or even a "They" to "Him" or "Her" and eventually to "Thou" and "We."

Fourth, mystical spirituality is a pattern of life in which we attempt fully to integrate the bodily, mental, emotional, social and religious aspects of experience in order to realize the human capacity for transcendence in loving union with God. It is the deliberate cultivation of mystical experience as an aspect of the whole of life.

Fifth, this effort requires the restriction of conceptual thought in favor of enhanced intuition and holistic perception, directed and perfected by the power of love, both for God and as compassionate concern for all living creatures. Mystical spirituality is a lifestyle devoted to loving service, eventuating in prophetic social action.

Sixth, as a contemporary style of life, mystical spirituality will be in true dialogue with the modern world, utilizing, but not subservient to, the findings of science, medicine, theology and philosophy as well as the means of mass communications and direct social action. It will promote the health of both individuals and society in a holistic manner.

All this may sound abstruse and as remote from the fuel crisis, peace in the Middle East and inflation as from the Interior Castle and the Cloud of Unknowing. In fact, however, if we turn to the teachings and achievements of the world's great mystics, we shall find that in time, their practice and theory of achieving union with God was little different in spirit, despite vast cultural differences and manners of expression.

And as we look back over the centuries of mystical spirituality, there is detectable a true evolution of the human capacity to experience the presence of God. Accordingly, whether as cause or effect, the *perception* of God has itself changed. Since all change is relative, process theologians may or may not be correct when they argue that God, too, has "changed." That remains a true *mysterion,* for, as the mystics tell us, we can never understand *what* God is in himself, including what he has revealed. It is enough, however, to know *that* God is, as the *Cloud* author states, and that he is *here, now*. For the main thing is to "know" experientially, not speculatively. That means to love, and love leads to service in this world and everlasting happiness in the next, as we were taught as children. Beyond that, there is nothing we need to know.

TYPE B CHECKLIST:

"You possess Type B Behavior pattern

1. "If you are completely free of *all* the habits and exhibit none of the traits we have listed that harrass the severely afflicted Type A person.

2. "If you never suffer from a sense of time urgency with its accompanying impatience.

3. "If you harbor no free-floating hostility, and you feel no need to display or discuss either your achievements or accomplishments unless such exposure is demanded by the situation.

4. "If, when you play, you do so to find fun and relaxation, not to exhibit your superiority at any cost.

5. "If you can relax without guilt, just as you can work without agitation."

From *Type A Behavior and Your Heart,* p. 103.

SUGGESTIONS FOR FURTHER READING

Meyer Friedmann and Ray Rosenmann, *Type A Behavior and Your Heart,* NY: Fawcett Crest, 1974.

Reginald Garrigou-Lagrange, OP, *The Three Ways of the Spiritual Life,* Rockford, Ill.: TAN Books and Publishers, 1977.

William Kay, *Moral Development,* London: Allen and Unwin, 1970 ed.

Daniel J. Levinson, *The Seasons of a Man's Life,* NY: Ballantine Books, 1979.

A. H. Maslow, *The Farther Reaches of Human Nature,* NY: Viking, 1972.

Evelyn and James Whitehead, *Christian Life Patterns,* Garden City, NY: Doubleday and Co., 1979.

Chapter 5

MYSTICISM AND THE BODY

The Word became flesh. . . .
John 1:14

What could be more characteristic of the human condition than our bodies? Corporality is the most obvious thing about us—the key to all our inner attitudes, experiences, hopes and memories. The body is our way of being present in the world—really our only way, especially to each other, but also to the realms of society and nature.

Our bodies share in the whole history of creation, the nobility of *matter*. The chemical components of our bodies were once the stuff of stars. It may well be that in the microcosmic laboratories of our cells, the atomic structure of the elements themselves are constantly being transmuted, and one day we shall be the stuff of stars again.

The body also provides the great metaphor for all our transcendent experiences, from "membership" in the body politic to "incorporation" into the Mystical Body of Christ. Similarly, the workings of our bodies have given us models for the tools and technologies that have extended and secured our presence in a universe of vast distances, incredible complexity and incomprehensible smallness—hammers and wheels, telescopes and microscopes, pumps and computers, cameras and cyclotrons, the State itself. Our houses are extensions of our skin, and what is a space station but a house in space?

Scientifically, the human body has probably been the most studied of all phenomena, yet it remains the most mysterious item in the universe. We know far more about the atom than we do about the human brain, which is the most complex object known to science.

When the body ceases to function properly, we weaken and may die. Birth and death and all the processes described in such terms, from the "life" of stars to love affairs, are measured by the history of the human body. How we deal with each others' bodies after death is the measure of the value we place on life. Anthropologically, it is the first evidence in history of what we recognize as a religious attitude.

TEMPLE OF GOD, TOMB OF THE SOUL

Understandably, then, spirituality and corporality have always been closely associated in Christian life and thought—though not always positively. The source of the negative associations, such as the Pythagorean-Orphic conception of the body as the "tomb of the soul" or as a prison of matter from which ecstasy and death provided escape, did not only stem from Hellenic influences. Jewish spirituality also had powerful body-phobias, especially those connected with sexuality, food and grooming. The Greek bias stemmed largely from a philosophical disdain of matter. The Jewish attitude was mainly a moralistic puritanism, a reaction against the hedonism of the surrounding pagan cultures.

We should remember, however, that Greek culture even more characteristically venerated bodily beauty, health and skill in its athletes, soldiers and citizens, immortalizing them in sculpture, painting and poetry. The art of medicine was a Greek invention as were the Olympic games; both were deeply religious exercises. The Jewish attitude was similarly divided, partly as a result of its contact with Hellenic culture, and partly because of its family-centered, Middle-Eastern environment, where beauty, health and skill are considered God's blessings. Nevertheless, Jewish youths were forbidden to participate in the gymnasiums because, among other reasons, the athletes performed nude.

Mystics have not only shared in the religious ambivalence toward the body, but have sometimes exaggerated it, as they have with other elements of spirituality. The extremes of "mortification" undertaken by the desert monks and late medieval mystics were largely an exaggeration of the ordinary *discipline* taught by Jesus and the early Christians regarding the body. The rigors of desert asceticism, however, were also undertaken in deliberate imitation of the sufferings of the martyrs during the age of persecution. But an unfortunate connection was made between martyrdom and renunciation by defining the body as sinful and guilty, and thereby deserving *punishment*—a moralistic interpretation, not a spiritual one. By "mortifying" the body, many monks, too, hoped to "free" the soul, whether from future punishment or simply from the "bonds" of flesh—a notion they may have derived from Pythagorean elements in the teachings of the Gnostics, one of the hybrid sects of the period.

So regarding the body as the "enemy of the soul" is dangerous for many reasons. It is radically anti-Christian, an affront to the Creator, the work of whose hands is holy and good. It is no less a repudiation of the Incarnation: God's assumption of the human body in the person of Jesus. It is psychologically unhealthy, for it fragments the unity of human existence, creating a schizophrenic attitude toward the body and its processes. Spiritually, the unity of the religious life is also disrupted, and the resulting dualism parallels the psychological fragmentation of experience. The body becomes further and further removed from the "real" self, the "soul." It is likewise made the culprit of sin as the goad and tool of wrong-doing, either leading the "soul" astray or being its all-too-willing instrument.

This attitude is nothing but a recurrence of the old Manichaean dualism, inherited from Persian Zoroastrianism, which pitted spirit and matter against each other as good and evil, a view that weakened the Christian message of St. Augustine. The psychology of the dualistic attitude is admittedly seductive—since the "soul" is obviously unable to punish itself directly or liberate itself, the body becomes a ready "whipping boy." This attitude, however, is about as reasonable as denting a car's fender because "it" had broken the speed limit.

THE ILLUSION OF SELF-PUNISHMENT

The flaw in this approach is not that renunciation is itself wrong, but that we believe it possible to cleanse ourselves of sin and guilt by self-inflicted pain. Worse is the illusion that we can't afflict our "souls" directly. In fact, we do so, but largely unconsciously. In psychological terms, such unconscious self-torture is a form of mental illness, whether expressed as chronic anxiety, hypochondria, suicidal depression, narcissism, sado-masochism, etc. No less a symptom of spiritual illness is the vindictive attitude that we develop toward ourselves in order to avoid God's wrath. The fact is that God does not inflict revenge like a petulant schoolchild, and we have no right to do so either. Self-hatred is not a sign of holiness, but of personal disintegration based upon a mistaken notion of our relationship to God.

So it is really unnecessary for God to punish us; we do that ourselves, whether by unconscious injury or setting in motion forces that will eventually turn against us. God did not "create" hell; it came into being as a consequence of sin. God, on the other hand, is forgiveness itself. Penitence, then, is a voluntary acceptance of the consequences of our misdeeds *as a sign of our recognition of responsibility and as proof of our receptivity to both divine and human forgiveness.*

No one can really forgive herself or himself, and herein lies the root, perhaps, of the illusion of self-punishment. Forgiveness always comes from others, because sin is always a social reality. We especially cannot redeem ourselves by making the body a scapegoat for our neurotic desire to escape responsibility for seeking real forgiveness.

MYSTICS AND DENIAL

What then of the mystics' "self-naughting," all the talk of unworthiness, of self-abandonment, self-lessness and so on?

The main point to note here is that no great mystic for long mistook the fragility and precariousness of the human condition for sin and guilt themselves, nor did they identify the body with either. Furthermore, weakness and dependence, including bodily limitations and mortality itself, were not interpreted as God's *punishment*, but as the creaturely condition of the human person.

Sin and evil are part of the human condition, of course, and bodily frailty is partly an effect of sin. But the body is not the sinner; the whole *person* is. Thus, the "sorrow of being" so poignantly described in *The Cloud of Unknowing* is fundamentally a recognition of our *metaphysical* and *spiritual* separation from God, experienced as a profound longing for complete union with God as the ultimate source of meaning and existence. Sin not only ratifies but compounds our distance from God *morally*. All these aspects of closeness and distance from God are closely associated because of the unity of the human person, *but they are different.*

And thus, like penance but in a different manner, renunciation ("purgation") has its place in the spiritual life, a very important one, but *not* as a renunciation of embodiment or as an expression of radical self-hatred, which are both wrong-headed. Further, renunciation is not itself penitential, but rather only the negative aspect of the toughening process needed in every dimension of human life—bodily, mentally and spiritually.

Like weight-lifting, dieting or the abstinence from alcohol and even sex during athletic training, "spiritual exercises" in the sense used by that old soldier, Ignatius of Loyola, are meant to strengthen us and integrate our experience. Thus any renunciation undertaken without a positive intent and without positive results is to that extent unhealthy spiritually and as such un-Christian.

AUTHENTIC MYSTICAL SPIRITUALITY

An authentic mystical spirituality for today (and tomorrow)

recognizes the inherent goodness and dignity of the body as the epitome of God's creation and the "manifestness" of the human spirit (Aquinas). The Self is not a "soul" *in* a body, it is the identity of the body-mind-spirit operating as a whole. Your body is an unrepeatable, unique aspect of the Self that *is* you. Consequently, a healthy spiritual attitude requires *tending* the body, taking care of it as an expression of the authentic self-love at the heart of all religious life and all mental health, not the perverse self-centeredness which is the root of all sin and mental and even bodily dis-integration.

Conversely, the cultivation of the body as the "temple of God" hardly means indulging every whim and desire, which is a truly selfish and destructive attitude. Rather, just as good bodily health requires a degree of deprivation, discipline and exercise to prevent deterioration and to rid us of flab, so does spiritual health. *Genuine* health always involves the integration of bodily, mental and spiritual functions to begin with—which is to say that health is *holistic*, manifesting itself in all dimensions of life.

"Holistic" is a current catch-word attached freely to medicine, spirituality and psychology. Based on the Greek *holos*, it means "entire, whole." *Integral* is another way of saying it. A closer look at the heritage of this and related words can be instructive, in that it reveals how our ancient ancestors regarded the integrity of life—bodily, mental and spiritual.

The words just referred to (except "integral") stem from the same Indo-European root, *SA-*, which seems to have meant "entire or whole." It appears in four major groups of words, each of which blossomed into a host of connected words and concepts in Latin, Greek, Gaelic and Germanic languages: *SAC-*, *SAL-*, *SAN-*, and *SAR-*.

Thus the Latin word *salvare*, "to save, to preserve whole" corresponds in structure and meaning to the Sanskrit *sarva*, the Indo-Germanic *solwo*, the Greek *holos*, the Old Latin *sollus*, the Irish *slan* and the Welsh *holl*. The Old English equivalent was *hàl*, from which we get the following words, all of which fundamentally connote "wholeness" (the *w* was added to "hole" in the 15th century): *hail, hale, hallow, heal, health, holly* and *holy*. (*Holly* or *holy* is the old adjectival form of *hallow*, "to make whole" in the sense of *sanctify*. It is also interesting that the Germanic greeting *heil*! corresponds to the English *hail*!, the Latin *salve*! the Spanish ¡*salud*! and the Irish *slànte*!—all meaning "good health!")

English derivatives of Latin words such as *sacer, salus, salvus, sanctus* and *sanus* are also illustrative: sacred, safe, saint, salvation, salvage, salve, sanatorium, sanction, sanctity, sanctuary, sane, sanitary, save and savior. All refer basically to the same thing: "preserving" *wholeness of body, mind and spirit*—personal integrity.

I strongly believe that given the stresses of contemporary urban and suburban life, the "asceticism" of the future will not consist of odd tortures from bygone ages, such as hair-shirts or prolonged fasts, knee-scraping pilgrimages and the like, but rather in the ordinary and proper care of bodily health, mental integrity and spiritual vitality. For the forces of disintegration—materialism, institutionalism, literalism, conformism, consumerism and the avoidance of pain by imbibing pills and potions in quantities—have never been greater nor more insidious.

THERAPIES

In the inescapable presence of such disintegrating inner and outer forces, the path of spiritual integration, whether direct or indirect, will thus necessarily include primary elements of *reintegration*. And since spirituality is a developmental process, its reintegrative character will often appear as a therapeutic or healing function. (Interestingly, members of a Jewish mystical sect in the Egyptian desert about the time of Christ were known as the *Therapeutae*, or "Healers.")

Some of the therapies evolved to counter the stresses of the modern world are effective, others are illusory. But most are as fragmentary as the society that produced them. Jogging and biking have caught the American imagination recently as ways to get back in shape and to "develop," just as have food fads, crash diets and health clubs. Yoga, aikido and tai-chi are taught everywhere. While all these forms of "asceticism" are potentially beneficial, they are also potentially hazardous. To someone used to years of too much stress, too much rich food and drink, too little exercise and too little common sense, any one of these can invite disability and even death. For many people, jogging is just another name for suicide.

A holistic spirituality, on the other hand, involves an integrative approach to all areas of life. That is, it not only reflects the authentic Christian tradition of the integrity of mind-body-spirit, it prescribes a *systematic* effort to get the whole, interconnected system of systems working together harmoniously. To do so, it will make good use of scientific, medical and spiritual research. For many areas of current investigation in psychology, neurology and physiology, as well as medical therapy and religious study have provided new insights into traditional practices such as "purgation" and meditation. A better understanding of the elements and processes involved in our psycho-physiological and spiritual makeup can thus improve the *practical* side of our spiritual life.

THE MIND-BODY AND SPIRITUALITY

Five new areas of discovery are of particular significance to a holistic, mystical spirituality: body rhythms and bio-feedback, the process of "deautomatization," the dialectic of right and left brain processes, the dual modality of consciousness and the two fundamental kinds of brain activity associated with ecstatic and contemplative states. Several implications of these areas of research bear directly on the body, some on the body-mind interaction, while others primarily concern mental processes or consciousness and will be treated more fully elsewhere.

MYSTERION

THE TIME BODY

St. Bernard took as his spiritual motto the Socratic injunction "Know Thyself." To know ourselves adequately, we must know ourselves bodily, for as I noted earlier, our bodies are the most obvious and accessible aspects of our selves, if often the most unconscious.

One of the most exciting and valuable areas of recent investigation concerns the biological rhythms of the human body and some of the applications of these rhythms such as biofeedback training.

Physiologists tell us that there are nine *major* interacting systems that combine to form the somatic unity we call the body: the nervous system, the respiratory system, the digestive system, the urinary system, the reproductive system, the endocrine system, the circulatory system, the muscular and the skeletal systems. Each system can be subdivided into component systems.

The harmonious interaction of all these systems is what we mean by "health," that is, *good* health. Further, each of these systems, and all of them in combinations and as a whole, operate in a rhythmic cycle of cycles, which we experience as a temporal *ebb and flow*, or *up and down*, or even *in and out*, that is, as an alternation. Anyone who has felt her pulse or who gets hungry at regular intervals, or falls asleep about the same time every night is aware of the "rhythmicity" of the human body.

Importantly, however, many of our cycles are not apparent, and most of them vary in length, that is, in their "period." Further, some of these systems go "out of phase" at times, which may result in unusual patterns of behavior or consciousness. For instance, the sleep rhythm of the body may go into a phase of "free running," in which we fall asleep and awaken an hour later each day for about three weeks, until the system has regulated itself again. We may *experience* this about halfway through the cycle as "insomnia," and probably reach for a sleeping tablet.

Thus, we lose an important chance to learn something valuable about ourselves.

Appetite, sexual drive, irritability, vitality and mental acuity also fluctuate in a generally regular pattern. They, too, sometimes go "out of phase"—fortunately, not all at the same time—and it is therefore helpful to know ourselves well in this respect, if for no other reason than to prevent our mistaking external factors for internal ones when we unexpectedly experience drowsiness, loss of appetite, irritability, etc.

Unfortunately, most of us have been taught from childhood to ignore our body-feelings and have become anesthetized from the neck down, experiencing our bodies only when something is sufficiently haywire to hurt. We would probably starve to death if we were not slaves to schedules of eating or aware of "hunger pains" caused by a lowering of blood sugar. But we are generally insensitive to the ordinary workings of our bodies, and thus ignorant of the profound effect they have upon our consciousness and spiritual awareness. We are even embarrassed by body "signals" such as when our stomach is suddenly heard "growling" or when we sneeze or cough, for all of which, and many other bodily sounds, we automatically apologize.

In the East, for the most part, there seems to be a much greater sensitivity to the importance of the body in spirituality. In beginning a program of spiritual training, attention is usually directed *first* to posture, breathing, to feeling one's bodily *being*—an attitude Westerners lampoon as "navel-gazing." Western spirituality has too long tried to forget the body, with disastrous results. After all, even monks get ulcers.

BODY RHYTHMS

Knowing the natural rhythms of our bodily systems can help us integrate our lives more harmoniously, but it takes some time and skill. It is impossible here to do more than illustrate a few examples.

First, our body temperatures rise and fall every day in a 24 hour pattern or "period," the *average* or "mean" being approximately 98.6° F. During our most active time of day, our inner temperature will be higher by as much as a degree or more, and about that much lower during our most inactive period. Ideally, we should be asleep during the low ebb and hard at work at the peak. However, for many people, this is not the case.

For the fact is that the time of day at which temperature peaks and ebbs varies from person to person. Two large groups of people can be differentiated, however—those whose temperature cycle peaks early in the day, and those whose cycle peaks later. The first group, the "larks," love to rise early, celebrate the dawn, eager to get to work and finish their day "early" in the evening—around 10:00 PM. The second group, the "owls," sleep later, are active longer in the evening, and retire later.

Both groups are normal. However, for centuries, "owls" have been discriminated against by schedules based on available daylight, such as those in monasteries, convents, prisons, schools, etc. But "early to bed, early to rise" does not make an "owl" anything but sluggish and irritable, if not an insomniac and coffee-dependent for lucidity before 8:00 AM!

Cycles such as temperature and appetite are to some degree malleable—people can modify them by force and habit. But altered cycles tend to revert naturally back to their normal period when given a chance. "Jet-lag" similarly shows that our built-in "biological clocks" are set to our own distinct rhythm. Knowing that and cooperating with nature can save a good deal of wasted time and energy in structuring a livable schedule.

Discovering your activity-rest cycle is fairly simple. Just take your temperature with a conventional thermometer every hour of the day and night for about six weeks. Keep a record and note the high and low points on a daily basis. The six weeks is important, because the daily pattern itself may also shift slightly according to a *monthly* rhythm. (These two rhythms, daily and monthly, are the most common, but there are many others!)

Another way is to note when you fall asleep *naturally* and when you awaken—for instance when on vacation—and to match this against your most alert, active time of day. But this is a less accurate way of telling, especially for people addicted to alarm clocks and sleeping pills.

Our emotional, intellectual and spiritual conditions or moods are greatly affected by these physical cycles. Knowing them better will permit a greater harmonization of mind-body-spirit dimensions of experience. However, I have little faith in what are popularly called "Biorhythms." This system of computerized cycles of physical, emotional and mental conditions is based on some highly questionable research done in the 1880's by Wilhelm Fliess, whose sole claim to fame otherwise lay in being Freud's nose surgeon!

About as valid as newspaper horoscopes, "Biorhythm" charts may sometimes "work," but not because there is anything like a universal pattern of body cycles. Each person's biological rhythm is a complex series of patterns synchronized to their own biological clock, and the *only* way to find out what "time" you're on is to check it out empirically. Only *experience* can really supply the information you can use to integrate biological rhythms into a coherent lifestyle.

BIOFEEDBACK

A more sophisticated self-study and mastery is called biofeedback, which refers to the use of instruments which monitor various bodily systems and supply information that can be "fed back" to the systems consciously and alter them. The medical and psychological benefits of biofeedback have been tremendous with regard to persons suffering from migraine, heart problems, hyperactivity, epilepsy, Reynaud's disease, sexual dysfunctions, physical handicaps and other disorders. Significantly, once mastered, the relative control over various body systems is not dependent upon continual use of the monitors, but becomes a real skill.

Almost any system or subsystem in the body can be thus monitored and voluntarily controlled by biofeedback training under the supervision of competent medical personnel, including the so-called "autonomic" (i.e., "automatic") systems controlling heart rate, blood volume, muscular stress, acid secretion, circulation and nerve response, such as the perception of pain.

One of the most interesting areas of biofeedback research concerns the ability of people to learn to recognize and to control various rhythms of the brain. In non-medical applications, by learning to increase or decrease brain activity by shifting the modes of conscious attention, people can acquire control over processes that formerly took years to learn without accurate feedback. The use of biofeedback equipment in meditation training is therefore very promising, if somewhat expensive unless one belongs to a training center. Of course, biofeedback training has nothing directly to do with thought *content*, and the use to which it is put will vary with the attitudes of those who practice it.

"DEAUTOMATIZATION"

This tongue twister has been identified by researchers such as the psychiatrist, Dr. Arthur Deikman, as the central psychological function of the mystical experience. In some respects similar to the sensitization process of biofeedback training, deautomatization (or dishabituation) refers to breaking down automatic or habitual modes of perception, thinking and behavior and reinvesting them with attention. Typically, the exercises of mystical development, such as purgation, "mortification," meditation, and ascetical practices in general are meant to achieve this effect—to "cleanse the doors of perception," in Blake's phrase.

By deliberately suppressing our usual modes of living, feeling and thinking, such as we might experience more spontaneously on retreat or vacation, the world (ourselves included) can take on new beauty, new meaning, new adventure. For the mystic, who has again learned how to see, judge and act *freshly* by freeing himself of accumulated habits, creation appears in some of its original glory, and persons—as well as the transpersonal Field of all experience—are revealed in all their potential and loveliness.

Perhaps the easiest way to become "deautomatized" is to practice some kind of deprivation. Any kind of sensory deprivation, for instance, increases our sensitivity to what we have deprived ourselves: food, drink, sound, motion, sleep, companionship, sex, work, play—almost anything. But all the deprivations and abstinences are only the negative stage of a dialectical process which is radically positive, aimed at increasing our understanding and appreciation of the *mystery* of Creation and the Creative Love at the heart of it all.

Any detachment not undertaken for greater and purer attachment is thus an affront to the Creator and (to repeat) unspiritual and un-Christian!

TWO BRAINS, TWO MODES, TWO FUNCTIONS

Our understanding of the structure and operations of the human brain has probably increased more in the last 20 years than in the previous 2000. One of the most recent and exciting discoveries is that this vastly complex nerve center is *structurally a double system.* And with this discovery of the "bilateral brain" about 20 years ago came a new appreciation of *two kinds of mental experience* correlated to it (the "bicameral mind"). Research has also shown us that there are *two fundamental forms or "directions" of brain activity* which correspond to the ecstatic and contemplative modes of consciousness.

These discoveries are truly revolutionary. Their primary spiritual importance lies perhaps in their implication for meditation and life-style, and we will meet them again in due course. Here, it is sufficient to note that the *problem* of most previous spiritualities (and life in general) is that about half the processes and experiences of our nervous systems and minds were either ignored or discounted. Our ability to integrate our lives was thus hindered proportionately.

For almost all of us, our "left brain," which is connected to our "right brain" by a bundle of fibers called the *corpus callosum,* primarily attends to items of discrete verbal awareness—rational, linear, time-bound thought processes, "objects," logical relations, mathematical reasoning, etc. The "right brain" by contrast is largely non-verbal, dealing with spatial relations, holistic patterns, poetic and musical perceptions, intuitive, non-verbal processes, global awareness, and so on. Despite our cultural bias for "left brained" process, a "whole" person in fact utilizes both brains and both kinds of experience, combining intuition with logic, patterns with sequences, objects and contexts. Significantly, much "mystical" training, especially in the East, traditionally emphasized aspects of right brain consciousness and reality, not so much to deny left brain processes, but to develop the latent powers of the "minor" hemisphere. A truly holistic spirituality will always tend to coordinate the bilateral aspects of human experience, whether as a goal or a result.

The other relevant areas of brain research concern the mental correlates of certain brain states, or, rather, functions. As Deikman and others have shown, the "active" and "receptive" modes of awareness are based on physiological as well as psychological structures and operations. Thus, the mystical dialectic of action and contemplation is based on a biological rhythm subject to voluntary control. That is, it is neither an autonomous process nor a wholly spontaneous one. Again, however, the pressures of coping and competing in a stressful world have largely resulted in the suppression of the receptive, contemplative mode of consciousness and with it the restful, healthful aspect of a holistic lifestyle. For its own sake as a valuable experience, as well as its bodily and mental benefits, we have to relearn the art of contemplative meditation.

Finally, it is now fairly clear that the ecstatic and deeply contemplative states of consciousness associated with developed mystical lifestyles are themselves alternative *ranges* of consciousness coordinate with certain kinds of brain activity—either the extremely rapid, or the extremely slow. We can now understand better why the great mystics like Teresa of Avila and Ignatius of Loyola resisted ecstatic states and developed contemplative ones. For not only are these states incompatible, but the deepest state of human awareness, our most radically open attitude toward the mystery of reality, is much more surely achieved by the practice of contemplative meditation.

Genuine ecstasies can sometimes pass by a kind of "rebound effect" to the *samadhi*-like repose of a true contemplative master. But the physiological, psychological and spiritual demands are much more draining, and the whole process is fraught with physical, mental and spiritual risks. Not the least of these is confusing "brain-ecstasy"—the result of uncontrollable nervous activity—with the rapturous vision of God's presence.

NON-VERBAL SPIRITUAL EXPRESSION

When we turn to the practice of meditation, we shall again consider these aspects of the brain-mind-spirit process again. But how we evaluate these new approaches to an understanding of mysticism is connected with our general attitude toward embodiment—our somatic existence. Further, a large part of a holistic spiritual program must be devoted not only to recognizing the basis of our awareness in the body, but also to enhancing our ability to perceive and *express* our spiritual sensitivities and experiences through the body, especially nonverbally, as in dance, music, art, gardening, and play. These expressions of spirituality are far too important to relegate to "mere" recreation. To eliminate them from our lives puritanically as "distractions" or "vanities"—or worse yet, as sinful amusement—is itself a sin against bodily and indeed human integrity.

A PERSONAL CHECK-LIST

At this point, therefore, it might be useful to conclude with an attitude checklist: how *do* you feel about yourself bodily?

1. How do I feel when I look in the mirror at myself for a period of 3 or 4 minutes? What is my first reaction at seeing my own face?
2. How much care do I take to prevent illness? Am I aware of disease-causing attitudes in my lifestyle and behavior?
3. What would I change about my body if I could?
4. How do I feel about taking time for exercise? How much time per week do I devote to physical development?
5. How do I feel about bodily processes such as digestion, elimination, reproduction?
6. Do I consider bathing a regrettable necessity, a luxury or an occasion for personal care and reverence?
7. How do I look on cosmetics and adorning the body? (Using eyeshadow, lipstick, aftershave lotions, deodorants, hair transplants and wigs?)
8. How do I feel about bodily expression of emotional states and attitudes—dancing, singing, touching, hugging, kissing, shouting, hitting, etc.?
9. How do I regard the use of clothing and jewelry to adorn the body?
10. How do I feel about good grooming? How much time do I spend each day grooming myself?
11. What do the contents of my medicine cabinet tell me about myself?
12. Do I eat as a task or a celebration? When do I eat?
13. Am I eating well? How do I feel about the kind of food I take into my body? Am I aware of the facts of basic nutrition? Have I tried to integrate diet into lifestyle?

13. How do I feel about "ordinary" drugs—coffee, tea, alcohol?
14. What is my attitude toward "junk foods"? Ethnic foods? Do I enjoy finding out what and how other people cook and eat?

15. How do I regard the Christian doctrine about bodily resurrection?
16. How much sleep do I need? How much do I get?
17. What do I do on vacation?

SUGGESTIONS FOR FURTHER READING:

Barbara B. Brown, *New Mind, New Body,* New York: Harper and Row, 1974.

Arthur M. Deikman, "Deautomatization and the Mystic Experience." *Psychiatry*, Vol 29 (1966).

Gay Gaer Luce, *Body Time*, New York: Bantam Books, 1973.

Robert Ornstein, *The Psychology of Consciousness*, Baltimore: Pelican Books, 1975.

John A. T. Robinson, *The Body: A Study in Pauline Theology*, London: SCM Press, Ltd., 1952.

Chapter 6

MYSTICISM AND THE WORLD OF NATURE

> *Creation waits with eager longing for the revealing of the children of God; for the creation was subjected to futility, not of its own will, but by the will of him who subjected it to hope; because the creation itself will be set free from its bondage to decay and obtain the glorious liberty of the children of God.*
>
> Saint Paul

From its earliest remembered expression in the sacred Vedas of ancient India, the religious response to life which we call mysticism has acknowledged the special place of Nature, the natural world, in our experience of the presence of God. The biblical vision of the Near East has interpreted this relation as one of true encounter with God, mediated by what is not God, yet filled with his presence:

> The world is charged with the grandeur of God.
> It will flame out, like shining from shook foil;
> It gathers to a greatness. . . .
>
> From "God's Grandeur,"
> Gerard Manley Hopkins

When we speak of our perception of nature as Creation, we are acknowledging, however poetically, the theological principle underlying the Jewish, Christian and Islamic sense of God's primordial revelation to humankind. The natural world is the creative manifestation of God in time and matter. It is also our "habitat," the sacred environment in which we find ourselves most fundamentally in the living presence of God—the Garden of Eden, our "Paradise Lost." Part of the discipline required to regain that paradisiacal awareness of the natural world is the mystical purgation the poet William Blake described as "cleansing the doors of perception."

Today, the specific challenge presented to a mystical spirituality in terms of Nature stems from our contemporary attitude toward our natural environment, as well as that toward history and culture. For Nature has become a problem for modern humanity.

In this century, apparently for the first time in history, it has become possible to fulfill what many Christians have considered to be a divine command: to conquer and subdue the Earth as if it were an enemy (see Gen. 1:28). Nature has been stripped, gouged, exploited, ravaged and altered in vast and sometimes devastating ways—so much so that some scientists fear that we may well be close to triggering an ecological cataclysm. We are suffocating in industrial waste while simultaneously depleting irreplaceable resources. Hundreds of species of animals and plants face hopeless extinction at our hands. It is hard to think of such predation as what God had in mind when he made Man and Woman the gardeners of Eden.

Many people, especially those trapped in the urban "jungles" of our major cities, have very little if any contact with Nature as we commonly think of it: clean, running water, clear skies, fields of grass, flowers and grazing animals. Extreme poverty, cultural deprivation and the consequent lack of opportunity have conspired to prevent thousands of children in Chicago and New York, for instance, from ever seeing Lake Michigan or the Atlantic Ocean, much less the soaring mountains of the West, the rippling grain belt, the rolling hills of the Southland—except, perhaps, on television.

Why, we ask, should this be a problem? Aren't there parks and zoos and picture books as well as television?

The answer is complex, perhaps. But if the mystics are right, and Nature does mediate the presence of God in its own special way, then it is no more possible to experience God naturally through books and television programs *about* Nature than it is to encounter God personally by reading books about the lives of the saints. If mystical spirituality means anything, it means that first hand, direct experience is not only possible, but necessary if we are to know, love and serve God in this riotous world. Parks and zoos, gardens and game preserves are at best a compromise, if a highly important one. For it is in the *wilderness* that the salvation of the world is readied.

Today, we are perhaps more inclined than in the past to seek and find God's presence in social, interpersonal and introspective experience than in Nature, if only because our experience of Nature has become narrower and more limited than before. This attitude is reflected not only in our heartless and senseless exploitation of the environment, but also in a kind of antagonism on the part of professedly religious people—often those particularly committed to social justice—toward the natural world. Animals, especially pets, are scorned and forbidden; plastic plants and flowers and mere pictures of animals increasingly replace the more demanding "live" ones in convents, rectories, monasteries and schools. Flowers and even lawns are becoming rare around religious establishments. It is increasingly hard to find Nature itself in such places, and, I fear, the God of Nature as well.

In Catholic Christianity, the most naturalistic Western religious tradition (excepting Native American religions), "rogation days" have all but vanished from memory. A positive religious attitude toward Nature has survived in some ceremonial activities such as the blessing of crops and fishing boats. But such celebrations are becoming increasingly rare as well as commercialized in places where they do survive.

All this is to say that if experience can be described, as William Hocking did, as a triadic relationship of the Self, the World and Other Selves, grounded in a divine Field of reference, then by eliminating or restricting one of these elements, our experience of God will be proportionately obscured. This is, I believe, exactly what has happened in the West since the rise of Cartesian thought and the Industrial Revolution. The *natural* dimension of religious experience has been increasingly reduced, and, whether as a result or a contributing factor, Nature itself has increasingly become prey to ruthless exploitation.

The "It" or Worldly dimension of the "I-It-Thou" relationship refers to *both* Nature and Society—all the institutions and human relations not characterized by "I-*Thou*" awareness. It is not surprising, then, as our awareness of Nature as a medium of divine and human encounter has declined, that the balance of our I-Thou and I-It relations has also become tilted, as Buber witnessed 20 years after Hocking's pioneering work. That is, with the degradation of our *natural* experience of God, our social, interpersonal and introspective experience of God has been proportionately disturbed. A closer look into the *mysterion* of Nature might help us understand this problematic situation.

THE GOD OF CREATION

St. Paul, echoing the primal experience of the race, stated simply in his letter to the Roman Christians: "What can be known about God is plain . . ., because God has revealed it. . . . Ever since the creation of the world his invisible nature, namely his eternal power and deity, have been clearly perceived in the things that have been made" (Rom. 1:19-20).

All ancient religious traditions first conceived of God in terms of Nature, only slowly humanizing those ideas, and, only in the advanced forms, coming to realize that all such notions are still radically inadequate. Yet the thought that God was present *in* Nature, if not identifiable *with* Nature, persisted in even the most advanced of all religious traditions, at least until the modern era.

God was spoken of in terms of fire, thunder and storm; as a rock of salvation and of destruction; as a mighty flood and a gentle rainfall. His brilliance and power were found in the sun and the stars. Animate creation also gave us conceptual "handles" by which to grasp this elusive Presence, often active in our experience: sturdy and enduring as the great cedars of Lebanon, beautiful as flowers and fields, fierce like the lion, strong like the bull and bear, wise as the serpent—even wiser.

Humankind gave perhaps the most enduring character to the concept of God—just, loving, vengeful; of mighty arm and warlike valor; jealous, forgiving, ironic. Like earthly kings, God had his court, his courtiers and his laws; messengers, plans and secrets. He made war and peace, governing the cosmos wisely and well. He called human beings not only to serve and worship him, but to be his friends and companions. Alliances were made and remade; sometimes, marriage.

Accordingly, human beings related to the God they first so dimly perceived in storm and drought, volcanic upheaval, earthquake, flood and prosperity. Sacrifices of food, of crops and animals were offered to appease, to cajole, to honor. Even human life, so precious and valuable, was offered in sacrifice—whether in bloody ritual or ethical dedication.

Not all of this awareness was lost as Nature increasingly became more the plaything of man than the haunt of God. In the ancient traditions, water, oil and bread, salt, wine, wax and milk, flowers, incense and branches were consecrated for use as instruments, *media* of God's commerce with his creatures. The sacraments are necessarily material signs, Thomas Aquinas tells us, because human beings are of the earth, fleshly. And in their use, creation is again hallowed where it had been desecrated. But for those who can see, all water is holy water. . . .

Theologians, looking back on this rich and sometimes bloody history, have been able to perceive patterns or levels of our awareness of God's presence in creation, in Nature. He is present and active, as Paul insisted, sustaining everything that is. Julian of Norwich saw that all God made, he loved, even though it were no more than the quantity of a hazelnut in the palm of his hand. And because he loved it, he kept it. God is first present, then, in *power,* but invisibly—manifesting himself in ways our senses can barely fathom.

God was more clearly perceived in *life,* that mysterious quality of plants and animals expressed in movement, growth and fertility. Animals were more alive, and therefore more holy, than plants—they were made totems as well as privileged sacrificial victims. And life was in the blood, which therefore belonged especially to God. Pouring out blood was consecration, an act of power, immediately invoking God's presence. Shed blood, such as that of the Paschal Lamb, gave protection from the angel of death. The blood of Christ, bringing eternal life, streams through the universe, as Marlowe said in *Dr. Faustus.* Human blood, human life, is the most sacred of all. It is in our relation to God as humanly alive, breathing the breath of God, that we are created *ruach, pneuma, spiritus:* "breath." We are created spirit by being made in the image and likeness of God, who breathed upon the waters and into the clay. We are spirit because we are created in the presence of God, open to receiving and transmitting life.

Yet another level of presence is found in *grace*—God's free giving of his own life to us, our share in his spirit. This is "original" grace, sanctifying grace. We are graced with God's presence in special ways throughout life, in addition: the "actual" graces of individual situations, the "charismatic" graces of special purposes. We are told, moreover, that grace, God's personal presence to us, may come in the guise of material support and favor. Similarly, it is structured and shaped by sacramental signs, concretely for life's major needs.

In all these manifold ways, the God of Creation becomes manifest within our experience, dimly or clearly as we are made less or more sensitive to that presence, as we learn again to "see." Furthermore, it is in discovering the reality *within our experience* of what the theologians have discerned that we mark the boundary, or rather, the transition, from theology to spirituality, the *practice* of the presence of God.

MYSTERION
THE EXPERIENCE OF GOD IN CREATION

The connection between mystical spirituality and the world of Nature has, we can safely assume, a contemporary aspect only slightly different from its more "classical" context. In the Jewish-Christian tradition, Nature was frequently and obviously a vehicle or medium for the *experience* of God's presence. We read of Abraham and the moving torch among the slaughtered beasts and stars; of Moses and the burning bush; Elijah's "still, small voice" after the tornado; the Holy One appearing in the form of a dove and of tongues of fire. St. Francis of Assisi has reminded us for seven centuries of the dignity and greatness of animals. St. Martin de Porres echoed him. We recall St. Hubert and his deer, Don Bosco and his dog, and the anchoresses' cat in the *Ancrene Riwle.*

There was John of the Cross in his secret glen, Richard Rolle in his forest, the Fathers (and Mothers) of the Desert, Jesus on the mountain, by the sea, in the garden. At one time or another, almost all the great and little mystics have perceived and celebrated the presence of God in its natural setting.

Similarly, in the thousands of case histories in the file of the Religious Experience Research Unit at Oxford, founded by the great zoologist, Sir Alister Hardy, I have read of instance after instance of a person being moved to *realize* the unifying presence of God by means of a single blade of grass, a flower, a sunset atop the Great Orme's Head in northern Wales, a suffering cat, a dying fish leaping upward against the blazing Moroccan sky, the stars that one night "sang," an aged dog's loyalty. Often people have described experiences of intense spiritual awareness coming upon them while standing quietly in a glade or on the shore, walking amidst a cloud of Wordsworth's golden daffodils.

Sometimes, people recount experiences of a sudden transformation of their surroundings, as if they were suffused with light, or experience *each* leaf on a tree, *every* grain of sand on the beach or snow crystal on the field, thrilling to the particularity of what was, an instant before, a blur of green or gold or white.

PAN-EN-HENIC VERSUS PAN-EN-THEISTIC EXPERIENCE

Are such experiences of the unity of all things, even in their atomistic particularity, *also* an experience of the presence of God? To put it another way, is a "natural" mystical experience capable of mediating the presence of God, even if God is not recognized *as* God for some reason?

More conservative writers, such as R. C. Zaehner, insist that such natural experiences—what he calls "pan-en-henic" or "all-is-one-ish" (from the Greek)—are not only distinct from but different from the authentic experience of God known by the great mystics. This is because "ultimate" Reality *excludes* all non-ultimate realities in this view. "This means a total and absolute detachment from Nature, an isolation of the soul within itself either to realize itself as 'God,' or to enter into communion with God. The exclusion of all we normally call Nature is the *sine qua non* of this type of mystical experience . . ." (*Mysticism Sacred and Profane,* p. 33). Passages from the *Cloud of Unknowing* in which the author enjoins his followers to put all things ever created under a cloud of forgetting might be interpreted along the same lines.

On the other hand, "liberal" authorities such as William James, Teilhard de Chardin, William Ernest Hocking and writers of the temper of Aldous Huxley and Nikos Kazantzakis would insist with equal force that there is *no* pure and absolute experience of God apart from some medium of consciousness. All our experience is *mediated,* but the intermediaries, as Hocking would say, can be rendered "transparent." This, in fact, is the art or skill of mystical awareness. If so, it is not only impossible to detach ourselves from Nature in any real sense in order to experience God "alone," but in attempting to do so, we risk *losing* contact with the God of Creation.

The mystical poets, certainly, would not agree with Zaehner. In Blake's "Auguries of Innocence," for instance, we find the sentiment stated, as it were, once for all:

To see a World in a grain of sand,
And Heaven in a wild flower,
Hold Infinity in the palm of your hand.
And Eternity in an hour . . .

Similarly, Francis Thompson, whose most famous analog of God was the "Hound of Heaven," magnificently wrote in "The Mistress of Vision,"

'When to the new eyes of thee
All things by immortal power,
Near or far,
Hiddenly
To each other linked are,
That thou canst not stir a flower
Without troubling of a star;
. . . seek no more,
O seek no more!'

Such a vision has rightly been called "pan-en-theistic," a term apparently coined by Friedrich von Hügel to convey the sense of God's presence *in* but not identity *with* Nature. (*Pantheism*, by contrast, would imply the identity of God and Nature, a charge brought against Meister Eckhart and Spinoza, for instance.)

To the "panentheist," which is to say, the mystic, the God of our inner awareness is not different from the transcendent God we discover in the world of Nature or of History, much less the God we encounter in our interpersonal relations of love and justice. Rather, it is the identity of God as we discover him present in all three dimensions of experience that grounds our perception of unity, that All is One. And it is because All is One in the depths of existence that *any* element of our experience can be a medium of our becoming aware of God's presence. God's presence in Nature has special importance for us, however—one that finds its meaning and complement in our social and interpersonal experience. A still closer look will help explain.

SPIRITUALITY AND PETS

Undoubtedly, one of the most sensitive and thus instructive areas of discussion regarding Nature and spirituality concerns the place of personal pets. During feudal times, when animal pets were the playthings of the aristocracy, disdain for them among religious writers might be understandable. In fact, there seems to be none. Then, as always, human destiny was inevitably tied up with animals as companions and even as moral analogs, as witnessed in literature from Aesop's fables to Dick Whittington's cat up to Black Beauty, Lassie and Ring of Bright Water. Merchant or peasant, beggar or princess—pets, especially dogs, have had an affectionate as well as useful place in the human order of things.

Pets, like house plants, are our primary source of ordinary contact with Nature. If the mystics are right, and this contact is a special medium of our awareness of God, then we should find it pre-eminently in the pet world. Far from being a substitute for or a distraction from divine or human concerns, pets have an important capacity of humanizing and divinizing our experience. Far from degrading us, the cultivation of plant and animal "friends" ennobles us by activating our sense of creative concern and responsibility as well as giving us *joy.*

Pets humanize us by relating us inescapably to the world of Nature, to which we belong, if not wholly. We, too, are animals, and in our wholly animal friends we find something of ourselves, something humble and innocent. But as our association inevitably reveals (and Genesis 2:18-25 reminds us), no animal can ever fully satisfy the longing of the human heart for companionship. Only other persons can—both human and, ultimately, divine. By their limitations, animals remind us of our need for others.

Our care for pets, which is immediate and direct, as well as our general concern for wildlife and wilderness areas, also reminds us of our divine task as God's stewards. Our creative "management" of the natural world reminds us that we are made to *operate* in his image and likeness. We are, as Hocking said, "apprentices in creativity." Sir Alister Hardy observes that our relationship to the natural world of animals, and theirs to us, especially that of dogs, provides the closest analogy to our relationship with God.

The dog, unlike any other animal, transfers its pack-allegiance from one of its own kind to a human being while still a pup. This biological anomaly finds its only known correlative in the human love of and devotion to God. Hardy, an eminent biologist as well as authority on religious experience, cites both Francis Bacon and, more to the point, Baron von Hügel: Dogs, he wrote, "require their fellow dogs, the shallow and clear, but they also require us, the deep and dim; they indeed require what they can grasp; but they as really require what they can but reach out to, more or less—what exceeds, protects, envelops, directs them."

Further, "if God be real, then this Reality, as superhuman, *cannot possibly* be clearer to us than are the realities, and the real qualities of these realities, which we have been considering. The source and object of religion, if religion be true and its object be real, *cannot,* indeed, *by any possibility, be as clear to me as I am to my dog*" (*Essays and Addresses,* pp. 102-103).

Hardy's analysis is much more detailed, following the evolutionary history of the dog's choice of man as, in Bacon's sense, his God. Hardy's conclusion, well worth pondering, is a tribute not so much to canine devotion, as to the integrity of Nature and the widsom of God: "The relationship of man to what he calls God is a biological one, in just the same sense that the association of the dog with man is a biological one. This is what I mean when I speak of the biology of God; *this* is what my book is about. What we call God must be related to man who, in turn, is very much a part of the organic system. That is why, to my way of thinking, the behavioral relation of the dog to man is not just an illustrative analogy; it is a clear demonstration that the same biological factors, resulting from the same kind of social development (that of the pack), have become involved in the formation of man's images of God" (*The Biology of God,* pp. 169-70).

HUMAN DEVELOPMENT, THERAPY AND PETS

More concretely yet, the importance of pets in spiritual, as well as in psychological growth and healing, has been cited by several eminent scientists. Dr. Boris M. Levinson, in his book *Pet-Oriented Child Psychotherapy,* argues demonstratively that "contact with the inanimate and particularly the animate world via the pet is most important to a wholesome emotional development" (p. XIV).

A summary statement from Levinson's *Pets and Human Development* is worth quoting in this regard: "A child exposed to the emotional experiences inherent in playing with a pet is given many learning opportunities that are essential to wholesome personality development. His play with the pet will express his view of the world, its animals, and its human beings, including his parents and peers. Further, through play with the pet, the child may learn to resolve some of the problems of relating to his peers and of achieving a wholesome balance of dependence and independence with regard to his family" (pp. 78).

The power of pets to evoke true humanity in their "owners" suggests that a child prevented from having pets during its formative years has been deprived of a privileged developmental guide. I am convinced that a healthy attitude toward Nature and Nature's God, as well as other persons and society in general, can only be enhanced by the proper handling of pets, as early in life as possible, as well as care for plants and the environment in general. Dr. Ashley Montagu remarks succinctly in his masterful book on tactility: "Interestingly enough child-battering and abusing parents, who were themselves neglected and abused as children, rarely report having had a childhood pet" (*Touching,* p. 279).

The power of pets to enhance development indicates their equal, perhaps greater ability to heal. Traditionally, "well-wishers" have given plants and flowers to patients recovering from illness or surgery. Similarly, persons recuperating from serious illness or surgery are greatly assisted by the presence of pets. The type of pet is less important than its presence—dogs, cats, birds, goldfish, gerbils and hamsters, among others, have demonstrated the basic capacity to heal. That power resides in the mutual care and attention exchanged, however passively, by person and pet, whose non-threatening availability provides a passage back into the social world by gradual stages. The pet becomes a medium of human (and, I believe, divine) love and trust at a time when the recovering patient is too vulnerable and weak to endure the full effort and risk of reaching out to other persons. This is especially true in custodial institutions. Dr. Montagu reports that in an experiment conducted at Ohio State University with institutionalized patients ranging from adolescents to the aged and infirm, pet therapy succeeded where human therapy had failed.

The use of pets, particularly dogs, in psychotherapy is now a well-established, if unfortunately infrequent, practice. Pet therapy has succeeded in helping both children and adults, whether emotionally disturbed, retarded or delinquent. In a recent issue of the *British Journal of Psychiatry* (133:550-555), Dr. E. K. Rynearson of Seattle's Mason Clinic reported that animal pets may be of crucial importance in therapy for patients who have lost trust in human persons. Schizophrenic patients as well as disturbed children have shown marked improvement when their therapy has been assisted by the presence of their pets.

Boris Levinson urges increased use of pets in day schools for both normal and exceptional children as well as in nursing homes. For patients in such facilities, "pets can satisfy vital emotional needs by helping these patients to hold on to the world of reality, of productive activity, and of intense emotional relationships. Through the assurance that the pets they care for love them in return, an image of themselves as worthwhile persons can be restored to nursing home patients. Through the activity involved in caring for pets, the physical health of aged people can also be improved and deterioration retarded" (*Pets and Human Development,* pp. 204-05).

MAN'S (AND WOMAN'S) BEST FRIENDS

Francis Thompson, like Sir Alister Hardy and Francis Bacon, Boris Levinson and Friedrich von Hügel, Drs. Montagu and Rynearson, and thousands of recovered patients, not to mention millions upon millions of people everywhere and at all times, knew well that the image and likeness of the humble dog was more than an apt metaphor for the love and fidelity of God. Far from sentimentality, in the man-dog relation, we catch a glimmer of the God-man relation. But only a glimmer. For if a human person is the dog's God, God is much more to humanity. In God we have the real possibility of friendship and thus of *equality,* of divinization. No man ever became a dog. . . .

Nature, then, in general—and as specifically as your goldfish—is a sacrament of God's presence. All we need to do is learn—or, rather, *re*-learn—how to see, feel and understand.

The next time you are at a loss for a meditative concern, try dwelling on the miracle of the *mouse*—still enough to stagger ten thousand infidels: the wonder of that tiny brain, its central nervous system, that powerful, fluttering heart, the keen eyes and sensitive ears, the harmony of that system of systems which glorifies God in every instant of its being. God loves you through that diminutive creature.

MYSTERION

SUGGESTIONS FOR FURTHER READING

Conrad Bonifaci, *A Theology of Things,* Philadelphia: J. B. Lippincott and Co., 1967.

Matthew Fox, *Whee! We wee All the Way Home . . . A Guide to the New Sensual Spirituality,* Wilmington, N.C.: Consortium Press, 1976.

Alister Hardy, *The Biology of God,* New York: Taplinger Publishing Co., 1976.

______, *The Divine Flame,* Oxford: The Religious Experience Research Unit, 1978.

Boris Levinson, *Pet-Oriented Child Psychotherapy,* Springfield, Ill.; Charles C. Thomas, 1969.

______, *Pets and Human Development,* Springfield, Ill.: Charles C. Thomas, 1972.

Ashley Montagu, *Touching: The Human Significance of the Skin,* New York: Harper and Row (second ed.), 1978.

R. C. Zaehner, *Mysticism Sacred and Profane,* New York: Oxford University Press, 1961.

Chapter 7

MYSTICISM AND PARAPSYCHOLOGY

From the earliest recorded instances of what we now call mysticism in ancient India and Greece, mystical experience and psychic phenomena have been closely associated in the popular as well as the religious mind. The same is true of the occult with regard to both these dimensions of the human experience. Yet I am convinced that despite some shared elements, mystical, psychic and occult experiences and phenomena are radically different.

To begin with, if by the occult we mean the magical arts, astrology, witchcraft, divination, necromancy and the like, neither mysticism nor parapsychology (by which I mean the scientific study of psychic experiences) has much to do with occultism. (Strictly speaking, *occult* merely means "hidden" or "mysterious," something not evident.) Mysticism, once again, refers to the direct and immediate experience of God in human consciousness, or, more simply, the practice of the presence of God, together, as William Ernest Hocking would say, with the theory of that practice.

Taken in the sense of a lifestyle centered on the awareness of God's presence, mysticism is an extension of the ordinary forms of religious experience, particularly that of worship. It is not in itself exotic, extraordinary or "paranormal." Nevertheless, in Christian mysticism as in that of other religious traditions, there often occur extraordinary events or experiences, especially in the lives of the great mystic saints. Some of these phenomena are similar to or even identical with the events and experiences now increasingly studied by scientists and philosophers under the categories of extrasensory perception (ESP) and psychokinesis (PK).

What is the significance of this connection? To answer this, we have to try to understand the place of the paranormal in ordinary human experience, religious and otherwise. We also have to have some idea of what we mean by parapsychology and psychical research. Equipped with even a minimal understanding of these areas of human inquiry, we will be better able to understand mysticism, for they have contributed significantly to its study. Further, we will be less likely to confuse essentially distinct forms of experience merely because they share some common features.

THE SCIENCE OF THE PARANORMAL

As formal disciplines, psychical research and parapsychology are not yet a century old. The Society for Psychical Research (SPR) was founded in England in 1882. The American Society for Psychical Research (ASPR) was established three years later. These first groups were composed of scientists and philosophers intent upon a truly scientific investigation of paranormal phenomena such as clairvoyance and post-mortem apparitions.

Perhaps the most prestigious body of its kind in the world, the SPR included among its early members William James and Sigmund Freud. James served as president in 1894-95. Other illustrious presidents were Lord Balfour, Sir William Crookes, Sir Oliver Lodge, Sir William Barrett, Charles Richet, Henri Bergson, Lord Rayleigh, William McDougall, Hans Driesch, G. N. M. Tyrrell, Gardner Murphy, S. G. Soal, Sir Alister Hardy, Dr. John Beloff and Prof. A. J. Ellison. In all, three Nobel prize winners, ten Fellows of the Royal Society, a Prime Minister, and, as Arthur Koestler remarked, a "galaxy" of professors of physics, psychology and philosophy.

In this century, other professional societies were formed in the U.S. such as the Parapsychology Foundation (1951), the Parapsychological Association (1957) the Psychical Research Foundation (1960) and the Foundation for Research on the Nature of Man (1962). Several major universities have departments or divisions of parapsychology, both here and abroad. In 1969, the Parapsychological Association was admitted to the American Academy for the Advancement of Science amidst heated debate, some of which still continues.

Parapsychology and psychical research are not entirely the same. Parapsychology represents an effort to subject psychic phenomena and other paranormal occurrences to precise observation and even experimentation, usually in a laboratory where strict controls can be enforced. In this respect, parapsychology is a kind of hybrid between experimental psychology and physics.

Psychical research, on the other hand, refers to a much larger field of inquiry and a wider methodological spectrum. In this respect, psychical research is more like natural history or ethnography than laboratory experimentation. Occasionally, it is a little like detective work, and because of its romantic treatment in the media, tends to be considered somewhat unscientific by professional scientists. Strictly speaking, psychical research is like any kind of original research. It is explorative, inquisitive and flexible. But it is no less scientific when properly conducted than laboratory experimentation. In some respects it is even more valuable and heuristic.

Paranormal is a word coined rather recently to indicate certain events or experiences which are considered by their observers or participants to be "beyond" or "aside from" normal events and experiences, that is, those of ordinary, everyday perception and behavior. Unlike "abnormal" or "subnormal," *paranormal* does not imply pathology, inferiority or even the supernatural.

By definition, then, paranormal experiences are those which are extraordinary or unusual in that they depart from our ordinary understanding of causality but are not supernatural or harmful. Infrequency is not a defining characteristic, although we can assume that paranormal incidents will not be frequent, despite their commonness. On a statistical basis, they can happen to anyone at any time.

Like any experience, paranormal events have multiple dimensions. It is important to know, for instance, whether the paranormal aspect is a quality of perception, of the appearance of the phenomenon, or of the transaction between them. An altered state of consciousness, like rapture or a clairvoyant experience, is not paranormal in the same sense that sighting a UFO or the Loch Ness Monster might be.

In the present context, the word "paranormal" will be employed primarily to refer to the subjective aspect of experience—perception and behavior. We will not be concerned with "objective" phenomena such as UFOs, Abominable Snowpersons, or the Bermuda Triangle, despite their possible reality.

COMPARATIVE MYSTICISM: PARANORMALITIES

Some insight into the possible significance of paranormal experience for both mysticism and parapsychology has resulted from comparative investigations such as Dr. Lawrence LeShan's pioneering work *The Medium, the Mystic and the Physicist.* LeShan's work concerned the remarkable similarities of worldview shared by traditional mystics of East and West, psychics such as Eileen Garrett and contemporary subatomic and astrophysicists, from Einstein to Heisenberg.

Among the more significant areas of agreement were the perception of the universe as an integrated whole and the relativity of space, time, matter and energy. Thus, one function of paranormal experience can be to awaken us to dimensions of reality we tend not to see because of our customary, unexamined presuppositions about the nature of things.

Experience itself provides important information about psychic and mystic capabilities. Recent studies seem to indicate that in terms of mental processes, at least four kinds of people can be linked together: psychics, artists, mystics and schizophrenic patients. Together with the nuclear physicists and other scientists, this assembly provides a rich resource for investigation, to say the least, but hasty generalizations should be avoided. However, a few hints concerning the place and value of paranormal experience in human life can be obtained from a careful reading of the studies presently available.

Several years ago, Dr. Frank Barron reported that artists and schizophrenic patients both tended to score highly with regard to "abnormal" experiences on conventional personality inventories. In fact, they tended to have the same *kind* of experiences, including definite instances of ESP and other psychic events. The major difference between the artists and the schizophrenic patients lay in the ability of the former group to *integrate* these experiences into a coherent life-pattern.

About the same time, another researcher, Dr. Kenneth Wapnick, published a striking account of the structural similarities of mystical experience and schizophrenia, observed in terms of a developmental process.

Wapnick indicated that from a psychiatric perspective, the content of the experiences of mystics and "mad" persons tend to approximate each other. But structurally, the mystic's development is organized and even systematic, while the schizophrenic patient's is aimless and chaotic. In some respects, many schizophrenic persons may well be disintegrated or unintegrated mystics. Conversely, mystics are persons who are preserved from fragmentation by the force of what are truly schizoid experiences (for example, the "Dark Night of the Soul"), by the strength of their personal integrity, which is simultaneously mental, emotional and physical, and both individual and social. Their "identity" is secure because they have anchored it not in their own precarious existence, but deep in the "ground" of their being, God. Further, for both the mystic and the artist, a community and tradition seem to have a crucial role to play in preserving integrity, while the schizophrenic patient has weak social ties.

Again, it is a fact of observable record that both mystics and madpersons report various psychic experiences, which, like many others, resemble those of the artist group in Barron's study. Their remarks or impressions concerning the cosmos are also similar and no less baffling to the "ordinary mind" than the physicists' accounts of black holes, quarks and quasars. It should not be overlooked that many psychotic patients report religious events of tremendous personal significance to them, such as visions and revelations, voices and the like. Many claim to be directly in touch with God, or to be one with him.

One way of relating these types of experience in terms of common factors is to see them as forming a continuum of levels or degrees of brain activity—the approach of the noted psychoneurologist, Dr. Roland Fischer. Fischer observed that it is possible to arrange various mental states progressively in terms of increasing or decreasing levels of brain activity, beginning with ordinary waking consciousness. Problem-solving and creativity show a manifest increase of brain-wave frequency, followed by states of anxiety, artistic inspiration, schizophrenic or other psychotic episodes and, finally, mystical rapture. (Psychic experience is not represented in this scheme.) Schizophrenia, significantly, represents a kind of "jamming," in which the rate of sensory-motor "input" exceeds the possibility of mental "processing."

The mystic's ecstasy represents a breakthrough experience in which the brain, as it were, goes into a higher gear, resulting in a kind of mental "overdrive." The outside world vanishes from consciousness, as awareness shifts wholly to the interior process. Further, the ecstatic state cannot last long, for, as in the case of an epileptic seizure, which it resembles, the nervous system cannot long endure so great an expenditure of energy. (Some forms of epilepsy, by the way, could thus be considered a kind of rapture frustrated by a physiological impairment of the brain.) Ordinarily, the mystical rapture is transformed into a trance state of very *low* brain activity, almost a form of sleep.

The same state of intensely peaceful psychophysiological "rest" can be achieved by deliberately attempting to *decrease* the level of brain activity from that of ordinary waking consciousness. This route is traditionally that of meditative contemplation, culminating in the state of utter tranquillity of spirit called *samadhi* in the East. If not identical to the "prayer of quiet" in Western spirituality, it is approximate.

Importantly, in this respect, psychical experiences, such as clairvoyance, telepathy, precognition and levitation are as likely to occur in moments of rapture as well as of trance, and in both extremes, consciousness of the world vanishes. Only Zen Buddhism seems to have elaborated a contemplative style of meditation in which the meditator stays closely in touch with the physical environment while attaining states of deepest tranquillity. But even Zen acknowledges moments of rapture when enlightenment *(satori)* is attained. And some forms of meditation, especially those cultivated in the tantric traditions of India and Tibet, appear to have been developed precisely to engender certain psychic experiences.

SENSORY SELECTIVITY

Another way of approaching extraordinary experience stems from a brilliant insight of the philosopher Henri Bergson, which has been expanded and developed by C. D. Broad and others. Bergson, who was keenly interested in mysticism, suggested that our ordinary senses are not "windows" onto the world, but rather, shutters or filters that screen out the world except for a very meager but essential bit of information required for immediate utility. Thus, the eye does not so much "let in" electromagnetic waves of a particular length but keeps all others out.

Bergson's point recognized the fact that we are continually bombarded with light and sound waves and other sources of information which, as a whole, are useless for survival or anything else. We have to learn to discriminate by shutting out unwanted information. Similarly, our memories and thoughts have to be limited by forgetting and concentration so as to free us to accomplish particular tasks. Our minds must restrict available information to a minimum, including, perhaps, vast amounts of telepathic or clairvoyant communication. But occasionally they break through. This would especially be the case in moments of mental relaxation such as sleep or meditation, when we attempt to revert to the "whole."

Still another way of dealing with the common elements of experience is based on more recent studies of the bilateral functions of the human brain and the "bicameral" nature of human consciousness. "Right-brain" activity (as we have seen before) is not less conscious than "left-brain" functions, but less able to be verbalized. These right-brain functions tend to be more intuitive, musical, poetic, pattern-sensitive, global, etc. Many of the experiences corresponding to these brain functions are not "translated" into left-brain modes of awareness and thus remain inexpressible or, in the classical term, ineffable.

The right brain may therefore be aware of many aspects of reality that we do not normally "recognize"—for instance, qualities of the universe itself, instances of telepathic communication, the presence of God. We might have faint "hunches," intimations or "presentiments," as we once called them, but our left-brain tendency is to discount them. However, in dreams, meditation and altered states of consciousness such as ecstasies, visions and auditory "hallucinations," these dimensions of experience may suddenly flood into left-brain consciousness. This would especially seem to be the case with urgent or impressive information such as disasters, danger to loved ones or solutions to problems. Then, the force of the information or feeling overcomes our psychophysiological "censor."

This "filtering" function of the brain-mind may well have developed as Bergson surmised, and Freud and Julian Jaynes later proposed, to enable human beings to adapt to immediate situations requiring specific, limited information. Interestingly, in the Bible as in the parapsychology laboratory, dreams remain the most common form of extrasensory perception, especially precognitive experiences.

A similar case can be made for PK phenomena such as healing—or its reverse, harming or cursing, as in the legendary "evil eye." Our minds may well harbor incredible stores of power which can affect the material environment directly. But as with extrasensory perception, we ordinarily suppress the operations at some primordial level of the psyche—a "skill" we perhaps acquired at a primeval stage of human evolution, again because of the unpredictability of such powers, their erratic nature and the precise demands of the immediate situations on muscle and bone.

These unusual powers of obtaining information or affecting the material environment could conceivably be expected to operate in the lives of the mystics, especially the greater ones, as a function of their greater integrity and openness. They could also be activated in someone accidentally, when the censoring function was impaired or suspended. In the first case, the effect of the mystic's experiences would probably conform to her or his overall attitude and disposition. But in the second instance, almost anything could happen, and sometimes seems to in the lives of psychics and mediums who have not developed a general moral or religious orientation to life which could safely guide such powers. (The films *Carrie* and *The Fury* deal rather sensationally with such possibilities.) The former instance can be illustrated by the life of St. Catherine of Siena, according to her biographer, Raymond of Capua. He tells artlessly but not uncritically, that inanimate objects "obeyed" her, that she healed diseases, "read hearts," and knew future happenings at times. But all of these events were integrated into a lifestyle of intense single-mindedness.

MYSTICISM AND PSYCHIC POWER

These hypotheses share a fundamental belief that all of us

apparently have access to unlimited realms of information and efficacy that we ordinarily—appropriately—do not utilize. We know as a fact that people suddenly experience these realms of meaning and power, whether by accident or design. The mystics do so perhaps more readily than anyone, including many psychics. This may be because of the greater integration of their personalities and their greater openness to experience. We don't know. But what seems to be the case is that whether it is rapture and ecstasies on one hand, or visions, "locutions," "touches," prophetic (i.e., precognitive) awareness and healing abilities on the other, the mystics *typically* discount these events even while performing them, and sometimes actually resist them.

The biography of St. Ignatius of Loyola recounts that he learned to avoid ecstatic prayer because it kept him from the necessary work of his destiny. Similarly, Teresa of Avila and St. Joseph of Cupertino sometimes vainly resisted being levitated during prayer. The author of *The Cloud of Unknowing* cautions against taking any physical sensations as signs of God's presence or favor.

In many instances, it seems that the mystics oppose these powers or "gifts" for reasons of humility. They attract too much attention to the mystic and distract people from the more important gifts of love, justice, reform and compassion, and from the mystic's *message.*

What the mystics do not say, at least in most cases, is that these powers and their employment are evil or wrong. Their place in the mystic scheme of things may in fact be very important. But their importance lies in their utility in building up God's kingdom, not in drawing attention to their possessors, who, like all human beings, are susceptible to vanity and egoism. This is true of both Eastern and Western traditions. It is one thing to have such experiences and quite another to seek them. Such gifts are thus regarded as dangerous, not so much physically, but morally and especially spiritually. Seeking them is a form of distraction, an illusion and a kind of idolatry. For the ultimate objective of all true mysticism is union with God and only that. Everything else is only a means to that end or a consequence of it.

VARIETIES OF PSYCHICAL EXPERIENCE

The paranormal phenomena studied by psychical researchers and parapsychologists can be roughly categorized in two main divisions, here following the approach of Dr. J. B. Rhine. There are perceptual phenomena or ESP and motor phenomena or PK.

Extrasensory perception is perhaps too extreme a term, however, for the experience is always mediated by ordinary modes of sensory awareness. Thus, some writers prefer the term "quasi-sensory" experience. Basically, both refer to information about persons or events acquired by means other than direct and immediate sensory perception. There is usually a dimension of separation or distance involved, whether spatial or temporal.

We can indicate here some major types of ESP:

1. *Clairvoyance* and other "sentient" experience—seeing, hearing, etc., at a distance, that is, without independently verifiable objects at hand. It usually involves mind-object cognition or awareness. It may also be a simple sensation of warmth or chill indicating an event or "presence."
2. *Precognition* and *retrocognition.* These terms refer to knowledge of future or past events without recourse to sources of information such as records of the past or inferences based upon present observation or knowledge.
3. *Telepathy* refers to mind-mind contact, rather than mind-object or object-mind contact, as in psychometry.
4. *Out-of-the-body-experiences* (OOBE's). Called "traveling clairvoyance" in the 19th century, OOBE's refer to the experience of apparently leaving one's body and "traveling" some distance from it, often seeing the body itself remaining "behind" in a state of sleep or stupor. Bilocation may be a form of OOBE.

5. *Apparitions:* the visual (or auditory, or audio-visual) experience of a departed (or sometimes living) person, such as a relative, friend, a saint, etc.
6. *Psychometry:* the ability to intuit information about a person or event by contact with something once in that person's possession or at the scene of the event. In some respects this resembles the awareness of the presence of relics or other holy objects by saints, demoniacs, and so on.
7. *Celestial Music:* For centuries known as the "music of the spheres" or "the song of the angels," people have heard sounds which can range from a simple humming to a full "orchestra" of unearthly instruments. A type of the former can be found in the writings of Rosalind Heywood, and the latter in Michael Whiteman's *The Mystical Life.*

The second class of paranormal or psychic experiences include instances of psychokinesis—the ability to influence material objects by the mind alone, sometimes at a great distance (telekinesis). We can classify instances in terms of the objects:

1. *Effect on stationary or moving objects:* causing something to move or change, or to stop moving or changing.
2. *Levitation:* the ability to move one's own body from the ground, often done in a state of trance or rapture. Perhaps a kind of weightlessness rather than true psychokinesis.
3. *Healing, harming:* affecting living tissue positively or negatively, such as Jesus' curing the lame and blind or his withering of the fig tree. The Evil Eye (Mal'occhio) may belong to this category.
4. *Poltergeist activity:* now often referred to as "recurrent spontaneous psychokinesis" (RSPK), this indicates physical effects wrought in the material environment unconsciously and probably by a displacement of psychic energy. Once attributed to mischievous spirits or lesser demons, RSPK is generally destructive if not usually seriously so. A minor manifestation may be found in people with "brown

thumbs," for whom plants will not grow, or people in whose presence machinery tends to break down.

In the literature of mystical experience, the most common psychic experiences are probably precognition, clairvoyance, healing, levitation and apparitions. In some cases, such as that of St. Joseph of Cupertino or the Curé of Ars, these may appear more or less together. Other saints, such as Joan of Arc, may be aware of only one kind of phenomena, such as her "voices."

MYSTICS AND PARAPSYCHOLOGISTS

From the earliest proceedings of the societies for psychical research, the lives of the mystics provided historical antecedents of paranormal phenomena to the reciprocal advantage of both parapsychology and mystical studies. The authenticity of contemporary instances is supported by historically verified cases, while the likelihood of the antecedent instances is strengthened by similar if not identical cases today. Further, the scientific study of paranormal events not only illuminates many shadowy areas of human nature and experience that trouble both scientists and theologians, but it also sets in bold relief the primacy of the ordinary.

For paranormal events acquire meaning and value only in a setting of normalcy. William Ernest Hocking once realized with a shock that if he had a truly telepathic glimpse of another person's mind, it would only be meaningful (not to say interesting) if the person had something in it! That is, if she were thinking about the common world we already share. Paranormal experiences have little if any value in themselves. On the other hand, as the "frame" of the ordinary, they establish limits, criteria and norms, thus advancing our understanding of the meaning and value of all human experience.

In *Philosopher King,* her warm and absorbing biography of Prospero Lambertini (1675-1758), Renée Haynes relates how as *promotor fidei,* the future Pope Benedict XIV established scientific criteria for evaluating the miraculous deeds attributed to candidates for beatification and canonization. His major work on canonization procedures occupies some eight volumes. Called "the humanist pope," Lambertini was a skilled scientist, having in his possession an early microscope and telescope. He founded chairs of chemistry, mathematics and physics at the Sapienza University of Rome. In Bologna, he established a school of surgery and an anatomical museum. He also fought for the rights of women scholars to lecture.

Miss Haynes, who was the secretary of the Society for Psychical Research for several years, calls Lambertini "the father of Christian psychical research." He personally investigated many cases of alleged miracles, sometimes disproving them by logical traps or simple empirical tests, as would William James and Harry Houdini two centuries later.

For Lambertini, no event, however extraordinary, is to be considered a miracle if natural causes can be traced or even inferred, for he was aware that many were not yet known. He also maintained that "natural prophecy" (ESP) could exist in persons who were not particularly holy. Similarly, visions, voices, dreams and apparitions could happen to anyone, often for their benefit, but sometimes to their physical or spiritual detriment. In other words, while never discounting authentic miraculous events, Prospero Lambertini was well aware that natural paranormal events were in fact common and should be studied scientifically for what they reveal to us about human nature.

CONCLUSION

What have psychical research and parapsychology contributed to the study of mysticism and human nature?

Fundamentally, we have learned that human capacities of knowing and doing are not limited to the five conventional senses or motor activities involving direct contact with external objects. That is, the mind can receive information that is not mediated by the physical senses nor limited by spatial or temporal proximity. It can, further, effect change in the material environment directly, without the necessary intervention of touch. *How* the mind operates in the paranormal dimension remains largely a mystery as well as a problem.

Similarly, "reality" cannot be limited to the rather prosaic model which we take for granted in everyday life, but is in fact a social-cultural presupposition. For, occasionally, hidden depths of yet undiscovered meaning and value, even the structures of the universe itself, are suddenly opened before us by the creative insight of a nuclear physicist, a microbiologist, a painter, writer, lover, mystic or even a "madperson."

What is the benefit of such insights for our everyday life? I think it is manifold, but at least this can be said. These glimpses confirm our intimation that there is far *more* to this mysterious cosmos than our dull senses and wits can properly fathom, that we will continue forever to plumb the inexhaustible depths of its creative potential and its omnipotent Creator. We are thus prevented from foreclosing our accounts with reality prematurely, as James remarked.

We are also reminded that the *human* mystery is similarly deeper and richer than our behavioralism, materialism, political totalitarianism and fatalism will ever enable us to grasp, much less control. The human psyche is not only structurally "open" to the universe, it is also the realm of *spirit.*

Several specific conclusions can be drawn from this interface between mysticism and parapsychology:

First, it seems evident that the human psyche must be considered to be something "else" than matter in motion. We cannot account for observed PK effects or ESP from a purely materialistic perspective.

Second, the mind or psyche (including emotional states and feelings) extends beyond the physical limits of the body and in some sense operates independently of it. Thus, "out-of-the-body-experiences" are no more unlikely than survival of bodily death.

Third, the integrity of the mind-body-spirit unit is nevertheless affirmed by the mysteriously complete interactions of these three aspects in normal as well as paranormal perception and motor operations. For instance, the imagery and "mechanics" of ESP experiences are the same generally as those of ordinary perception; ghosts look like living people, and the "voices" heard speak recognizable languages.

Fourth, the psyche is able to control in some manner not only the ordinary processes of human physiology, but also the material-energetic systems of the physical world.

Thus, it is not surprising from a developmental viewpoint that as a person seriously committed to a mystical lifestyle progresses in integration and self-mastery, various psychic phenomena would occur. We should, in fact, expect them to. For the mystical life effects a transformation of ordinary human experience in which "normal" perceptions of reality and behavior are systematically disengaged, purified, integrated and re-engaged in a dynamic lifestyle for the betterment of the individual, the society and the world.

Thus, too, we should be neither alarmed nor elated if clairvoyant, precognitive or psychokinetic episodes occur in relationship to our progress in the spiritual life. They happen at times anyway, and, apart from their immediate utility (if any), they are, if anything, signposts—not the rainbow's end.

SUGGESTIONS FOR FURTHER READING

Frank Barron, "The Creative Personality: Akin to Madness," *Psychology Today,* Vol. 6, No. 2 (July, 1972), pp. 43-44, 84-85.

Roland Fischer, "A Cartography of the Ecstatic and Meditative States," *Science,* Vol. 174, No. 4012 (Nov. 26, 1971), pp. 897-904.

MYSTERION

Renée Haynes, *The Hidden Springs,* London: Hutchinson, 1973.

______, *Philosopher King,* London: Weidenfield and Nicholson, 1970.

Rosalind Heywood, *The Sixth Sense,* London: Pan Books, Ltd., 1971.

Lawrence L. LeShan, *The Medium, the Mystic and the Physicist,* New York: Viking, 1973.

______, "Psychic Phenomena and Mystical Experience," in *Psychic Exploration,* Edgar D. Mitchell, ed., with John White, New York: Capricorn Books, 1974, pp. 571-577.

H. Richard Neff, *Psychic Phenomena and Religion,* Philadelphia: The Westminster Press, 1971.

Kenneth Wapnick, "Mysticism and Schizophrenia," *The Journal of Transpersonal Psychology,* Vol. 1, No 2 (Fall, 1969), pp. 49-66.

J. H. M. Whiteman, *The Mystical Life,* London: Faber and Faber, 1961.

Chapter 8

MYSTICISM AND MEDITATION

For thousands of years in both the West and East, meditation in some form has been recognized as an indispensable element of the spiritual life. The relative inattention to this dimension of life by Western Europeans and Americans in the last century and more is thus a departure from our heritage, not typical of it. This forgetfulness, moreover, has had serious repercussions in the texture of social life as well as individual consciousness.

Within the last two decades, however, there has been a gradual recovery of the practice of meditation in the West. Significantly, this renewal of interest has come not so much from organized religion—the monasteries and convents where the contemplative aspect of Christianity somehow managed to survive the industrial revolution. Rather, it has emanated mainly from the incursion of oriental spiritualities into the West on one hand, and, on the other, the scientific study of altered states of consciousness. In particular, I would mention Transcendental Meditation (TM)—a form of Hindu yoga practice, Zen and Tibetan Buddhism, and Sufism—the mystical tradition of Islam. Transpersonal and humanistic psychology have provided the other major impetus to the revitalization of meditation in our time.

Today, books, seminars, lectures and training courses in meditation are widespread. Recently, a new interest in traditional Christian forms has begun to emerge, not only among professed "contemplatives," but also among laymen and women.

Little agreement exists, however, as to what meditation is or how it functions in human experience. Its religious significance is particularly open to debate. Some proponents deny that religious motivation, content or context have any necessary connection with meditation as a practice. For example, TM instructors routinely deny that the Hindu veneer of *bhakti* ceremony associated with initiation is actually religious or that TM is itself religious.

Many meditation techniques, such as Dr. Herbert Benson's "Relaxation Response" and other methods, are specifically designed to avoid any religious implications. In their studies, both Drs. Ruth Carrington and Lawrence LeShan carefully distinguish even the techniques evolved within religious traditions from the content of these traditions themselves. Similarly, in their now classic work, Naranjo and Ornstein disconnect the *practice* of meditation from religious frames of reference and value systems, while granting them due acknowledgment.

From the viewpoint of Christian mystical theology, however, meditation and contemplation are elements in an integrative style of life centered on the mystery of God's presence to us. As such, they cannot be divorced from religious faith or practices without disintegrating the whole—the entire personal style of living as well as the integrity of the tradition. This is the split we are, in fact, attempting to overcome in this program.

WAYS AND MEANS

Traditionally, in Christian practice as well as theory, meditation and contemplation have been considered as a form of prayer, as a way toward closer union with God. They are not "ends" in themselves. But neither are they mere *means*. They must be approached in an attitude of mind very different from that which, in left-brain fashion, tidily divides the realm of action into ends and means—a merely instrumental, non-contemplative, much less holistic attitude.

A "way" in the mystical life is more like a trip, a journey, than a road. The path is inseparable from the goal, the quest from the conquest. Thus meditation and contemplation must be approached for what they *are,* not for what they can do for us. Otherwise, paradoxically, they won't do much of anything, because they can't. For, far from being mere "means," they are *media,* agencies through which persons communicate. Meditation and contemplation are the media through which God's presence is more fully realized in human experience. They represent the "way" in which our conscious awareness of that presence is organized and simplified.

EFFECTS AND BENEFITS OF MEDITATION

Despite their privileged place in mystical development, there is little doubt today that meditation and contemplation contribute valuably to human well-being on many levels other than the religious or even spiritual planes alone. Their applications seem to grow daily. In terms of human integrity as we have been considering it, meditation has produced remarkable benefits in accelerating both physical and mental healing when combined with appropriate therapies. General psychosomatic functioning is enhanced in the direction of greater integration. The rate of metabolism is lowered, oxygen consumption is reduced, cardiac output is lessened, and the lactic acid content of the blood diminished; all of which produce a sense of quiet, calmness and a greater feeling of reality contact or "objectivity." Discriminatory abilities are sharpened, sleep and other bodily functions are improved. In general, there seems to be increased right and left brain synchronization, improved memory, lowered anxiety and a heightened sense of optimism and well-being.

Full human integrity is, of course, another way of saying "spirituality." Thus, whatever contributes to human wholeness has a spiritual value and religious importance, apart from any doctrinal implications. And even apart from all these obvious benefits in the body-mind realm of human experience, meditation was, again, from the beginning a discipline developed in and until very recently confined to mystical religious traditions. One of the most remarkable works of Western mysticism, *The Cloud of Unknowing* is essentially a treatise on the art of meditation, seen, importantly, within the context of the whole spiritual life. Less well known is an equally remarkable work by the Catalan layman and Arabic enthusiast of the fourteenth century, Ramon Lull, *The Art of Contemplation.*

In brief, bodily and mental integration (health) are enhanced and promoted by meditation, but it is the area of spirit, the transcendent dimension of human experience that seems ultimately to benefit most, as we shall see.

STYLES OF MEDITATION

One of the less edifying aspects of the reappearance of meditation in the West is the competitiveness between different, often rival schools. This, in turn, springs from another problem, the commercialization of meditation—its "packaging and promotion," what Christmas Humphreys calls the prostitution of great wisdom for personal gain.

A hallmark of competitive and commercial approaches is the fallacy that a specific style of meditation is the "only way." Dr. LeShan writes: "One of the reasons the formal schools of meditational practice have such a high percentage of failures among their students—those who get little out of the practices and leave meditation completely—is that most schools tend to believe that there is one right way to meditate for everyone and, by a curious coincidence, it happens to be the one they use." (LeShan, p. 3)

As there are different personalities, so there are different spiritualities and different kinds of meditation. A person should select that form which suits him or her best, not that which promises the quickest or most glamorous results. As Dr. Ruth Carrington observes, "the personality of the meditator is the most important factor of all when judging the 'merits' of any of these techniques." (Carrington, p. 16)

Similarly, in *The Cloud of Unknowing,* the author advises his disciple(s) to try the method he suggests, but if something better turns up, to use that, and to let him know about it so that he can try it as well.

It is important, however, to stay with a style of meditation once it has been selected, even if the way becomes difficult (as it will). Abandoning a style of meditation should be done only very carefully and with proportionate reason: because it no longer "works," not because it has become challenging or even boring.

A PRELIMINARY NOTE: CENTERING AND MEDITATION

Given the frequent confusion of terms such as meditation and contemplation, often used in exactly opposite ways by different authors, a few words about each might be helpful.

First, not only are meditation and contemplation different, but each differs from what we can call "centering," "mind control" or "concentration." *Centering,* according to Carrington, is "a reinstatement of a sense of inner balance through the use of devices which serve to focus the person's attention on some single point" (Carrington, p. 4). *Concentration* or mind control, similarly, "is only the mental counterpart of physical training, and there is nothing particularly spiritual or mysterious about its practice or technique. It calls for no special hours nor place nor posture, and the only apparatus needed is the daily round" (Humphreys, p. 8).

Meditation, by contrast, is more holistic and developmental. It involves not only discipline, but set times and, preferably, a regular place. It concerns, Humphreys notes, "the whole strength of the mind turned inward to find the Self, and only then turned outward to apply the Wisdom so gained in the service of all that lives" (Humphreys, p. 7). He cites the Zen master Hui-Neng: "To meditate is to realize inwardly the imperturbability of the Essence of Mind" (Humphreys, p. 10).

The difference here is not exact, however, but a matter of degrees of development. Meditation can be best seen, I think, as a systematic and progressive employment of centering practices leading toward a condition of mental integrity marked by much greater receptivity or attentiveness than we experience in ordinary life, a form of "passive concentration." Carrington writes, "When I speak of meditation . . . I will be referring to the centering techniques that constitute what I call 'practical meditation' " (Carrington, pp. 7-8). What these practices have in common, she believes, is "the ability to bring about a special kind of free-floating attention where rational thought is by-passed and words are of far less importance than in everyday life" (Carrington, p. 3).

So close is the rhythmic, positive-negative interconnection between centering and meditation, that the psychologist Claudio Naranjo suggests that "for each type of concentrative meditation one is likely to find a corresponding state of expressive meditation" (Naranjo and Ornstein, p. 114).

CHRISTIAN CONTEMPLATION

In Christian spirituality, contemplation is wider in practice, as well as being older than the term "meditation." Equivalent in some respects to the Greek notion of *theoria* inherited from Plato, contemplation means much more than a certain kind of mental activity (or, rather, receptivity), especially with regard to abstract concepts or disembodied "idealizations." It not only refers to a whole style of life, it was taken by early Christian teachers to mean what today we call "mysticism" or the whole mystical life. In medieval works such as *The Cloud of Unknowing,* in which a modern word such as "mysticism" never appears, "contemplation" is still employed in that original fashion.

The Latin word *contemplare* means, roughly, "to look at something with continued attention," to "behold." It is based upon a more ancient combination, *con-templum*—attending to an open space on the earth or even in the sky, marked out by the augur with his staff for the purpose of divining the god's will.

(*Templum* meant a space or section marked off or separated, and generally a place inhabited by a divine being.)

Thus, to contemplate something (or, rather Someone) means to be aware of *presence*, not to think or reason. Even meditation, Naranjo tells us, "is concerned with the development of a *presence*, a modality of being, which may be expressed or developed in whatever situation the individual may be involved" (Naranjo and Ornstein, p. 8). In classical Christian usage, contemplation meant loving attention to the presence of God.

Thomas Aquinas, in the thirteenth century, cited the following definitions from Richard of St. Victor, who wrote in the previous century, "Contemplation is the soul's clear and free dwelling on the object of its gaze; meditation is the survey of the mind while occupied in searching for the truth; and cogitation is the mind's glance which is prone to wander" (*Summa Theologiae*, II-II, Q. 180, a. 1). While a conscious activity of the mind and heart, contemplation signifies a whole attitude toward existence, one that can pervade every activity and needs no "time" for its execution. The *Cloud* author tells us that we can direct our attention toward God as often as there are instants in an hour, something (by medieval computation) on the order of 23,000!

The earliest use of the word "meditation" in English, however, (about 1225) referred to mental consideration, in fact, to written or spoken *discourse*, presented in a manner to help a person arrive at contemplation. Apparently, the word derived from the Greek *medesthai*, "to think about something."

While the historical careers of these words, with their odd reversals of meaning (Carrington suggests that "contemplations" "create an atmosphere where thought is directed in a disciplined manner to a specific theological problem or religious event." Carrington, p. 21) are less important than the way in which we use them today, it is important to remember that from the beginning, meditation and contemplation were seen as distinct but related aspects of the mystical life. Especially as we use the term today, *meditation* implies a discipline of the mind which takes time not only to develop but to exercise. From a traditional Christian point of view, it is a preparation for the more effortless, spontaneous gift of contemplation.

"Contemplative meditation," therefore, can be considered either as an intermediate form between meditation and contemplation, or as a term embracing both. As it develops, however we conceive it, the would-be mystic becomes freer, less deliberately controlled, and more receptive in turning attention to the divine presence, the Field of all our experience, with an attitude of love and reverence.

MEDITATION IN PROCESS

Contemplative meditation, as an art as well as a gift, is a process rather than an act; it develops therefore in time. The psychological aspect of this process has been variously described. For William E. Hocking, it consisted of a shift of attention from particular objects of experience of whatever kind to the Field which grounded and contained them. In this, it is the reverse of centering, or, rather, the *transcendence* of centering, "decentering." A more recent psychiatric writer, Dr. Arthur Deikman, identifies the psychological function in meditative contemplation as a process of "deautomatization," one in which we disengage our attention from ordinary objects of consciousness by various kinds of voluntary activities of renunciation or deprivation, followed by a reinvestment of our actions and perceptions with full awareness.

Both views are, I think, correct, and fundamentally the same. Deikman points out that the *effect* of shifting our attention from ordinary objects of consciousness is to experience these same objects *later* in a wholly "new" way when our attention is shifted back to them. Hocking called this "objectivity," a new "innocence of the senses."

One of the principal effects of meditation is this "refreshening" of experience, "cleansing the doors of perception" by sensory or mental deprivation followed by refocused attention. Meditation in this regard is the mental-emotional equivalent of fasting, sexual abstinence or other forms of bodily renunciation. We deprive our busy, discursive left brain of its customary objects of consciousness for a time, giving the right brain a chance to function in a more holistic manner. The net effect, as we shall see, is an integration of our mind-brain perceptions and behavior. The experiential correlative is a "new" perception of reality as well as a "new" sense of the wholeness of personal existence, united in the field of God's presence.

The integration of the mental-emotional dimensions of experience can be envisioned as a progression from initial centering attempts, through the mastery of states of consciousness at the direction of the will, leading to a condition of receptive awareness, more "passive" than active, but highly alert. It is in regard to this phase of meditation that Edward Maupin writes, "Meditation is first of all a deep passivity combined with awareness" (Maupin, p. 184).

And thus meditation, as a process in time, occupies the middle ground between centering and mind-control on one hand, (which, from a religious perspective, are ways of simplifying mental prayer), to contemplation on the other. Classically, contemplation is distinguished into "acquired" and "infused" forms, the difference being in the source of primary agency; in the first instance, still mainly human, despite increasing efforts to become receptive, but "wholly Other," in the second, the work of God's grace. "Contemplation," Hocking wrote, "as used by the medieval mystics implies that the effort of 'meditation,' in which one holds the object before the mind by force of will, gives way to a state in which the object attracts and holds attention without further conscious effort" (*The Meaning of God in Human Experience,* p. 371). The mystic, he added, "must render himself passive and wait in hope that God will vouch-safe to reveal himself" ("The Mystical Spirit," p. 190).

From an integrative or holistic viewpoint, this process of

development not only coincides with the "three ways" of Purgation, Illumination and Union; they are identical. In both the first and second phases of mystical development, the "passages" from active but negative efforts at renunciation to positive attitudes of effortless receptivity are accurately described, in the famous idiom of St. John of the Cross, as the "dark nights" of the senses and the spirit.

The effort to achieve voluntary passivity in order to enable God's indwelling presence to manifest itself fully, without hindrance or interference, must be transformed into an *involuntary* passivity through which every obstacle has at last been removed. Possible only at that point, "God accepts and lifts to himself the prepared soul" (*The Meaning of God in Human Experience*, p. 386). And thus, the negative phases of the spiritual life are only half its history at most, and "its history is that of an activity of self-suppression which must itself be suppressed." (Ibid.)

Ultimately, contemplation, as distinct from centering and meditation, cannot be learned. It is an experience that is "given," a *grace* which gradually pervades the whole of life. But it can only be wholly given when the mystic has accomplished all in her power to render herself receptive by no longer hindering the active presence of God from full manifestation in the foreground as well as the depths of consciousness.

The "passivity" of the contemplative is thus not idle inaction, but total receptivity. In Shakespeare's phrase, "the readiness is all." To this end, the *Cloud* author urges us to

Let it be the worker, and thou the sufferer;
do but look upon it and let it alone.
Meddle thee not therewith as though thou wouldst help it,
for dread lest thou spill all.
Be thou but the tree,
and let it be the wright;
be thou but the house,

and let it be the husband dwelling therein.
Be blind in this time,
and shear away desire of knowing,
for it will more hinder thee than help thee.
It sufficeth enough unto thee
that thou feel thee stirred likingly
with a thing thou knowest not what,
save that in thy stirring
thou have no special thought of anything under God,
and that thine intent
be wholly directed unto God. (Chapter 34)

PRACTICAL STEPS

Meditation and its culminating stage, contemplation, must be situated in the context of an integrated lifestyle if they are not to become "wild" elements. They will thus have organic or "systematic" connections with other aspects of life. Traditionally, meditative contemplation is the characteristic feature of the "Illuminative Way" and must be preceded by "purgative" exercises or, in Deikman's sense, "renunciation."

Important in this respect is the *moral* development of the meditator, the quality of actions and relations which reflect personal integrity and "rightness." A skewed moral disposition could have very destructive effects when magnified by the catalyzing power of contemplative meditation. Humphreys writes, "Meditation develops considerable power in the mind, and if this new force is used for selfish ends the effect on the individual seems to be disastrous. This is 'black magic' leading to spiritual death" (Humphreys, p. 7). And in *The Cloud of Unknowing,* we are reminded that "the Devil hath his contemplatives as God hath his."

Thomas Aquinas taught, almost in passing, that among the predispositions necessary for a true contemplative, chastity has a place of great importance, for reasons we shall explore in greater detail in a subsequent chapter. But it should be added here that the emotional and mental strength and purity of heart gained from the honest expression and restraint of human sexuality is a necessary element in all spiritual development. Without them, the clear vision of "living truth"—the "object" of contemplation—is all but impossible. Just as important, the intensification of human sexuality likely to result *from* meditation will require control and direction according to a person's situation in life—the work of chastity as "virtue."

Deikman observes that the typical elements of renunciation undertaken to help develop the mystical life are poverty, chastity and the solitary way. It is also important to see such efforts at attaining personal freedom from possessions and possessiveness as a *positive* attempt to grow, rather than a rejection of the world of nature and human society.

THE VARIETIES OF MEDITATIVE EXPERIENCE

Various authors, in paying homage to the incorrigible and wonderful plurality of human personalities, diverse traditions and the multiple spiritualities spun off from their encounters, identify many "ways" of meditating. LeShan articulates four "paths" toward enlightenment based roughly on yoga philosophy: through the body, through action, through the emotions and through intellect. Each has its own program and characteristics. A prerequisite for choosing one or more of them is the achievement of sufficient personal integrity to "know" one's own personality, its needs and abilities.

LeShan further distinguishes meditations themselves into formal, structured approaches and informal, unstructured ones. Similarly, Naranjo groups types of meditation into three main categories: the Way of Forms, the Negative Way and the Expressive Way, or (alternatively) the Apollonian, the "Middle" and the Dionysian ways. Carrington speaks of "permissive" and "non-permissive" forms.

SOME PRACTICAL ADVICE FOR WOULD-BE MEDITATORS

It would be impossible here to pursue all the possible permutations of these systems, or even to describe those just mentioned adequately. Hence, the first advice I would give the potential meditator is to read widely and critically among the sources available. Or, better, find a good teacher, one who will respect your individuality and who has a good grasp of the varieties of meditative techniques. Try out as many "ways" as seem profitable, then select the one which best suits your individual need and temperament—at least provisionally. It is probably a good idea to avoid schools or methods making claims of being the only or even the best possible way.

As regards the process of meditation, I would suggest the following by way of simple advice:

1. Find out whether you meditate better in the morning, afternoon or evening. Utilize the time you have available to best advantage—when you are neither sleepy nor most active, neither hungry nor stuffed. Meditating immediately after arising or before retiring, or before or after meals, is thus (probably) self-defeating.
2. Some simple warm-up exercises should help prepare you by invigorating the body. But don't overdo it.
3. Find a quiet spot where you will have the fewest distractions, either indoors or outdoors. It should be neither completely dark, nor totally silent, but restful.
4. Having a regular time and place to meditate helps set up favorable physical and psychological conditions. The use of incense might help. If it does, use it.
5. Various positions are equally beneficial, depending on your own style, needs, age, etc., whether sitting, lying prone, standing, walking or kneeling. The main thing is to keep the spine straight and to be able to breathe easily. Wear loose clothing so as not to impede circulation.

6. Keep alert. If you tend to doze, walk around for a few moments. If that doesn't work, try shifting the time for meditation or get more sleep at night. The use of coffee is not really helpful.
7. A 20 to 60 minute period is generally adequate for a single session. Shorter or longer periods can be either inadequate to achieve the necessary psychosomatic stillness or too long to sustain a state of relaxed attentiveness without becoming either sleepy or restless. Find your own best time period.
8. Don't be worried about "itches"—bodily, mental or spiritual. All sorts of buried memories, resentments, fears, hopes, embarrassments and events of the past will probably bubble up to the surface of consciousness a short time after you begin meditating regularly. This is a natural and even healing process. Find someone to help you sort it out.
9. Expect to change, but don't be anxious about it. Every organism ages at its own rate. Boredom is probably inevitable; make the most of it. You are changing faster than you think.
10. Remember: meditation is a time *not* to think, but to still the mind, and eventually to shift attention away from all discrete objects of consciousness to the frame of the Whole. Learn to be receptive.
11. Take a few minutes to readjust after finishing your meditation period. Come back to normal consciousness gradually. Now is *not* the time to have a cigarette or to jog! Try to preserve your tranquillity into the rest of your day.

Meditation, like adulthood, is only a phase you are going through. Keep your heart fixed on your goal. And remember the advice of the sage, Hakuin:

Do not meditate only hidden in a dark corner,
But meditate always, standing, sitting, moving, resting.
When your meditation continues throughout waking and sleeping,

MYSTERION

Wherever you are is heaven itself.

from the *Song of Meditation,*
cited by Humphreys, p. 17.

SUGGESTIONS FOR FURTHER READING

Patricia Carrington, *Freedom in Meditation,* Garden City, N.Y.: Doubleday Anchor Books, 1978.

Christmas Humphreys, *The Search Within,* New York: Oxford University Press, 1977.

Lawrence LeShan, *How to Meditate,* New York: Bantam Books, 1975.

Edward Maupin, "On Meditation," in *Altered States of Consciousness,* ed. by Charles Tart, Garden City, N.Y.: Doubleday Anchor Books, 1972, pp. 181-202.

Claudio Naranjo and Robert Ornstein, *On the Psychology of Meditation,* New York: The Viking Press, 1971.

Chapter 9

MYSTICISM AND SEXUALITY

The worship of God is not a rule of safety—it is an adventure of the spirit, a flight after the unimaginable. The death of religion comes with the repression of the high hope of adventure.

Alfred North Whitehead

When the great mystics, many of them great poets, express their feelings of closeness to God, they tend to use the language of erotic love. This "bridal" mysticism or *Brautmystik* identifies a current of mystical literature from the *Song of Songs* to the outbursts of St. Paul and the lyricism of Underhill, Eliot and Hammarskjold. It is striking in medieval Christian mysticism, in St. Bernard, Dante, Eckhart, Catherine of Siena, Jacopone da Todi, Ruysbroeck, Teresa of Avila and John of the Cross. It is no less dominant in Hindu, Jewish and Sufi mysticism, if not in Buddhism.

Similarly, great lovers, many of whom are also great poets, employ the language of religious enthusiasm to describe their experiences—they sing of adoration, worship, idolatry. Consider the poetry of Shakespeare, the *Carmina Burana,* the works of e.e. cummings, as well as the content of any half-dozen traditional love ballads.

Veneration and *venereal* stem from the same root. For the ancient Jews, idolatry was adultery.

Such an exchange of idioms opens wide the doors of speculation—sometimes too wide. Psychiatric analysts from the time of Freud, and perhaps James Leuba most eloquently, have considered religious mysticism in fact to be the result of thwarted sexuality. Leuba observed, "many of the curious phenomena to which most great mystics owe in great part their fame or notoriety are due to perturbations of the sex function consequent upon its repression" (*The Psychology of Religious Mysticism,* New York, 1926, p. 119).

Such skeptics delight in analyzing the erotic imagery of the mystics' language for evidence of pathology, considering their case won when they uncover a passage of particular ardor or directness. The problem is compounded, however, by the typical stress the mystics lay upon chastity and purity of heart, which far from abating the psychiatric critique, sharpens it. Here, surely, is evidence of repression. . . .

Outside the West, less fuss has followed upon the use of erotic symbolism to portray the further reaches of mystical experience and integrity. In the *Kama Sutra* as well as in the temple sculpture at Konarak and Khajuraho in India, sexual eroticism has been integrated directly into a spiritual vision of human life as a way of transcendence, as Alan Watts shows in his fascinating study, *Erotic Spirituality.*

Sufi poetry is likewise filled with erotic themes signifying the quest for union with God, the "Friend."

O my Joy and my Desire and my Refuge,
My friend and my Sustainer and my Goal,
Thou art my Intimate, and longing for Thee
sustains me.

Rabi'a

The Christian approach to sexuality and spirituality has been far more subdued for a variety of reasons, not least of which was a persistent influence of "angelism"—a prejudice against pleasure and especially sexual pleasure as being too "carnal." The roots of this bias are largely Manichaean, a form of Gnosticism that deeply influenced both Tertullian and Augustine, two fountain-heads of Christian spiritual teaching and theology. Such pessimism contaminated the wells of Christian spirituality for over a thousand years.

The obvious lack of sexual integration in Christian spiritual teaching for the past several centuries in particular has not, however, diminished the force of St. Bernard's passionate lyricism or the nuptial bliss of Catherine and Teresa. The *Song of Songs*, in all likelihood a pagan love song, was taken into liturgy and mysticism by both Jews and Christians. It is still sung in churches and temples. Paul's voice is also heard declaring that human sexual love is the great *mysterion* of God's love for his people, Christ's love for his body, the church: "This mystery is a profound one, and I am saying that it refers to Christ and the church. . . ." (Eph. 5:32). Here, Paul is commenting upon the classic text from Genesis: "For this reason a man shall leave his father and his mother and be joined to his wife, and the two shall become one flesh" (Gen. 2:24).

It is important to remember that in Genesis, as well as in the New Testament (for example, in Mt. 19:5, Mk. 10:7 and I Cor. 6:16), this passage reflects the innate desire for human companionship and love. The section begins with God's musing—"It is not good that the man should be alone . . ." (2:18). The Woman, Eve, is created to be a "helpmate," a companion who alone can satisfy the longing for union. And Adam says on beholding his "bride," ". . . this is at last bone of my bones and flesh of my flesh" (2:23). He recognizes her as being of the same nature as himself. And, as Genesis goes on to comment, "it it for *this* reason that a man . . . cleaves to his wife . . . ." Jesus and Paul concur.

The unitive stages of the mystical life are, in fact, couched in erotic imagery because no other language can begin to do justice to intimacy experienced with God. Spirituality and sexuality are not inimical. They are neither antithetical nor even complementary; they are virtually identical, both springing from the same radical capacity of the human heart. Spirituality *is* sexuality.

SPIRITUALITY AS SEXUALITY

This possibly surprising statement may appear less provocative if we take a closer look at both spirituality and sexuality.

Spirit, pneuma in St. Paul's Greek, as we are told by J. A. T. Robinson, "when it is used of man, is that in virtue of which he is open to and transmits the life of God (Rom. 8:16, cf. I Cor. 2:10f.). . ." (*The Body: A Study in Pauline Theology,* London: 1952, p. 19). What makes a human person spiritual, then, is the radical capacity to be open to another Person, and to be a channel of life, to go out *to* others, to be *related.*

This capacity, at once both a receptivity and an agency, is actualized in concrete encounters with men and women from birth onwards—encounters in which there is always a "third" presence, recognized or not. This is especially so with regard to the Christian's participation in the life of Christ, with and in whom we are one body.

As a *spiritual* capacity, which makes us spirit in the first place, this receptive-ecstatic character of the human person is the way in which each of us is created in the image and likeness of God, *ikon* and *paradeigma*: "So God created man in his own image, in the image of God he created him; male and female he created them" (Gen. 1:27). For God is *likewise* a spirit, infinitely open, giving and receptive. God is, in Christian terms, a community of *persons* perfectly related by mutual giving and receiving, a community that is One in virtue of the divine love that exists among "them."

In human terms, our ability to receive and give is also the radical basis of sexuality, and it is in this sense that *as* male and female we represent the image and likeness of God. We are referring here, however, not to mere biological gender, for every person, *each* man and woman, is God's ikon and paradigm. Rather, human spirituality is an integration of the masculinity and femininity of the whole person. It is this complementarity *within* each of us that enables us to achieve true intimacy with each other on the sexual level and otherwise.

For this reason it is *not* surprising that throughout the Hebrew scriptures and in the New Testament, spirituality and sexuality were so closely associated. This is no less the case in later Christian teaching, whether expressed positively or negatively, as we shall see. As late as 1934, Teilhard de Chardin, in an essay "On the Evolution of Chastity," could write with *traditional* emphasis as well as prophetic relevance, "At the point at which life, in the present world, has arrived, the spiritualizing unification of human monads is governed by two attractive forces, which are the same in nature but differ in value. These are the mutual love of man and woman, and divine love. As each element seeks to find fulfillment in unity, it is courted simultaneously by the forces of passion and by mystical forces, working *in association.*" (Teilhard, p. 83)

The close tie between spirituality and sexualilty is perhaps nowhere more acutely if mysteriously described than by St. Paul's comment on the Genesis passage we have just examined. That passage, in fact, not only represented the foundation of sexual equality as well as sexual psychology for Jesus and Paul. It was also utilized by Christian writers from the earliest times to establish the dynamic structure of spiritual development—again pointing to the mystical connection between sexuality and spirituality in the Judeo-Christian tradition.

In the 14th century, Walter Hilton, in his *Scale of Perfection,* for example, constructed the "therapeutic" dimension of his spiritual doctrine in terms of the *imago Dei* in human persons, an image deformed by sin, both actual and "original." The "reformation" of the *imago Dei* is a process of increasing conformation to Christ, the exemplar as perfect image of God *and* humankind, the new Adam. We are conformed to his likeness by grace, as he had been formed in our image by his "descent" into *sarx*—sinful flesh, the full but fallen human condition. And by conformity to Christ, we are conformed to God. We are renewed in *spirit.*

The connection of the male-female dimension of human sexuality to the image and likeness of God has had a tumultuous history in Christian thought. Fundamentalists and neo-orthodox interpreters such as Karl Barth argue from the Genesis passages that the spiritual perfection of humankind can *only* be realized in heterosexual marriage—thus eliminating at a stroke both celibacy as a Christian lifestyle and other-than-heterosexual married love from the spiritual realm.

Other commentators have argued (with not measurably less cogency) that God, by this token, must therefore be androgynous—having *both* male and female characteristics—if men and women are created *as such* in "his" image and likeness, being complete only in pairs.

While it is worth considering with St. Ambrose and Julian of Norwich that God is indeed our "mother" as well as our "father," it is also important to remember that applying physiological attributes to God is a *metaphorical* device. God is neither male nor female, nor, indeed, both. How then does the famous Genesis passage refer to God?

ANDROGYNY: DIVINE AND HUMAN

As it stands, the Genesis text tells us very little about God, and what it does tell us is experienced through the filter of human self-awareness as men and women. What it really describes in intention and in fact is what it means to be a true human person, male *and* female. *Both* are created in the image and likeness of God. A woman is no less the ikon and paradigm of God than a man is. And each is so by virtue of the power and capacity they have to receive and transmit the life of God itself. (And it is well to recall that for the ancient Jews, *all* life was God's.)

Such giving and receiving becomes truly creative when the bond of mutual love grows between persons, not merely as males and females. Here we find, I think, the mystical link, an androgyny that points in two directions.

First, the radical giving and receiving that constitutes the spiritual character of the human person is *symbolized* and *realized* in the sexual intercourse which, as unitive, is thus the *mysterion* of God's love for humankind. It is this aspect which the mystics celebrate by appropriating the whole process of love, courtship, engagement and marriage to describe their developing union with God. Sexuality provides the *only* truly appropriate metaphor.

Similarly, the sexual love between men and women is a mystical enactment of God's love, and thus the language of worship is the only truly appropriate way to describe the wonder and mystery of human love. In God's *mysterion*, they are the same.

Secondly, when we envision *God's* nature, the human mind naturally appeals to the highest human experience of personal integrity and growth—sexual love, the *total* giving and receiving of persons—spiritually, mentally and physically. If the doctrine of the Trinity means anything in human terms, it means this: that the inner life of God is also and *primordially* an intercourse of persons productive of love itself both personal and real, the bond which unites. The Holy Spirit, then, is truly "a living bond of Love."

In transcending the biological *difference* between men and women in order to sketch in even so rudimentary a fashion the inner life of God as a communion of persons, we have touched upon the unique Christian contribution to sexual freedom as well as theology. Jesus first, and after him, Paul and the early church, clearly understood that the *transformation* of human sexuality demanded by the in-breaking of the Kingdom of God did away with all human distinctions based on gender, race or social condition: "There is neither Jew nor Greek, there is neither slave nor free, there is neither male nor female, for you are all one in Christ Jesus" (Gal. 3:28).

In the same spirit, John Macmurray wrote of this transforming liberation over forty years ago: "What is the moral problem of sex? It is the problem of subordinating the functional relations of the sexes to their relation as persons. It is the problem of taking the sexual aspect of life up into the personal aspect and making it one of the differences between persons through which their personal life in relation to one another is enriched" (Macmurray, p. 113).

Further, this "creative transformation of human love" (Teilhard, p. 85) was not a rejection of the body, pleasure or matter itself. It was, rather, a true transcendence, a "going beyond by going through," establishing the celibate way as a *mysterion* of that Kingdom-to-come. As a symbol that also realizes, celibacy is sacramental, if not a sacrament in the technical sense—*part* of the total dedication and transformation of human energies, desires and abilities which from the human side bring the Kingdom to realization.

Androgyny, while only a metaphor of God's total love and care for us, is applicable to men and women in a way perhaps remote from the Genesis text itself (but perhaps not too far at that). Modern depth psychology, particularly the analytic psychology of C. G. Jung, has emphasized the radical "bisexuality" of the human psyche. That is to say, every truly integrated man and woman is *both* masculine and feminine in the depths of their identity, their "nature."

Just as each of us has both male and female hormones and vestigial traces of rudimentary undifferentiated sex organs, so also we are a mixture or a compound of masculine and feminine characteristics in the psychological order. For Jung, each man has a feminine "soul" or "anima," and each woman an "animus." Integrity requires the complementarity of anima-animus in each human being. This is psychological (and spiritual) androgyny. As experienced, human wholeness requires a man's developing his "feminine" capacity for tenderness, receptivity, nurturing, attentiveness and so on. A woman, likewise, must integrate elements of "masculine" characteristics such as strength, agency, fostering and providence.

A man who has rejected or ignored his feminine side is not more but less a man, because less whole. Similarly, a woman who cannot accept her masculinity is less a woman. Neither will be able to relate with full comfort with other men or women, for they will incline toward rejecting the femininity or masculinity of others as well as their own.

Sexual complementarity is not a function of heterosexual differentiation but of human, personal individuality. No one can achieve true sexual harmony with another until he or she has achieved it within him- or herself.

Thus the sexuality of the great mystics—those who were celibate as well as those who were or had been married—was not thwarted or frustrated or repressed. It is transformed, developed beyond biological functions and even ordinary human desires for companionship and ecstatic union. The mystics use sexual language because they are sexual beings whose sexuality has achieved a new level of integration and power. It is this integration and energy that is the meaning and effect of that much abused and little understood mystical quality, chastity.

CHASTITY

Sex, from the Christian viewpoint is, in short, a way in which persons love each other. As human, it is not primarily a biological process, a means for perpetuating the species, nor even of satisfying basic instinctive needs for contact and release. As *distinctively* human, sex is a spiritual process of development to full humanness, and it is the work of chastity to qualify that process as spiritual.

Chastity manifests the mystical connection between sexuality and spirituality as a quality of relationships necessary for full human development in every state and condition of life. Thomas Aquinas made this abundantly clear in his treatise on the contemplative life (a document remarkable for its integrative approach).

In writing of the elements constituting the contemplative life, Thomas singles out chastity for special attention: ". . . the moral virtues belong to the contemplative life dispositively. For the act of contemplation, wherein the contemplative life essentially consists, is hindered both by the impetuosity of the passions which withdraw the soul's attention from intelligible to sensible things, and by outward disturbances . . ." (*Summa Theologiae,* II-II, Q. 180, a. 2.). He goes on to say, ". . . the moral virtues dispose one to the contemplative life by causing peace and cleanness of heart." Further, ". . . the virtue of chastity most of all makes man apt for contemplation, since venereal pleasures most of all weigh the mind down to sensible objects, as Augustine says."

We know from Thomas' teaching elsewhere that it is not sexual pleasure itself which disturbs contemplative awareness, but the weakness of our attention, which passion so easily overcomes by its force. This weakness is the result of "original sin," a loss of control that otherwise would have made sexual pleasure even greater (Cf. I, q. 98, a. 2 ad 3.).

For Thomas, chastity is the virtue or habitual power of regulating, that is to say, integrating, human sexuality. It pertains to an adult person, one who has become sexually aware of her or his powers and needs. Most properly, it is a quality of sexual *relations,* not a restraint of bodies. Further, chastity is a quality of *spirit* as well as of mind: ". . . if the human mind delights in the spiritual union with that to which it behooves it to be united, namely God, and refrains from delighting in union with other things against the requirements of the order established by God, this may be called a spiritual chastity. . . . The essence of this chastity consists principally in charity (i.e., divine love) and the other theological virtues whereby the human mind is united to God" (I, q. 145, a 4).

For Thomas, too, then, sexuality and spirituality are closely linked, a connection revealed by our use of language. For a holistic theology of the human person, this would follow by logical necessity. But for Thomas, as for other great mystics, it follows from *experience;* Thomas was known as the Angelic Doctor for his purity of mind as well as his chaste sexual attitudes.

In such a view, which is, I think, the common Christian and

universal mystical vision, chastity is not so much a "virtue" which regulates the use of bodies as the quality of detachment and freedom that humanizes, that is, spiritualizes sexual *relations.*

To regard chastity as having reference only to one's own body or sexual pleasure is to fall back into the trap of subjectivism or solipsism. Morality, like spirituality, is primarily a social process dealing with the relations among persons—justice, courage, common sense decisions, restraint, etc. Biologically, sexual "functions" remain about the same no matter who the participants are. But there is a world of difference between adultery and marital intercourse—a difference constituted by the character of the relationship established between persons.

Even within marriage, the *quality* of sexual relations makes a vital and spiritual difference. Selfishness, cruelty, indifference, even prostitution—using sex as a commodity for barter—can exist in, and corrupt, married life. Similarly, sexual relations among persons who are not officially married may well be loving, generous, supportive, healing and sustaining. Such sexual relations, moreover, need not imply actual intercourse or any overt genital behavior for that matter. But by the same token, chastity may be corrupted without any physical contact between persons: ". . . I say to you that anyone who looks at a woman lustfully has already committed adultery with her in his heart" (Mt. 5:28).

As a disposition necessary for the contemplative life of true mystical spirituality, chastity stands, then, for all the attitudes and patterns of behavior that integrate sexuality constructively in human experience as a whole. Three areas in human relationships stand out in this regard and thus warrant particular attention: emotional honesty or intimacy; poverty of spirit or purity of heart; and personal freedom.

INTIMACY AND CHASTITY

True intimacy refers to the emotional, mental and spiritual

closeness that can exist between adult persons as well as the physical proximity so obviously a part of sexuality. Such closeness requires an openness of spirit, a willingness to share what and who we are. Eric Berne described intimacy along these lines in an important passage from *Games People Play* (a book on how we avoid true intimacy): "Intimacy means the spontaneous, game-free candidness of an aware person, the liberation of the eidetically perceptive, uncorrupted Child in all its naiveté living in the here and now" (p 180). In this sense, intimacy *means* chastity, chastity as sexual honesty. Another way of putting it is "emotional sincerity"—a phrase taken from a remarkable essay by John Macmurray in his book *Reason and Emotion*—". . . if honesty is expressing what you think, chastity is expressing what you feel" (p. 129).

CHASTITY AS EMOTIONAL SINCERITY

In explaining this enigmatic phrase, Macmurray used our ordinary understanding of honesty as truth, showing that there is also a truth of the emotions:

"Negative untruthfulness is simply expressing what you do not think; that is lying. But sincerity in the mind is more than this. It is positively expressing what you do think and believe. To refrain from expressing what you think or believe or know to someone, if it is to his advantage or to someone else's advantage that he should know it, is positive dishonesty. We call it dissimulation—the suppression of the truth. In the same way, there is a positive and negative insincerity of the emotions. This negative insincerity is to express a feeling that you do not feel. The positive is to fail to express what you do feel when it makes a real difference to the person from whom you conceal it. It is, then, a failure in chastity to express a feeling to someone that you do not feel; to express love for a person, for instance, when you do not feel it. It is equally unchaste to conceal your feelings from someone to whom it makes a real difference" (pp. 129-30).

Aquinas and Macmurray are in full accord here because both recognize the place of truth in human life, truth as the living object of contemplation, and truth as the expression of what we are, think and feel. Thomas speaks of honesty in this sense as an integral part of the virtue of temperance, the larger realm of human integration of which chastity is an aspect. Further, for Thomas, honesty in human relations is a kind of spiritual *beauty*, it is a quality worthy of respect and therefore *honor*. And as for Macmurray, emotional sincerity is inseparable from reason and mental sincerity. (See *Summa Theologiae*, I, Q. 145, a. 4.)

CHASTITY AS SPIRITUAL POVERTY

Chastity, as the mystical aspect of sexual relatedness, constitutes for the spiritual life at its highest point of development the element of *renunciation* necessary to have true freedom for union with God. It does not entail a renunciation of love, nor of sex, nor of persons, but of *self*, specifically of the deep selfishness that inclines toward possessiveness in human relations. Chastity is poverty of spirit in the realm of human relationships, especially in the sexual order, whether genital or not.

As a kind of personal poverty of spirit, chastity prevents our attempting to "own" or control another person, as if he or she were a personal possession of ours. Similarly, it prevents our succumbing to the lure of becoming a possession of someone else.

As a voluntary renunciation of the attempt to own someone, chastity is a negative attitude, but as a liberating force that allows both members of a relationship to be free, it is positive.

CHASTITY AS FREEDOM OF SPIRIT: THE TRANSCENDENCE OF SEX

Liberation, both as Berne described it and for the great mystical traditions (particularly in this respect, Buddhism), is virtually synonymous with enlightenment or mystical integrity in the mental dimension of life. In the West, it is no less associated with the final development of human spirituality, as the fully-alive person not only achieves true independence of spirit, but fosters individuation in others as well.

This independence of spirit can only be attained by a voluntary renunciation of self that leads to an *involuntary* self-renunciation, a further purification that reaches to depths hidden from our limited self-awareness. This ultimate purgation is a cleansing fire of God's love which sublimates but does not destroy our human loves. The mystic returns from the negative path, as William Hocking insisted, not less a lover of men and women, but more.

Such a love will never rest content until it has expended every available moment and its last reserves of energy in helping others become free. The control and power of this incredible outpouring of liberating activity is another way of describing chastity. It also describes *prophecy*.

Chastity is freeing love, a passion for "souls" able and willing to become what they have been called to be: whole persons, united not only in themselves, but *among* themselves. There is no freedom which is not social freedom.

Such a passion realizes itself historically in the pursuit of *justice*—the correlative of, as well as condition for, eternal friendship. And such a passion results not from an intellectual conviction of ideal possibilities—the philosopher's idle dream. It emerges *only* from a transformation of human sexuality, a conversion which places the greatest power in the universe at the disposal of God's friends for the building of the Kingdom of Heaven:

> *The day will come when, after harnessing the ether, the winds, the tides, gravitation, we shall harness for God the energies of love. And on that day, for the second time in the history of the world, man will have discovered fire.*
>
> *Teilhard de Chardin*

MYSTERION

SUGGESTIONS FOR FURTHER READING

Eric Berne, *Games People Play,* New York: Grove Press, 1967.

Shelley Gross, ed., *The Mystic in Love: A Treasury of Mystical Poems,* New York: The Citadel Press, 1966.

John Macmurray, *Reason and Emotion,* London: Faber and Faber, 1967.

Pierre Teilhard de Chardin, *Toward the Future,* trans. by René Hague, London: Collins, 1975.

Alan Watts and Eliot Elisofon, *Erotic Spirituality,* New York: Collier Books, 1974.

Chapter 10

MYSTICISM AND SOCIAL ACTION

In our era, the road to holiness necessarily passes through the world of action.

Dag Hammarskjöld

In the East and West alike, the mystics' withdrawal from society and the receptive, waiting aspect of mystical development have earned the scorn of those committed to a lifestyle of active involvement in the world. This is especially true when seen in its most extreme forms—attitudes such as Taoist *wu-wei,* "non-action," the Buddhist *za-zen,* "just sitting," the Hindu *ahimsa,* "non-violence," or, in its Christian expression, "abandonment to divine providence," the development of "Quietism" from the teachings of Miguel de Molinos and Madame Guyon (in the 17th century), and the Quakers' silent waiting for the Inner Light.

Reacting against Quietism, the Catholic Church discouraged the pursuit of mystical spirituality by moving it to the periphery of religious concern as an elite and extraordinary side-road to heaven. Early Protestantism was even more antagonistic toward mysticism and, despite exceptional manifestations, had all but stifled it in Germany, England and the Netherlands by the end of the 17th century. George Fox's "Society of Friends," the Quakers, were hounded, outlawed, persecuted and sometimes executed in England and the American colonies. Madame Guyon was condemned; Molinos died in the dungeons of the Inquisition.

In the 19th century, as the need for increased and widespread missionary activity became more apparent, Protestant theologians such as Ritschl, Troeltch and Harnack, following the lead of Immanuel Kant, launched a heavy attack on mysticism, especially as developed in the writings of Friedrich Schleiermacher. In America, the Social Gospel movement, led by Walter

Rauschenbusch and further developed by Reinhold and H. Richard Niebuhr, was no more open to mysticism. Neo-orthodoxy, represented by Karl Barth, Emil Brünner and Hendrik Kraemer, repudiated mysticism in strong terms as a world-denying, Hellenic intrusion into the pristine Jewish faith of early prophetic Christianity. Heiler, Nygren and other influential Protestant theologians were similarly antagonistic.

Despite such attacks, the mystical element in Christianity survived, defended by a minority of important figures like Rudolf Otto, Baron von Hügel and William Inge. As William James, William Ernest Hocking and other non-theological writers attempted to show, mystics were often women and men of tremendous social activism, including the supposedly heretical Madame Guyon. One of the greatest Protestant mystics of our time was also a scripture scholar, theologian and ultimately a man of direct social action, Albert Schweitzer, who became a medical missionary in Africa.

But despite evidence to the contrary from history and current events, to many of our contemporaries, mysticism is still synonymous with passivity and withdrawal. Thus, given a new interest in mysticism today, as well as a reawakening to the need for social involvement, the question stands open again: are mystical spirituality and social action opposed to each other?

MYSTICAL DEVELOPMENT AND SOCIAL ACTION

It is undeniably true that, as a rule, mystics tend to drop out of social life. In India, such renunciation is classically expected of the higher caste males who have finished their studies and established a family. Buddhist monasteries harbor hundreds of thousands of monks and nuns. Hasidic rabbis are forbidden to engage in ordinary business and social life. Christian mystics are often found "fleeing" into monasteries and convents, if not into the desert or forest, becoming hermits like Richard Rolle or recluses like Dame Julian of Norwich. According to writers like

Thomas à Kempis, the world is a distraction and temptation. Anyone serious about the spiritual life abandons it.

Plotinus, held by some to be the intellectual fountainhead of Western mysticism, considered action to be a "weakening" of contemplation. For this reason, however, the great French philosopher Henri Bergson considered the Greek mystical thinker, noble soul that he was, less advanced than the great Christian mystics. As a whole, he wrote, "mysticism in the absolute sense in which we have agreed to take the word, was never attained by Greek thought" (*The Two Sources of Morality and Religion*, p. 221). Bergson likewise claimed that Hinduism and Buddhism, while achieving true mysticism, never attained the complete mysticism of action, creation and love. This occurred, according to the great philosopher, himself never a Christian, only with the advent of Christianity (Ibid., p. 227).

Evelyn Underhill had previously noted in her monumental work, *Mysticism,* that the great mystics, following their unitive experience, typically involved themselves in lives of continual activity. Like Bergson, she saw such a return to action as a result of the mystics' heightened compassion, an outpouring of love. But even less than Bergson, she did not see action as *part of* the mystics' developmental process, which for her culminated in Union. Thus, action could be considered an incidental by-product of mystical development.

Such a situation would not only be open to the attack of the liberal and neo-orthodox theologians, since action could just as easily *not* result from contemplative union, it also failed to account for the fact, as was becoming obvious, that there was a *tendency* for the mystics to become vitally active late in their careers. This often happened, as in the cases of Catherine of Siena, Ignatius of Loyola and Teresa of Avila, after they had completed the main body of their writings and thus was not noted in their teachings.

Several recent writers have followed Underhill and Bergson in characterizing the turn to action as a feature of the mystic's development. Dr. Kenneth Wapnick, in a seminal article entitled "Mysticism and Schizophrenia," went so far as to adapt Underhill's paradigm of the mystical stages. She had included sudden conversion, purification, illumination, the "dark night of the soul," and union (Cf. *Mysticism,* pp. 169ff). To these, Wapnick, on the basis of his studies of Teresa of Avila and other mystics, added a sixth, a "return . . . to the requirements of social living," which, he claimed, "constitutes the most important part of the [mystic's] path" ("Mysticism and Schizophrenia," p. 53). In a striking passage, Wapnick explained the integral nature of this return in terms of the mystic's inner development:

"The mystic now no longer finds his involvement with the world to be abhorrent, but, in fact, seems to welcome the opportunity to move in the social world he had abandoned. This seeming paradox becomes understandable when one considers that it was not the world the mystic was renouncing, but merely his attachments and needs relating to it, which precluded the development of his personal, asocial experience. Once he was able to abandon these dependent, social needs, and felt freed of the pull of the social world, he experienced the freedom to live within society in conjunction with his inner strivings, rather than experiencing society's customs and institutions as obstacles to his self-fulfillment" (Ibid.).

MYSTICS AS REFORMERS AND REVOLUTIONARIES

Another recent discussion of the social dimension of mystical development can be found in William Johnston's study of meditation and mysticism, *Silent Music.* Even more than Underhill, Bergson and Wapnick, Johnston notes the integral character of social activity in the course of mystical development as reflected in the writings of St. Teresa compared to some twelfth century Chinese Buddhist texts, the famous "ox-herding pictures," which portray the mystical quest in terms of a man searching for the ox, which symbolizes the true self.

"Successive sketches show man lost in illusion until he gets a glimpse of the footprints of the ox; then of the ox itself. Next he tames the ox and rides it home. Then the ox disappears, leaving the man alone. But the drama reaches its climax with the eighth picture where not only the ox but also the man disappears and nothing remains" (*Silent Music,* p. 80).

Thus, the original set ended with a depiction of "a state of consciousness beyond subject and object in which it is impossible to make a statement or a judgment about anything" (Ibid., p. 81). Underhill's classic paradigm ended, similarly, with the ineffable sense of Union. But, as Johnston continues, "In twelfth-century China, however, other pictures were added, so that the series ended with the enlightened old man returning to the market-place to save all sentient beings . . ." (Ibid.).

Under the influence of Mahayana teachings, compassion is the force that brings the old man, the *bodhisattva,* back to the world, much as love is the usual motive attributed to the Christian mystic's return to society. But Johnston, like Underhill and Bergson, although identifying love as the impelling cause, does not *account* for this outcome as an intrinsic part of the mystical process itself.

Another contemporary philosopher, W. T. Stace, devoted several pages of his study *Mysticism and Philosophy* to a consideration of the ethical elements in mysticism. But although he adverted to the active character of the mystic's response to the oneness of All, repeating the judgment that Christian mysticism appears superior to other forms in this regard, Stace, too, failed to account for the active phase of mystical development in terms of the *structure* of that process itself in its social context.

Conversely, Wapnick's description of the social integration concluding the mystic's development, while aware of the *structural* aspect of the turn to action, does not relate it to the mystic's motive, that is, to compassion. This almost gives the impression that mysticism is a form of preventive psychotherapy evolved to promote social adjustment. In fact, however, the mystic returns to society as a reformer and revolutionary, not merely a more adequately adjusted wheel in the social machine.

HOCKING AND THE SOCIAL DIMENSION OF MYSTICISM

The observed tendency of the mystics to engage themselves in action, despite the strenuous accusations of the Protestant theologians to the contrary, also attracted the attention of one of the great religious thinkers of our time, William Ernest Hocking. A life-long student of mysticism, Hocking alone was able to identify the process by which the mystics returned to the world of social action, not as a by-product of their development, but as its end-product.

Waging a fifty-year campaign against his fellow Protestant opponents, Hocking succeeded, I think, in showing the connection between mysticism and prophetic social action to be one of structural continuity: "The prophet is but the mystic in control of the forces of history, declaring their necessary outcome: the mystic in action is the prophet. In the prophet, the cognitive certainty of the mystic becomes historic and particular; and this is the necessary destiny of that certainty: mystic experience must complete itself in the prophetic consciousness" (*The Meaning of God in Human Experience,* p. 511).

Hocking's point of departure was different from that of Underhill, Bergson and the more recent authors. Rather than considering mystical development as a fundamentally individual matter between "the soul and God," or even, as Wapnick did, a process enhancing the individual's participation in society, Hocking perceived mysticism to be an *essentially social process* as well as a "private" one.

For Hocking, the mystic is "selected" to represent the society itself, undergoing a strenuous process of discernment and evaluation with regard to basic social beliefs, values and behavioral standards *precisely in order to renew them for the sake of more effective social harmony and progress.* As the embodiment of the highest ideals and values of a society, the mystic is primarily a social person. Her message is to society, and the way she communicates it immediately is by way of direct action.

MYSTICS AS SOCIETY IN MINIATURE

Needless to point out, to appropriate authentically the deepest meaning and value of a society's fundamental tenets, the mystic must not only be deeply identified with his or her society, but also be capable of undergoing a rigorous process of surfacing, clarifying and appraising those values, ideas, beliefs and patterns of behavior prior to carefully reintegrating them in a lifestyle relevant to the society's larger quest for its own harmony and progress. From a social viewpoint, this is the process of purgation, illumination and union, negatively experienced as the "dark nights" of the body and spirit. As we have seen elsewhere, as a dialectical process, this development can be characterized as one of a systematic disintegration of *apparently* integrated social values, ideas, beliefs and behavior, followed by a reintegration, which prepares the mystic for a re-entry into the social world.

Such a process allows society to renew its awareness of its most authentic and deepest objectives, reconstruct its programs for attaining them, and improve its operation without the immobilizing process of "deautomatization" which requires the mystic, society's surrogate, to withdraw from the social world into a period of inactivity. It is in this sense, as Johnston remarks, that "mystical action flows from *wu-wei* or non-action" (*The Inner Eye of Love,* p. 155). The success of the project depends not only on the mystic's identification and the thoroughness of the clarification process, but also upon her ability to *communicate* and *motivate* once she has returned from her solitary excursion into the depths of her own personality and, by extension, that of the social group. For Hocking, this ability was truly a prophetic skill.

Thus, the compassion experienced by the mystic as a result of perceiving the identity of all things in God has as a previous condition a self-identification with the society out of which the mystic emerges. The process of development, as Wapnick observed, is one in which the mystic acquires true freedom or *detachment* from that society, becoming thereby a real individual, but an individual encapsulating the values, norms and ideals of that society. *The mystic has become the society in miniature.*

The change effected by purgation, illumination and union therefore does not destroy either the mystic's individuality or social identification, but extends them dramatically. True "individuation," the name given the process of mystical development by Jung, releases the authentic self, the natural self, from the confines of the artificial self, preoccupied in reflection on its own existence and controlled by social conventions. Further, the narrow identification with a particular culture, people, land and tradition is *universalized;* the mystic becomes a surrogate of all human persons everywhere and at all times.

Consequently, despite the selflessness and universal compassion characteristic of the "completed" mystic, she or he is commonly perceived as a distinctive individual, a "character," involved in a very timely way in the immediate concerns of the society in which they find themselves. This, of course, stands to reason: *all are one*—it makes less difference which group the mystic approaches than that things *move.*

It is also worth noting that the universal compassion and relevance of the mystic's message and work argue concretely that whether at the bottom or at the top, the hopes, beliefs and ideals of human beings are ultimately the same. Further, they are realizable as such, given the insight and willingness necessary to do so. This is the social value of the mystic's developmental process.

MYSTICISM AND PROPHECY

For Hocking, then, there was a vital connection between the mystic and society *prior to* the solitary withdrawal into the negative way. The completion of that journey toward full integration, of individuation, required a return to that society. "The mystic is a bearer in his own person of the questioning out of which he was born. When he joins his community in worship, he joins in its questioning—for worship when it is alive contains a new grouping of the soul, not a wearing deeper of old ruts. And if he finds an answer, he must bring it back into the context of the questioning to which the answer belongs. He must vest his insight in that particular historical campaign" (*Living Religions and a World Faith,* p. 46).

A mystic, then, is a person not "asocial" but supremely and sensitively social, even *hyper*-social. To live out the implications of that social sensitivity, the mystic must first become independent of society, however, or forever be at the mercy of what is essentially an adolescent identification. When expressed in the form of mature action and involvement, that social sensitivity becomes a force for reform and progress, what Hocking meant by "the prophetic consciousness." As we shall see, his view was not far from that of many biblical scholars.

Convinced that society depended upon the mystic for its essential well-being and development, Hocking's original rejoinder to those who pitted prophetic social action against mysticism was to assert their identity. For him, as we have seen, prophecy was the extension of mystical awareness in action: "The mystic in historic action is termed the prophet: in a study of the prophet we may span the final term of religion's work in the world" (*The Meaning of God in Human Experience,* p. 484). Prophecy is thus not merely a mode of social interaction or of precognitive vision, but the ripe fruit of a mystical encounter with God rooted deep in the meaning and structure of human experience.

The transition from mystical awareness to active social intervention is inevitable, given the prophet's impulse toward communicating what he has experienced despite its ineffable character. He is no less committed to leaving behind a permanent contribution to the world, as he feels he has been charged to do by a mysterious destiny. "Hence it is that the greater mystics have been great founders, great agitators, and have if not a heavenly immortality yet unquestionably a mundane immortality. There are no deeds more permanent than those of Buddha, of Mohammed, of Jesus. And innumerable lesser deeds of equal validity have completed the substance of these mighty frames. The deeds of the mystics constitute the hard parts of history; the rest has its day and passes" (Ibid., p. 512).

So it is that in the accounts and orders and sects left behind by the great mystics, the supreme values of society, refined and renewed by the personal transformation of the mystic who embodies them, are readjusted to their institutional form and rendered more accessible to those less able to endure the stresses of the negative path. Perhaps even more importantly, new values are also discovered, clarified and expressed by means of the mystical adventure. Thereby, the race moves forward slowly and raggedly but definitely toward the unification of history in a common spiritual vision, a mystical union of human persons with God which Teilhard de Chardin poetically described as "the Omega Point."

Contemporary biblical scholars have come round to an appreciation of the mystical aspect of prophetic action which clearly supports Hocking's embattled defense. H. H. Rowley, in his book *The Servant of the Lord,* defined a prophet as "a man who knew God in the immediacy of experience," and felt "an inescapable constraint to utter what he was profoundly convinced was the word of God." Further, "the measure of his experience was the measure of his receptiveness and his response" (p. 45).

John L. McKenzie even more explicitly recognizes the mystical aspect of prophecy: "The only satisfactory parallel to the prophetic experience is the phenomenon of mysticism as described by writers like Teresa of Avila, John of the Cross and others. They affirm that the immediate experience of God is ineffable; like the prophets, they must employ imagery and symbolism to describe it, with explicit warnings that these are used. They describe it as a transforming experience which moves one to speech and action beyond one's experienced capacities. It grants them a profound insight not only into divine reality but into the human scene. Thus the prophetic experience is such a mystical immediate experience of the reality and presence of God" (*Dictionary of the Bible,* p. 697).

THE DIALECTIC OF CONTEMPLATION AND ACTION

Not everyone will agree that the relationship between mysticism and prophecy is one of dynamic continuity. And in actual fact, the situation is not one of direct, linear development from contemplative union to action, from withdrawal to return. The mystic (and prophet) often withdraws again to contemplative solitude, having met rejection, hostility and denial, if not simple indifference. Typically, however, the dialectic continues.

Impelled by a heightened sensitivity to the betrayal, corruption or distortion of the fundamental values, most cherished beliefs and manner of life of a people, the mystic returns to prophetic action again and again, like an outraged conscience. Catherine of Siena, craving solitude to be with her Lord, like Isaiah, Jeremiah, John the Baptist and Paul, was driven repeatedly into hounding, nagging and cajoling her audiences—whether Pope Gregory XI, the citizens of Florence, or a leprous old woman named Cecca—until she overcame all resistance. Like Abraham and Moses before her, she even bartered and wheedled with God until she got her way—in more than one case, the special grace of conversion for a hardened sinner.

In his description of the mystic's re-entry into society, Wapnick not only did not account for the motive to do so, but also overlooked the pattern of rejection and hostility, especially on the part of the established religion and civil government, which characteristically involve the reformer in another dialectic of withdrawal and return.

Had the people not forgotten or squelched the fundamental elements at the foundation of its very existence, there would, of course, have been no need to recover them by the mystical dialectic. Further, the mystic-turned-prophet would have been welcomed as an honored guest instead of treated like a bad memory.

But in historical fact, such has not been the case. Today as ever, a real prophet finds little receptiveness in his own land and among her own people for the very reason that they are prophets: to reform, to disturb, to agitate and, above all, to remind and move people to action.

Far from implying that the mystics' identification with society is imperfect, the antagonism argues for the mystics' deeper perception and truer realization of the values, ideals and goals of the society than those of the most influential social leaders themselves. Entrenched by institutionalism, custom, habit and "enlightened self-interest," both shepherds and often the sheep become indolent, forgetting their deeper calling and ultimate objective. The mystics, having recovered these through a process of personal re-evaluation, become catalyzing agents for society, trying to induce a wide-scale "deautomatization" similar to what they had experienced along their solitary journey into the waste-lands of their own spirits.

JUSTICE, PEACE AND FRIENDSHIP

The mystics' return to the world of society after completing the preliminary stages of mystical development depends, then, upon two levels of awareness. First, the mystics' compassionate identification with people—all people—impels them to act in order to alleviate injustice, oppression, ignorance, disease and misery of all kinds. In short, to establish a kingdom of right relationships, a just society founded on unrestricted good will, that is, on *love*.

Secondly, on a different level, the mystics are recovering the original values, standards and hopes that had inspired the great founders of history, whether the Apostles, other religious geniuses such as the Buddha, Sankara and Mohammed, or even the civil partisans who began a new order of things to insure a better world for all—the Republicans of Florence, the constitutional democrats of 1689, 1776 and 1792, the Emancipator of 1863, the Suffragettes, Gandhi or Malcolm X.

The mystics are not returning to the past, however. They are attempting to recover and renew a past commitment, an original vision of a future bright with possibilities of peace, universal sisterhood and brotherhood, and justice for all. Thus, they are not only the pioneers of humanity, as Underhill called them, scouting ahead for new horizons to attain. They are *precursors,* anticipating that attainment, as Hocking would say, in their own persons, lives and careers. Further, they are the "party whips" of the race, spurring us all back onto the path toward a truly better world, a new humanity.

A mystic who does not act, therefore, who does not fulfill the vision of heroic possibility granted in the moment of insight, is to that extent incomplete, indeed un-holy. The perfection of the spiritual life, of passionate concern, is action. Both James and John bear eloquent testimony to this "law" of Christ: "If a brother or a sister is ill-clad and in lack of daily food, and one of you says to them 'Go in peace, be warmed and filled,' without giving them the things needed for the body, what does it profit? So faith by itself, if it has no works is dead" (James 2:15-17). "By this we know love, that he laid down his life for us, and we ought to lay down our lives for the brethren. But if any one has the world's goods and sees his brother in need, yet closes his heart against him, how does God's love abide in him? Little children, let us not love in word or speech but in deed and in truth" (1 Jn. 3:16-18).

It is for this reason, and because the inequities of the social system are so evident, that the mystics seem inevitably to turn their attention first, if not primarily, to those Franz Fanon called "the wretched of the earth." In the life of Jesus we see it as he proclaimed the good news (for a change) to the poor and downcast, cured the sick, cast out evil spirits and taught men to forgive sins. We find it in the commitment of Francis of Assisi, Alexis, John of God, Catherine of Siena, Vincent de Paul, Martin de Porres, Peter Claver, Jean Baptiste de la Salle, Dom Bosco, Charles de Foucauld, and Damien of Molokai. In more recent times, it finds fulfillment in the work of Dorothy Day, Albert Schweitzer, the Little Brothers of the Poor, Dr. Tom Dooley, Mother Teresa of Calcutta and Cardinal Leger.

In an important article on politics and contemplation, Segundo Galilea observed the same kind of thrust within the movement in Latin America toward a true "liberation theology": "Christ encountered and contemplated in prayer is prolonged in the encounter with our brother, and, if we are capable of experiencing Christ in our service of the least, it is because we have already encountered him in contemplative prayer. Contemplation is not only the discovery of the presence of Jesus in the brother ('you did it to me') but also a call to action in his favor, to the liberating commitment ('as you did it . . .'). The contemplation of Christ in the suffering, oppressed brother is a call to commitment. It is the historical content of Christian contemplation in the Latin American Church" (p. 25).

The mystical life, then, is the way, divinely human, of translating word into work, of transforming the all-embracing love found in the presence of God into humanly meaningful *action*. In so doing, it fulfills its own destiny and moves the world inexorably toward final unification in the revelation of the children of God. And *that* is prophetic.

MYSTERION

SUGGESTIONS FOR FURTHER READING

Henri Bergson, *The Two Sources of Morality and Religion,* trans. by R. Ashley Audra and Cloudesley Brereton, Garden City, N.Y.: Doubleday and Co. Anchor Book, no date.

Matthew Fox, O.P., *A Spirituality Named Compassion,* Minneapolis: Winston Press, 1979.

Segundo Galilea, "Liberation as an Encounter with Politics and Contemplation," in *The Mystical and Political Dimension of the Christian Faith,* ed. by Claude Geffre and Gustavo Gutierrez, New York: Herder and Herder, 1974 (*Concilium,* No. 96), pp. 19-33.

John C. Haughey, ed., *The Faith that Does Justice,* N.Y. The Paulist Press, 1977.

William Johnston, S.J., *The Inner Eye of Love,* N.Y.: Harper and Row, 1978.

______________, *Silent Music* N.Y.: Harper and Row, 1974.

Marie Augusta Neal, S.N.D. deN., *A Sociotheology of Letting Go,* N.Y.: The Paulist Press, 1977.

Evelyn Underhill, *Mysticism,* N.Y.: World Publishing Co., 1955 ed.

Kenneth Wapnick, "Mysticism and Schizophrenia," *Journal of Transpersonal Psychology,* (Vol. 1, No. 2), pp. 49-66.

Chapter 11

MYSTICISM AND THE MYSTERY OF EVIL

A theology of love cannot afford to be sentimental. . . . [It] must seek to deal realistically with the evil and injustice in the world—not merely to compromise with them.

Thomas Merton

Of all people on earth, at least those religiously inclined, mystics seem to be the most incurably optimistic; perhaps aware of the inescapable presence of evil about them, but, to many observers, seemingly unaffected by it. This attitude has earned them the unenviable reputation of romantics and idealists. Yet it was taken by Bertrand Russell, among others, as a characteristic feature. "Mysticism maintains," the great philosopher wrote in *Mysticism and Logic,* "that all evil is illusory, and sometimes maintains the same view as regards good, but more often holds that all Reality is good" (p. 26). Julian of Norwich's optimistic "all shall be well, and all shall be well, and all manner of thing shall be well" provides a noteworthy example *(Revelations of Divine Love,* ch. 27).

The mystery of evil becomes a problem for a mystical spirituality because of the mystics' awareness of, and unshakable faith in, the radical goodness of God and the world of his creation. For now, as in Julian's fourteenth century, we are daily immersed in tragedy and disaster. The morning news can easily cast a pall over our entire day, unless we indeed decide that such evil is an illusion. Or that we are uninvolved. But the mystics know better.

It helps little to reckon that evil has entered the world because of human (or even angelic) sin—the stock answer to the challenge evil raises with regard to God's goodness. If we are realistic at all, the monumental scope of human evil, revealed by modern communications media, itself seems to cry out against the goodness of creation, especially if we believe that humankind represents the crown of God's work (Gen. 1:31). Is freedom so valuable as to be worth all this suffering?

Apart even from human sin—the scandal and bane of the social world—the violence, destruction, waste and futility of the *natural* world argues that evil is somehow woven into the very fabric of creation:

When the stars threw down their spears,
And watered Heaven with their tears,
Did he smile his work to see?
Did he who made the lamb make thee?

Tiger, tiger, burning bright
In the forests of the night,
What immortal hand and eye
Dare frame thy fearful symmetry?

Blake, "The Tiger"
in *Poems from the Notebook, 1791-1792*

Whether we call it the effect of "original" sin or see it as a consequence of some primeval moral disaster, the problem remains: *if* God is good, if his creation mirrors his own image and likeness, *whence come these evils,* as the ancient Greeks inquired.

To deny that they exist is to court the charge of avoiding reality, if not sanity. To acknowledge them in all their horror casts a shadow over the sovereign goodness of God. How could so loving, so powerful and so *benevolent* a parent—more, a Lover—of humankind allow such catastrophes to occur?

Surrounded as it is by some of the most powerful and undeniable evils in human history, a mystical spirituality is *possible* in today's world only to the extent that it effectively acquits itself of the charges of romantic idealism and escapism to address itself to the reality of the common situation. And if it succeeds in this task, I am convinced it will become a *necessary* mode of being in the world of reality and of the future.

THE POWERS OF DARKNESS

The inevitability of tornadoes, taxes, death and the myriad lesser forms of destruction, pain and malice we group under the heading "evil" has been an obstacle to religious belief since the dawn of time. How can God, if he is all-knowing, all-powerful and all-good, do such things or allow them to happen?

The Psalmist, like Job, inquires morosely, "Why do the innocent suffer?" And adds, spitefully, "Why do the wicked prosper?"

The reality of evil, the threat it presents to faith, is not an abstract problem to be solved by mental agility. It is not a puzzle, but a true challenge. It is a mystery—perhaps an unfathomable one.

The classic attempts to answer this challenge philosophically and theologically have often left people disappointed, not so much because of their naiveté or inadequacy, but because of their *coldness.* Surely this has been the religious crucifixion of the world's Jews since the Holocaust in Nazi Europe. As Richard Cavendish observed with respect to a less mind-numbing example, "It makes no sense to tell someone trapped in a burning building and roasting to death that he is not having an experience of Authentic-Being. To call agonizing pain a negative or to say that a person born crippled is in a condition of lesser good is mere juggling with words" (*The Powers of Evil,* p. 6).

How can the slaughter of three million Cambodians be described as a "lack of due goodness" and still mean anything?

The references are, of course, to the definition of evil as a privation of being. Which is to say that evil as such has no reality of its own. It is always derivative, the corruption of something good. Evil is ruin. This view, the product of the genius of St.

Augustine and the anonymous mystic who called himself Dionysius the Areopagite, is perhaps the most brilliant and cogent conception of evil in human history. But for all its success, it is not very helpful.

Other thinkers, such as Spinoza, and idealists in general, have, like most Eastern philosophies and Mary Baker Eddy, decided that if evil has no proper being of its own, it must therefore be an illusion. It is this view that Russell attributes to mysticism.

Many mystics, caught up in their awareness of what Hopkins called "the dearest freshness deep down things," or in idealism, have indeed denied that evil has any proper existence, whether it "is" an illusion or a negation. As Mother Julian wrote, "I saw not sin."

CONCRETE EVIL

But merely identifying evil as an illusion is no more helpful for someone caught in a tornado, an earthquake or a mugging than is calling it a deprivation. For as we *experience* it, which for most of us (not to mention the mystics) is what counts, evil is not negative but very positive and very real.

That is, whether evil is a presence or an absence, we experience it as something *concrete*—toothaches, broken bones, acne, cancer, ingrown nails; hair and teeth falling out; we have belly aches from gluttony or starvation. We are prey to disease, accident, old age, and death. There are natural disasters such as flood, fire, hail, volcanic eruptions, lightning, hurricanes, drought, blizzards, and tidal waves. We can speak of social evils, such as the inequitable distribution of food, land, income and opportunity; crime, vandalism, political corruption, war, oppression and the collective insanity of ideology. And moral evil, such as sin and temptation in all their guises; ugliness or aesthetic evil; and the intellectual evil of ignorance and falseness, which seems endemic to human existence.

Perhaps to refer to all these as "evil" is already to beg the question. But to deny their reality is worse than blindness.

Beyond such "ordinary" manifestations of the wrongness we encounter in the world of nature and society, many persons, saints included, have reported experiences of superhuman evil. Accounts such as those of the desert fathers or St. Catherine of Siena, and those also of otherwise very ordinary people, describe "mystical" encounters with spiritual forces or "presences" so malignant and terrifying that our cinematic tales of possession and haunting are only dim reflections.

Even in the contemplative life itself, we find instances of the deepest corruption—the *miccha samadhi* or "contemplation of the left-hand path" William Johnston speaks of in the Orient, and the "devil's own contemplatives" that we read of in *The Cloud of Unknowing.*

Whence come *these* evils?

We find evil within our experience when we discover that things are not as they should be or that they are as they should not be. That is, as Russell remarked, when matters depart from our desires or expectations in a serious manner.

THE RELATIVE QUALITY OF EVIL

Such a view of evil is, of course, both subjective and relative. Are there things or situations that are evil in themselves, absolutely evil? Is a black hole in space evil? Is a tiger or a black widow spider? A tornado? A "poisonous" mushroom or an earthquake?

It was to such questions that the theologians (and mystics) replied, emphatically, "no." Nothing in God's creation is evil in itself, for all that God created is good, and there *is* nothing beyond what God created except God himself. In Meister Eckhart's concise phrase, "everything that is, is in God." For Mother Julian, also: "And after this I saw God in a Point, that is to say in mine understanding, by which sight I saw that he is in all things. I beheld and considered, seeing and knowing in sight, with a soft dread, and thought: *What is sin?*" (ch. 11.).

Evil, since it has no proper being, does not "exist," but that need not mean it is not real, an illusion. At least not entirely. True evil is real *in our experience.*

First of all, evil *is* relative because it is a relation. We call something evil when it is seriously out of harmony with the way we perceive things ought to be, the way they are *meant* to be. A blighted oak or a cat born blind is not evil, but their condition is, relative to what they should have been. For some mysterious reason, creation is marred with such accidents and imperfections.

The carnivorous appetite of the tiger is not evil, but the fate of the lamb is, in comparison to what the lamb could have been otherwise. But eating the lamb is not evil for the tiger. The evolutionary process which has developed tigers and scorpions is not evil; furthermore, nature has its own process of balancing animal and plant populations.

But surely, as C. S. Lewis observed, all the violence and bloodletting argues that somewhere, sometime, *something* went awry. It is not just sentimentality that causes us to wince when the lamb encounters the tiger.

If such misfortunes suggest a deeper malaise of Creation than suffering and loss alone, there is no doubt for the mystic that evil is also real as a quality of human behavior. Sin, that is, voluntary or moral evil, is so much a part of the human situation that *The Cloud of Unknowing* poignantly describes the process of self-discovery as finding oneself "a foul, stinking lump of sin." And yet, as Mother Julian realized, such evil has no proper being of its own. It is the corruption of our intentions, desires and actions which finds expression in human and animal suffering as either motive or consequence.

As we shall see, the mystics' perception of what ought to be, what can be but is *not,* is so profoundly moving an experience that they become agents of social change. For the mystics, evil in the form of injustice, disparity, cruelty, oppression, misery, ignorance, or sin is no phantasm, but a call to action.

EVIL AS ILLUSION

Nevertheless, much of what we call evil *is* illusory, because our desires and expectations are out of harmony with the order of things as God intended them. A weed is only a plant out of place in the *human* order. Similarly, animal "pests" such as weasels, rats, insects and other vermin are harmful only in relation to our needs or desires. Coyotes, wolves, bats, snakes, toads and tigers are among the most useful, marvelous and beautiful creatures God has given us to watch over (and out for). Even a spider is a miracle of engineering.

In the social order, even more than in the natural one, before a mystic—or anyone else—embarks upon a course of rectifying evils, it is therefore not only wise but really necessary to have gotten one's perceptions straight about what is and what ought to be. This is probably why, in almost all mystical traditions, there is so much emphasis placed on restraint and non-action. The process of mystical development is, in this light, one of gradual enlightenment, a path of purification in which customary attitudes and patterns of behavior, with their habitual assumptions about the order of things, are systematically clarified and re-integrated. This is especially true with regard to attitudes about good and evil, which so often are merely unquestioned notions based on personal or group whims and bias, custom and prejudice.

This is perhaps why, in the lives of the mystics, what those around them all too easily describe as evil, from dandelions to "infidels," gives way to a perception of *real* evil, particularly social injustice, oppression, and the wretchedness of the poor. The correlative of a new awareness of the goodness and beauty of Creation is a heightened consciousness of social evil.

Nevertheless, even the mystics replace baby robins in their

nest. And in this lies, perhaps, the ultimate rebuttal to Lord Russell.

Russell, I think, was wrong in taking as *typical* of the mystical vision the claim that evil is an illusion. For, in fact, being so acutely sensitized to God's presence and the goodness of his creation, the *intended* harmony of the world, they typically take evil very seriously—more so than did the venerable philosopher himself. As H. D. Lewis wrote, "Evil is only a problem in the proper intellectual sense for a religious view or for some form of metaphysics which finds supreme goodness at the heart of things" (*Philosophy of Religion,* p. 307). *How* the mystics address themselves to evil differs, however, from case to case.

OPTIMISM, PESSIMISM AND HOPEFULNESS

If Spinoza considered evil an illusion, Leibniz went a step farther toward optimism when he concluded that this must be the best of all possible worlds—a view which Voltaire so richly lampooned in *Candide.* The mystics are not optimists in that sense. They know that this is a world in process, one infected with evil, but perfectible by dint of tremendous effort. In this regard, they are *hopeful* rather than simply optimistic.

The mystics further differ from the academic philosophers in that they are concerned first, last and always with *experience,* not with concepts. Even here, as with regard to a fundamental attitude toward the world, they differ from each other in remarkable ways. Some are sufficiently less hopeful than others with respect to the world of nature and especially of society that they can accurately be called pessimistic.

The difference between mystical hopefulness and pessimism can be seen in the striking dissimilarity between two mystics who lived near each other in time, if not geographically: Dame Julian of Norwich, an Englishwoman, and Thomas à Kempis, a Dutchman.

Over the centuries the latter's *Imitation of Christ* came to have an importance in devotional literature next to that of the Bible itself. Julian's *Revelations of Divine Love* remained virtually unknown outside of England for almost six hundred years. Both works reflect the stresses and hardships of the fourteenth century, and both have much to offer our own similarly calamitous century.

Yet Julian's is the truer vision from a holistic Christian perspective, and she the greater mystic (if such comparisons are in any sense appropriate). For her message is one of hope overcoming evil, sin and death. Unlike Thomas, she neither feared the world nor fled from it. In her anchorhold at Norwich, she waited and prayed, and the world came to her.

While there is a spiritual message of true value in *The Imitation of Christ,* the author ultimately hopes to achieve the goal of salvation without having been sullied by a world which he perceives as a dangerous, immoral environment. There is little joy in his writing, and less awareness of the *grace*fulness of Creation. Thomas à Kempis was weary and world-denying.

"The greatest Saints," he wrote, "shunned the company of men when they could, and chose rather to live unto God in secret. As often as I have been among men, said one, I have returned less a man" (I, 20). His attitude toward human nature was fairly sour: "Nature inclines a man to creatures, to his own body, to vanities and to running to and fro. But grace draws to God and to all virtues, renounces creatures, flees the world, hates the desires of the flesh, restrains wanderings and blushes to appear in public" (III, 54). Friendship is hardly encouraged by such a spiritual melancholy: "We should have charity towards all men; but intimacy is not expedient" (I, 8).

Such an approach comes perilously close to cynicism and a fundamentally un-Christian devaluation of Creation: "There is nothing that so defiles and entangles the human heart as an impure attachment to created things" (II, 2). As for human beings, "Every man is a liar, weak, unstable and subject to fail, especially in words; so that we ought not readily believe even that which in appearance seems to sound well" (III, 45).

DAME JULIAN'S VISION

Far from underestimating the force of evil, Julian's soaring Christology rises above it in a vision of magnificent hope that returns us to the great mystical rhapsodies of the Cappadocian Fathers. Jesus tells her, as Lord, "See! I am God: see! I am in all thing: see! I do all thing: see! I lift never mine hands off my works, nor ever shall, without end: see! I lead all thing to the end I ordained it to from without beginning, by the same Might, Wisdom and Love whereby I made it. How should anything be amiss?" (Ch. 11). Puzzled over the problem of sin and evil, Julian returns again and again to the theme, and is told in various ways by Christ, "Sin is behovable, but all shall be well, and all shall be well, and all manner of thing shall be well" (Ch. 27). "Ah, good Lord, how might all be well," she asks, "for the great hurt that is come by sin to the creature?" (Ch. 29). Consolingly, Christ reminds her that he is the source of all strength and victory: "I may make all thing well, I can make all thing well, I will make all thing well, and I shall make all thing well; and thou shall see for thyself that all manner of thing shall be well" (Ch 31).

No matter how great or imponderable the mystery, whether of sin, evil, hell or damnation, Christ insists that despite all the pessimism of our theology, against all possibility as we know it, all shall be well in *him,* by and for *him:* "That which is impossible to thee is not impossible to me: I shall save my word in all things and I shall make all things well" (Ch. 32). Even sin has its place, for by his grace "the token of sin is turned to worship" (Ch. 38).

God's mercy, Julian realizes, "worketh, turning to us all things to good. Mercy, by love, suffereth us to fail in measure and in as much as we fail, in so much we fall; and in as much as we fall, in so much we die: for it must needs be that we die in so much as we fail of the sight and feeling of our God that is our life." Grace, however, "worketh our shameful falling into high, worshipful rising; and grace worketh our sorrowful dying into holy, blissful life" (Ch. 48).

The mystery of evil, for Julian, is transformed into victory by the power of God's love: "in this love He hath made all things profitable to us; and in this love our life is everlasting" (Ch. 76). Her message then, is one of hope, founded on God's promise that we shall not be overcome, but rather that we shall overcome. *How* we shall overcome is less urgent to her than the fact, which, for her, was an unshakable conviction. But her inkling that the victory lay in the transformation of evil into "worship" by the grace of Christ is surely the heart of the matter.

UNITY AND ACTION

Every student of mysticism is aware of the radical connectedness the mystic perceives beyond the manifold plurality of the social and natural world. If there is any cardinal principle of mystic teaching, surely it is this. As Francis Thompson reminds us, "Thou canst not stir a flower Without troubling of a star."

Similarly, Dr. Kenneth Wapnick defines mysticism "as the experience of Unity, or what Stace has called 'the apprehension of *an ultimate nonsensuous unity in all things,* a oneness or a One to which neither the sense nor the reason can penetrate' " ("Mysticism and Schizophrenia," p. 50, citing W. T. Stace, *The Teachings of the Mystics,* pp. 14-15). John Donne was only expressing Jesus' insistence upon the inescapable solidarity of all human beings (Cf. Matt. 25: 31-46) in his famous passage: "No man is an island, entire of itself; every man is a piece of the continent, a part of the main . . ." (*Devotions,* 17).

For the mystics, who have experienced the deep unity of the human family, the suffering of any one diminishes *them.* Injustice to any person, anywhere at any time, is not only a personal wrong to the mystics, it is also a corporate injury. It is *we* who are the oppressed and the oppressor. Far from being immune to evil done or suffered, the mystics are highly sensitive to both and identify with both in the persons involved.

Further, this perception of the part for the whole, the whole *in* the part, far from diluting the force of sin and suffering or immobilizing the mystics in some timeless absorption into the Absolute, spurs them on to action. And it is in *this* that we find, I think, the final clue to understanding the mystics' "solution" to the mystery of evil.

First, it is important to realize that the unity the mystics perceive underlying and binding together the untold billions of human lives, indeed connecting all things, is still a goal to be achieved even though it is a present reality in promise and potency. The mystics' vision is a prophetic one. This is why they are not immobilized in contemplative stupor but incited to a life of untiring activity. The City of God, the Omega Point, the Kingdom of Heaven, the "Restoration" *(apokatastasis)* of Creation—however we name the End Time, must be *achieved.* And it will be achieved but not, to be sure, by mere human effort. The times and seasons remain with the orbit of God's grace; the transformation of the cosmos will be the ultimate accomplishment of divine power. But like all gifts, this, too, must have its preparation. We must do all in *our* power to make ourselves receptive, to make ready the way of the Lord. Then we must abandon ourselves and all things into his hands.

William Ernest Hocking once wondered if there was any reform movement in history that did not have a mystic at the bottom of it. Here, it is enough to note that in Francis of Assisi, Catherine of Siena, Vincent de Paul, George Fox, Charles de Foucauld, Florence Nightingale, Maximilian Kolbe, Mother Teresa of Calcutta and others, the poetic insight of Donne has been translated into effective *action.* Such examples are, I believe, typical, not exceptional with regard to the mystics.

Because the whole is *known* to be within the part, the mystics' struggle to eliminate disparity and oppression, sickness, want and ignorance, must begin with the needing person at hand. Who, after all, is my neighbor, but the person next to me? If the mystics' perception is different from that of others, it is because they consciously recognize all of humanity and therefore the whole Christ, in the beggar, leper or child before them. The doors of their perception have been cleansed, their hearts opened along the journey of their inward purgation, their path of "self-naughting," of "de-automatization." The process has many names, but its product is the same—*compassion.* But the manifestation as well as the test of the reality of compassion is action.

THE MYSTIC'S ANSWER

The mystics' "solution" to the problem of evil is thus not an answer to a riddle, an intellectual achievement. It is found, rather, in a response to concrete needs. That is, evil is overcome *in our experience,* through our conversion to right action by the process of becoming compassionate.

In this regard, the mystics' value to humanity is twofold. First, they teach us that a merely mental solution to the challenge of evil can be at best only a partial response and therefore inadequate. For evil is real only in experience, and it must be overcome in experience if it is to be "solved." The theologians did not err when they defined evil as a deprivation of something good. They simply did not go far enough. For *real* deprivation is something *experienced* as pain, loss or diminishment, and it can be overcome only by action. The Lamb of God *takes away* the sin of the world by suffering, dying and rising, not by talking. Insight is never enough.

Second, if real evil is adequately answered only by action, since it is only by action that we truly enter the world of actual experience, the mystic shows us the way to effective action by *example* as well as by precept. *Motivation* is the key item in this equation. We must be *moved* out of our indolence and fearful immobilization in order to act. And only a motive sufficiently powerful to overcome the resistance we encounter in the face of overwhelming evil will be able to convert insight into action. That is, we must be able to overcome *ourselves* for the sake of others.

Such a motive is supplied by compassion, the mystics' essential and concerned feeling of the oneness of All. Evil, then, has this, at least, to "justify" its reality—it is the occasion for compassion, and with compassion comes the way to overcoming evil in experience, by right action.

To put it differently, God "permits" evils to occur in order that something might come about in human experience that could or would not happen otherwise—the eventuation of universally effective love through compassion. We realize the divine imperative not only by doing good, but even more by overcoming evil.

OVERCOMING EVIL

For the good we do is often negligible, half-hearted and transient. We are also prone to pride ourselves on our meager accomplishments as if they were momentous. Our struggle to overcome evil in human experience, motivated by compassion rather than self-regard or self-preservation, assures that we will not succumb to pride, but continue to rely on God's guidance and assistance, and also extend our compassion to all.

Our sights are generally too narrow as well as too low to be effective in advancing the Kingdom of God, the enterprise to which we were called in Eden Garden and which we cannot renounce by our failures or half-heartedness. But we are only apprentices in creativity, called out of the clayish desert of our nothingness to cooperate in the building of a cosmic city of universal love, peace, truth, and justice. Evil is the sacrament of our limitations and the occasion of our success—an effective sign that without God's present and future assistance, his grace, we can only engender nothingness, un-create the universe step by step.

The evil we have done remains until it is overcome; until the gap in being we have gnawed and hewn in selfishness and self-glorification is again filled up. But, with God's help, each fulfillment takes us not to where we might have been, or even to where we were meant to be, but to new heights once only the dream of God.

Mother Julian heard Jesus correctly when she perceived him to say not that all *is* well, but that all *shall* be well. The future is the kingdom of the will, the realm of hope—a City that must be won, or, rather, *built,* by action, not by wishes.

Evil remains a mystery to the human mind, a challenge in human experience so long as the City is unfinished. But it is no illusion. It is also a mystery not because it has no satisfying intellectual solution, but because it has been taken up into the *divine* mysterion, the "plan" hidden from all ages, where it has a place—one not meant, but consequent. The mystery also resides in the fact that, at least for those who can see and act, the consequence has been converted into a possibility, a condition for a future good greater than that lost in the past.

SUGGESTIONS FOR FURTHER READING

John Hick, *Evil and the God of Love,* London: Macmillan, 1966.

William Johnston, *Silent Music,* New York: Harper and Row, 1974.

Julian of Norwich, *Revelations of Divine Love,* ed. by Grace Warrack, London: Methuen and Co., Ltd., 1901.

Paul Ricoeur, *The Symbolism of Evil,* Boston: Beacon Press, 1969.

Bertrand Russell, *Mysticism and Logic,* 3rd edition, New York: Barnes and Noble, 1977.

Kenneth Wapnick, "Mysticism and Schizophrenia," *The Journal of Transpersonal Psychology,* Vol. 1, No. 2, pp. 49-68.

Richard Woods, "The Devil, Evil and Christian Experience," *Listening,* Vol. 12, No. 2, pp. 21-42.

Chapter 12

MYSTICISM, THEORY AND PROCESS

> *Every event on its finer side introduces God into the world. Through it his ideal vision is given a base in actual fact to which He provides the ideal consequent, as a factor saving the world from the self-destruction of evil. The power by which God sustains the world is the power of himself as the ideal. He adds himself to the actual ground from which every creative act takes its rise. The world lives by its incarnation of God in itself.*
>
> Alfred North Whitehead

As a whole, the world's great mystics appear to be primarily practical rather than theoretical in their approach to God, life, and even literature. Paradoxical statements, hyperbole, concrete imagery, symbolic thought and poetry characterize their writings and distinguish them clearly from thinkers devoted to logical precision, order, unambiguous discourse, and a rather abstract approach to reality. For the mystics' main concern is not to clarify our ideas, but to jar us out of our customary inattentiveness to the meaning of life and move us to seek a more immediate and experiential involvement with the Source of life.

Yet despite that fundamental difference, the mystics are not uninterested in theory. They have their own views of the nature of God, the meaning of life and the make-up of the world. They are often keen psychologists, and the ethical content of their teachings is either stated or clearly implicit. Many mystics have in fact been outstanding philosophers and theologians, among whom we could certainly include at least Plotinus, Augustine, St. Bernard, Bonaventure and Thomas Aquinas, Catherine of Siena, Pascal and Schelling.

In the Orient, philosophy, theology and spirituality are far less isolated disciplines than in the West. Thus, Lao Tzu, the Buddha, Dogen, Rumi, Sankara and Vivekananda each represent all three dimensions of endeavor. Similarly, two of the greatest Jewish philosophers of all time, Philo and Moses ben Maimon (Maimonides), were also mystics. The same is true of Al-Ghazali, the Moslem sage and Sufi mystic.

As acutely sensitive members of society, the mystics' theoretical reflections on God, humanity and the world also mirror to a greater or lesser extent the philosophical and religious presuppositions of their culture, whether positively or negatively. By comparative analysis, it is therefore possible to disengage at least some of these socially derived "superstructures" in order to expose the more fundamental elements of the mystics' vision of reality, which no one of them might wholly espouse, but which nevertheless represents a common view.

Several scholars have attempted to examine this basic philosophical and theological theory, among their works being Bertrand Russell's 1917 essay "Mysticism and Logic," Aldous Huxley's *The Perennial Philosophy,* R. C. Zaehner's sharp rejoinder, *Mysticism Sacred and Profane,* W. T. Stace's *Mysticism and Philosophy,* Illtyd Trethowan's *Mysticism and Theology* and Stephen Katz' anthology, *Mysticism and Philosophical Analysis.* William James, Josiah Royce and William Ernest Hocking were likewise preoccupied at the turn of the century. A more recent and provocative approach can be found in Lawrence LeShan's *The Medium, the Mystic and the Physicist.*

What these and many works like them primarily illustrate is the fact that there is a long way yet to go before we can speak of anything like a consensus regarding more than a few central tenets of mystical theory. In further chapters, we shall examine some of these basic notions. At this point, however, I wish to explore some aspects of mysicism in the context of contemporary thought, particularly process philosophy and theology. This appraisal will serve as both a resumé of what we have already considered and an introduction to subsequent treatments.

MYSTERION

MYSTICAL THEORY

Perhaps it is inevitable that the mystics become philosophers and theologians, for if they attempt to express their vision to others, they must necessarily do so in terms of some interpretation of "the way things are." Further, to articulate a coherent account of the meaning of God for human experience on the basis of one's own experience *is* theology, whether or not it is filtered through or corrected by traditional religious beliefs. Thus, *some* theory is inescapable, even though it may be reduced to a bare minimum, as in Zen Buddhism.

Several characteristics serve to differentiate the mystic thinker from his or her academic counterpart in addition to the emphasis on practice. The mystics speak with the conviction of personal acquaintance with the mysteries of God's encounter with humankind. In proof of their claims and reports, they appeal not to personal authority, however, but to *experience*: see for yourself, they tell us. Further, the mystics show a manifest ability to recognize their fellow mystics across ages and climes. Regarding this latter characteristic, Evelyn Underhill quoted Claude de St. Martin thus; "All mystics . . . speak the same language and come from the same country" (*Mysticism,* p. xiii).

William Ernest Hocking similarly observed in 1956, "Whatever their departure from one another in practice and theory, there is a tendency for the mystics in various traditions—selectively—to understand one another" (*The Coming World Civilization,* p. 141). (He went on to point out, significantly, "The primary identity involved in recognition of mystic by mystic is the essence of the religious worldview, the perception of Being as beatitude—God is, and God is One," P. 149.)

Given this ability to recognize and understand each other, it is nevertheless evident after a century of comparative studies of mysticism that in terms of their theoretical interpretations of reality, the mystics are often very far apart. Some are metaphysical monists, seeing all of reality as a manifestation of a single, undifferentiated unity, all differences being illusory. Theologically, such a vision, which we find in many Oriental traditions and in the philosophy of Spinoza, finds expression in *pantheism,* the belief that "All is God" (from the Greek *pan* = one, and *theos* = God).

Others, particularly but not exclusively in the West, are dualists, postulating a real difference in being between God and the created universe. Such a view, which is almost universal in western mysticism, may be either absolute or relative. Kierkegaard, Buber, and Bonhoeffer represent the tradition of absolute dualism. For them, as for classical Judaism and Islam, God is *wholly* Other, totally transcendent, communicating himself to the world from outside in. But there is no real inner connection. Relative dualism maintains, contrariwise, that although there is an essential difference between God and Creation, there is nevertheless a real inner connection, a *participation* in being.

For instance, in the 14th century *Book of Privy Counseling,* written by the author of the *Cloud of Unknowing,* we read: "he is thy being, and in him thou art what thou art, not only by cause and by being, but he is *in* thee both thy cause and thy being. And therefore think of God in this work as thou dost on thyself, and on thyself as thou dost on God: that he is as he is and thou art as thou art, so that thy thought be not scattered nor separated, but oned in him that is all; evermore saving this difference betwixt thee and him, that he is thy being and thou not his."

PANENTHEISM

Such a vision has rightly been called *panentheistic* ("All *in* God"), as we have seen before, for it recognizes the *interiority* of God's loving presence, his "immanence" in the very depths of being—not only as Creator, sustaining us in existence, but as Life-giver and Lover, sharing his very life with us. In this view, *all* created things share God's being according to the extent they are able, but they are not God by that participation—except in the case of *human* beings.

Our spiritual nature, according to the panentheistic mystics, is made in the image of God, and is thus open to a transforming infusion of grace that elevates us to a higher state of being than that proper to a creature. In the dangerous mystical language of the great Greek Fathers, this is the process of *theosis*—"divinization," in which, continuing the Incarnational dialectic, *we become* God. Still, however, the identity is not absolute. Only God *is* God. The transforming union which represents the goal of mystical development does not obliterate the distinction between Creator and creature. It does transcend it, however, in the *experiential* unity of Beloved and Lover.

Panentheism finds God wholly immanent, the same everywhere, pervading the manifest differences among real things. Absolute dualism finds God wholly transcendent, always and completely Other, the essential difference remaining radical and unbridgeable. Both views have the elegance of logical simplicity. Panentheism, or relative dualism, is neither elegant nor simple. It is paradoxical and illogical, caught between the absolutes of One and Two, Immanence and Transcendence. On one hand it knows that the abyss between creature and Creator is absolute, that we are nothing, God is All. Yet it knows also that God has overcome the existential distance once for all and even within individual experience.

The monist says "I," the Dualist says "I and Thou," but the panentheist says "We." It is the "we-consciousness" that spans the difference and which, as Hocking realized, constitutes the true realization of all mystical longing. As philosopher, he rejects the dichotomy between "Either/Or" and chooses "Both/And"—both immanence and transcendence, the One and the Twain. Although Monistic and Dualistic forms remain important strands of Western mysticism, from here on, by "mysticism" I shall mean panentheistic mysticism, the dominant and most representative Christian form.

Richard Woods

MYSTICISM AND PROCESS THOUGHT

One of the reasons that many philosophers and theologians have been unwilling or unable to deal very positively with mysticism is the divergence the mystics show with respect to the accepted canons of rational discourse and tidy metaphysical categories. But as the demands of modern life have rendered classical physics obsolete in many respects, the moral and existential dilemmas of today's world have also rendered classical philosophy and theology similarly irrelevant in many areas of concern. With respect to both their view of the world, their "Weltanschauung," and their reflective evaluation of it, the vision of the mystics has survived the collapse of the systems once so hostile to it. Nowhere is this truer, I believe, than in the development within philosophy and theology associated with process thought.

As an approach to both the physical world and its philosophical and theological interpretation, process thought is often identified with the work of the Anglo-American mathematician and philosopher, Alfred North Whitehead. No one figure has, in fact, contributed more to this view of reality. But Whitehead is not a solitary witness to the reality of cosmic process.

Fundamentally, process thinking differs from classical metaphysics and science in its tendency to conceive of reality in terms of constant development rather than fixed categories of being, like "substance" and "accidents." In this sense, old Herakleitos, Hegel and Marx could also be considered process thinkers. Darwin and Wallace realized the truth of evolutionary history, and Spencer popularized and developed their views philosophically. At the turn of the century, Henri Bergson first truly succeeded in articulating a coherent philosophy of "flux." Bergson, in turn, had a great influence on William James and his disciple, William Ernest Hocking, at Harvard. Whitehead was an avid follower of James, and on his coming to Harvard from Cambridge, he taught with Hocking.

Other important figures in the development of process thought include Hocking's students Charles Hartshorne, who next to Whitehead is the most influential process philosopher of our time, and Henry Nelson Wieman. The Canadian-American theologian and Anglican priest, W. Norman Pittenger, now of Kings College, Cambridge, is perhaps the most important process theologian. Yet proponents also associate the writings of the Jesuit paleontologist and philosopher Pierre Teilhard de Chardin with the theological and spiritual dimensions of process thought. Several more influential theologians should also be included in this group, at least as showing the effects of process thinking in their own development: Gregory Baum, Rosemary Reuther, Bernard Meland, John B. Cobb, Jr., and Schubert Ogden.

What these thinkers have in common is a creative openness to the findings of modern scientific method, tempered by a real humanism in the biblical tradition. Justice and compassion are no less important themes for them than are growth and energy. Process thought is far less abstract than classical metaphysics, and tends to value the real and systematic relations among concrete individuals, or, in process terminology, "events," which were neglected in the classical systems.

It was in this holistic respect that Whitehead characterized his philosophy as "organic." By this he meant not only that events are interconnected in time and space, but that *life* is the fundamental reality of the universe, and that life in abundance is the aim of universal development. In this he greatly resembles not only Bergson, but Teilhard, for whom all matter was en route to energy, life and consciousness, culminating in a transcendent cosmic awareness he called the "Omega Point," the goal and end of all evolutionary history.

Process theologians such as Teilhard and Whitehead envisage God as operating within universal process, not observing or even directing things from "beyond," occasionally intruding a bit by some miraculous interruption of the processes of nature. In this sense, process thought, like much Western mystical thought, is panentheistic.

Further, the God of process is no "unmoved Mover," but a loving, compassionate Presence who enters into the sufferings of his creatures and rejoices in their enjoyments. Here, the isolated, impassive God of the older philosophies and theologies has given way to a more biblical notion, that of a God capable of real *change,* such as loving implies. This, too, is the God of the mystics, a God who loves, who endures, who supports and suffers. In the case of Abraham and Catherine of Siena, he is the God who isn't above being prayed into acquiescence, if not submission.

This is the God *encountered* one night by the brilliant mathematician, Blaise Pascal, of whom he could only scribble on a scrap of parchment he kept with him until his death:

FIRE

God of Abraham, God of Isaac, God of Jacob,
Not of the philosophers and the learned.
Certitude. Joy. Certitude. Emotion. Sight. Joy.
Forgetfulness of the world and of all outside God.
The world hath not known Thee, but I have known Thee.
Joy! Joy! Joy! Tears of joy.
My God, wilt Thou leave me?
Let me not be separated from Thee for ever.

This is the God to whom the church prays on the 23rd Sunday of the year:

O Lord, look with favor upon your people and their gifts.

Let this offering move you to compassion, and grant us forgiveness of our sins and a quick answer to our prayers.

PROCESS MYSTICISM

Process thought and mysticism share several major characteristics, then, even apart from any doctrinal similarities or differences regarding the nature and structure of reality. For this reason it might be safely suggested that their mutual fortunes are connected. Mysticism has found in process thought a congenial metaphysical framework; process thought has found in mysticism a spiritual ally and concrete exemplification.

Fundamentally, taking a processive view of mysticism enables us to reconceive some of the basic elements we have been considering so far in terms more in accord with 20th century life than that of the 14th or 18th centuries. The difference is not so much a matter of interpretation as it is of translation. That is to say, the *way* in which mysticism is described has been brought into closer harmony with the dynamic actuality of lived experience.

To speak of process in the first place is to speak of some form of structural transformations in time, usually a natural phenomenon characterized by gradual changes leading toward a determinate result. The growth of an oak from an acorn is thus a true process. Cosmic evolution is also a process, although the goal, however determinate, is not immediately apparent because the scope is so incredibly vast and the gradual changes most often so incredibly fast or slow that they cannot be directly observed.

Mystical development is no less a process—a gradual series of changes leading to a specifiable result—ultimate integration. We may consider a particular instance of mystical insight, or an "experience" in the singular sense, to be an "event" in this process. Any process of development is composed of such events, each momentarily real, but passing inexorably into the past, which remains real only in its present effects. The mystic, as Hocking once said, may show disappointment at the passing of the moment of union, but not surprise.

Relations are also real components of process, representing the concrete ways in which events are connected among themselves.

Real events have real relations. The network of relations among the constituent elements of an event which give it its character or nature is its *structure*. A *system* is a structure in operation, a whole whose parts are so combined as to function in unison. A living system is an *organism*.

All this may seem very remote from the mystical ecstasies of St. Teresa. By using these descriptive terms, however, we can understand such lived experiences as part of a complete and operational whole which might otherwise make only partial sense not only to a contemporary reader, but even to a contemporary of Teresa's. A notable example of so creatively redescribing mystical experience can be found in Dr. Kenneth Wapnick's essay "Mysticism and Schizophrenia," in which St. Teresa's experiences are compared structurally and dynamically to those of a woman who had suffered a complete psychotic breakdown.

In psychiatric perspective, mysticism was revealed by Wapnick's analysis to constitute a systematic restructuring of life events to effect a determinate result—complete individual and social harmonization, interpreted as union with God. The psychotic breakdown, conversely, represented a fragmentation of personality resulting from the woman's inability to integrate life events structurally—events which were in many respects psychologically no different from those of the mystic saint.

The crucial difference between the mystic and the schizophrenic patient lies not in the identity of the persons, nor even in the final result, for both emerged from their respective processes as whole persons, if the psychotic woman did so only by totally succumbing to her madness for a period. Rather, the crucial difference lies in the process of development—in one case, organized and systematic, while in the other, uncontrolled and haphazard.

The mystical life, therefore, can be helpfully described as a process of development in which the elements of experience are *reorganized* in order to achieve a specifiable result—the complete and harmonious integration of the whole person—physically, mentally, emotionally, spiritually and socially. As an organic process, moreover, mystical development actualizes these human potentials most intensely and permanently, without the severe disruptions characteristic of a psychological breakdown and reintegration.

Thus conceived, the "mystic path" is not a linear passage from one set of adventures to another, like a Flash Gordon serial, in which the character of the individual remains fundamentally unchanged, despite acquiring new "experience." Rather, a *new* person emerges out of the process, much as a butterfly emerges from the cocoon spun by a caterpillar, to use St. Teresa's homely but appropriate simile. Mysticism effects a complete transformation; an oak has small resemblance to an acorn, but there has been an undeniable continuity of experience.

Such continuity is not that of a "substance" undergoing a sequence of accidental modifications, such as water becoming alternately steam and ice. This continuity of experience is one in which an event develops out of another according to a pattern itself subject to the particular variations of a concrete history. An oak may become a *bonzai* masterpiece or a dining room table.

The three "ages" of the interior life, accordingly, with their transitional "dark nights" of the body and spirit, are not "states" one passes through like Kansas, or phases such as a freshman undergoes being initiated into a sorority or fraternity. Such terms are titles given some of the typical states of development or events that constitute the ongoing process of a person's life as a mystic. In this, they are like "puberty," "adolescence" and "menopause." Strictly speaking, we are dealing with the effects of an encounter between a growing individual and her total environment when approached in an attitude of complete human openness to experience.

Another important aspect of seeing mysticism as a process is that it stands revealed as a program of gradual intensification of ordinary human abilities rather than the acquisition of strange and mysterious "powers." Even so, these abilities develop far beyond what would otherwise occur because of the power of their systematic re-organization according to a goal-directed pattern. In this regard, mystical development is a *natural* phenomenon, not an artificial "career" like military service. Nevertheless, the completion of the process goes beyond what the process can itself achieve. It is "finalized" by a transformation which truly transcends human abilities. Ultimate integration is a *gift* for which we can at most make ourselves receptive.

The process theologian, like the biblical prophet, the poet and the mystic, finds God and his grace *within* the process of world development. No matter how "super" natural the ultimate achievement of integrity, the gift of God's loving presence has been steering the process from the beginning. Only at the end does it assume complete command, thus finishing the process it has begun. But, as for Thomas Aquinas, grace is not an interference or a deflection. Because it operates within process, it "perfects" nature—guiding, enhancing, preserving and often, healing.

The culmination of the mystical quest occurs when the natural process and the influx of grace reach a maximal intensity of co-operation, and the human contributor, having reached the sum of his or her powers, becomes transformed into an agency of divine operation. It is thus that in the absence of perceived difference in operating, of self-conscious "friction," the still thoroughly human mystic can say with the Apostle, "it is no longer I who live, but Christ who lives in me!" (Gal. 2:20).

GOD AND PROCESS

There are other areas of contact between mysticism and process thought which will be valuable resources for further consideration. Like the mystics, the process thinker is uncomfortable with concepts of God, especially those enshrined in classical schemes. *That* God does not exist: the remote law-giver, observing and judging his world in passionless indifference; the masculine deity with white beard and all-male retinue; the Conservator of the status-quo, hostile to revolution and development.

Along with the mystic, the process thinker rejects the passionless God, the God who is wholly Other, and the authoritarian, "either/or" God. Their God is a lover, the root and field of experience, uniting all things in himself, paradoxical in nature and operation: reconciling, peace-making, enhancing our enjoyment of this shining cosmos by overcoming evil at every turn, so that goodness is in the ascendant, if not in absolute control.

In the second half of this series of essays in contemporary mystical spirituality, we will examine some of the more central teachings of the mystics regarding God, human nature and development, and the world-process, especially as further light has been shed on these teachings by contemporary thinkers of the caliber of Whitehead, Teilhard and Hocking.

We will also examine in more detail the concrete instances of mystical spirituality in the world's great religious traditions, which provide the field and testing ground for all mystical theory. For mysticism is first and above all a way of life, a practice which exists prior to all mystical theory. So much is this the case, that mystical theory, if authentic, is reflection on practice and the effects of practice. How such theory and practice have concretely evolved in the history of humankind is the story of the inner heart of religion.

SUGGESTIONS FOR FURTHER READING

John B. Cobb, Jr., and David Ray Griffen, *Process Theology: An Introductory Exposition,* Philadelphia: Westminster Press, 1976.

Ewart H. Cousins, ed., *Process Theology: Basic Writings,* New York: Paulist Press, 1971.

Richard Woods

Alfred North Whitehead, *Religion in the Making,* New York: World Publishing Co., 1960.

——————, *Science and the Modern World,* New York: The Free Press, 1967.

Chapter 13

HINDU MYSTICISM

. . . Samsara is just one's own thought;
With effort he should cleanse it, then
What is one's thought, that he becomes;
This is the eternal mystery.

Maitri Upanishad

Mystical spirituality is not only practical, it is concrete; it rests on principles for organizing behavior in order to reach a desired goal, union with God, and it exists only in the lives of real persons with real histories and real traditions. All the rest is to a greater or lesser extent abstract and of no immediate concern to the mystics, if of supreme concern to scholars.

In the following chapters, we shall explore somewhat briefly the origin and development of concrete mysticism in the traditions which still structure the beliefs and behavior of most of the world's peoples—Hinduism, Buddhism, Judaism, Christianity and Islam. Other cultural manifestations of the mystical spirit have great historical importance, and we should not forget that modern spirituality is also indebted to Egyptian, Persian, Chinese, Hellenic, Japanese, Celtic, Germanic and other less familiar traditions. American Indian and African religious traditions are equally important and will become more central in the future, as ecumenism and politics edge nearer each other in the great dialogue and sometimes debate among the world's major peoples.

Our approach to world religions will be schematic, since it is difficult to describe accurately in so small a space even the major elements of these traditions. First, we shall consider the collective development of the tradition—its foundation, teachings, history, permutations and modern forms. Second, we shall explore the particular development of persons espousing such a mystical tradition in terms of general patterns of integration and growth. Finally, we shall reflect briefly on the significance of the mystical element in these traditions for a contemporary Christian spirituality.

Religion accompanies the appearance of human culture wherever it is found, but "religion" includes a wide variety of forms of belief, worship, conduct and values. If by *mystical* religion or spirituality, we mean the belief in the possibility of personal union with the divine, together with ways of attaining to such union, then the appearance of mysticism as a more developed form of religious awareness can be appreciated more easily. It will be characterized by the religious tradition out of which it has developed, yet it will possess something in common with mystical spiritualities in other religious traditions.

Although forms of mystical religion have undoubtedly existed from the beginning of human history on this planet, the most evident manifestation possessing a continuous history and still a powerful influence in the modern world, is found in Indian religion, or "Hinduism."

HINDUISM

The ancient religion of Hindustan, or Northern India, that is, the region of the Indus river, is not only among the oldest religious and philosophical traditions of the world, it is also one of the most complex and extensive. Moreover, it is pervasively mystical in outlook and practice.

According to one of its most brilliant contemporary exponents, Sarvepalli Radhakrishnan, Hinduism "is not a 'founded' religion, nor does it center round any historical events. Its distinctive characteristic has been its insistence on the inward life of the spirit" (*A Sourcebook in Indian Philosophy,* p. 615). In its general aspect, however, Hinduism is a complex of mixed beliefs, values and practices: a seemingly endless tangle of polytheism, idols, temples, fakirs, juggernauts, incense, ritual, sacred animals, gongs, and throngs of bathing pilgrims in holy rivers.

In fact, Hinduism is much simpler than its manifestations seem to indicate. It is, first of all, a religion of *experience* and *fact,* incorporating widely diverse elements tested during centuries of experimentation. It is primarily *pragmatic* and *inclusive,* although possessing a richly profound philosophical tradition and recognizing the existence of heterodox forms such as Jainism and Buddhism. Even so, Hinduism is not a competitive or proselytizing religion.

Historically, Hinduism refers to that form of belief and conduct which developed between the end of the Vedic period and the beginning of the Epic period, roughly between 600 and 300 B.C. The Hindu "scriptures" are thus preeminently those comprising the "end of the Vedas," the *Vedānta,* being mainly the *Upanishads.* However, Hinduism retained a great deal of old Vedic influence, which has survived through subsequent developments, as has Hinduism itself, adapting, absorbing and adjusting itself and its newer components.

The historian, Louis Renou, distinguishes an "extrovert" and "introvert" aspect of Hinduism (although he does not use those terms). The first is manifest by the multitude of sects, external ritualism, *bhakti* (devotional) worship, the sacredness of animals and doctrines such as *ahimsā* or nonviolence. The "inward" aspect of Hinduism, its mystical side, concentrates on developing paths to spiritual perfection, the quest for liberation, renunciation as a way of life, and concern with certain metaphysical problems.

While perhaps accurate as far as it goes, other authors portray the essentials of Hinduism in terms different from this assessment. Some single out the pervasive belief in reincarnation, others consider it to be a commonplace of most "oriental" religions. Hinduism is said to reject the material world and to seek escape from self-hood and the evils of personal existence, especially as interpreted in terms of *karma,* the doctrine of works, which maintains that each person's destiny is the expression of good or bad actions in previous lives. Salvation is thus conceived as liberation (*mokṣa*) from the cycle of rebirth (*saṃsāra*), achieved by realizing the deep union of each self with the Absolute Self, Brahman. In order to attain this liberating union in personal consciousness, it is necessary for individuals to empty themselves of all traces of multiplicity, all attachment to this passing world.

Clearly, the theistic component of Hinduism is a distinguishing characteristic, especially in comparison with Buddhism, Jainism and the biblical traditions. The plethora of gods and goddesses in the Hindu pantheon is balanced by a profound realization that the Absolute is One—all these "others" being but manifestations of Brahman proportionate to human limitations of conceptualization and needs.

At its highest level, Hindu theology is professedly monotheistic, poised between affirming and denying the personal nature of God. In Radhakrishnan's words: "The difference between the Supreme as spirit and the Supreme as person is one of standpoint and not of essence, between God as he is and God as he seems to us. When we consider the abstract and impersonal aspect of the Supreme, we call it the Absolute; when we consider the Supreme as self-aware and self-blissful being, we get God. The real is beyond all conceptions of personality and impersonality. We call it the 'absolute' to show our sense of the inadequacy of all terms and definitions; we call it 'God' to show that it is the basis of all that exists and the goal of all" (Ibid., p. 629). He could, of course, have been quoting Meister Eckhart or *the Cloud of Unknowing*.

The development of Hindu monotheism has been credited, understandably enough, with the emergence of explicit mysticism for the first time in human history. William Ernest Hocking, in describing the inexorable process of bringing unity out of the many gods of the ancient world, explained, "the many gods cannot be independent; and a subordinate or dependent god cannot be the supreme Reality." Thus, "It was in accord with the genius of India that this logic [was] pursued relentlessly to its conclusion in the doctrine that the Real is absolute unity, whereas such unity rejects description: the One, as inexpressible, culminates for our thought in *Mysticism*. What we may describe as *the discovery of the Absolute* marks, I believe, the most important cultural achievement of antiquity" ("History and the Absolute," p. 433).

SACRED WRITINGS, SACRED WAYS

Historically, the major developmental stages of Hindu mysticism can be described in terms of the dominant scriptural and ritual traditions of those periods: Vedic, Upanishadic, Yogic, Epic and Bhakti—the devotional. Despite the fact that "Hindu" refers to the late Vedic period most properly, the term is generally used to refer to all these orthodox religious and philosophical systems indigenous to India, including Sikhism. It does not refer to Buddhism, Jainism or the various Moslem or Christian traditions of India, despite their antiquity.

The Vedas

In the third millenium B.C., India was invaded by progressive waves of lighter-skinned Aryan peoples from south central Asia. The culture and religious beliefs of the invaders were gradually imposed on the darker, less advanced inhabitants, although the more primitive religion of the original Dravidian peoples also influenced the development of Hinduism. Some forms of yoga may have been introduced in this manner. The most ancient strain of Hinduism, however, is connected with the great hymns of the *Rig Veda* and the charms, prayers and spells of the *Atharva Veda*.

Early Vedism is not generally associated with mysticism, but as S. N. Dasgupta has argued, there was a truly mystical element in the elaborate and to our mind impersonal sacrificial ceremonialism of the ancient Hindus. With Hocking, Dasgupta believes that Vedism represents the oldest form of mysticism in the world, prior to a developed belief in the possibility of personal union with God. He comments: "The assumption of the mysterious omnipotence of sacrifices, performed by following the authoritative injunctions of the Vedas independently of reason or logical and discursive thought, forms the chief trait of the mysticism of the Vedic type" (*Hindu Mysticism,* p. 18).

At a later time, the elaborate ceremonial sacrifices, which brought about harmony or operative unity with the order of things, were progressively internalized by a process of meditative substitution, much as the "clean oblation" of the Hebrew prophets was a "pure heart." The "mysterious power" that resided in the ritual activities became more and more associated with the inner life.

Slowly, the idea that Brahman, the Highest, was that power grew in the minds of the Hindus. Knowledge of and union with Brahman, was deemed possible by means of the inner discipline of meditation, the achievement of the next period of mystical development, that of the *Upanishads.*

The Upanishads: The Mysticism of Love and Service

The concluding parts of the Vedic literature are known as the *Vedānta,* and refer principally to a large collection of stories and expositions, only a dozen of which are considered to be "major." They were composed from about 800 B.C. to about 400 B.C. Perhaps the greatest achievement of Upanishadic mysticism was the realization that attaining oneness with Brahman was not a matter of joining disparate personalities. For Brahman was the essence of the self, much in the way God was the "ground of being" for Eckhart. "That art Thou," *Tat tvam asi—Atman* (the self) and Brahman are already one (*Chandogya Upanishad,* 6. 8-16).

Upanishad means something like "session," or "sitting at a master's feet" in order to learn. The 108 official *Upanishads* (there are in fact more than 200) thus constitute the authoritative teaching of Hindu philosophy and religion. Central to Upanishadic teaching is the supreme reality of Brahman, "One without a second," and one with the human spirit. Upanishadic thought generally tends to pantheism and monism—holding that God is the true reality of all that exists, surface differences being *māyā*, which is sometimes translated "illusion."

Māyā traditionally means "power," however, and refers to the creation of the world. *Māyā* is the phenomenal universe, the world of multiplicity which obscures the inner divine nature of all things. Liberation is thus conceived of in terms of transcending multiplicity by detachment from the manifest world of sense awareness, materialism, suffering and death in order to achieve non-dualistic integrity.

The Bhagavad Gītā: The Song of God

In contrast to the *Vedas,* and even to the *Upanishads,* the mysticism of this great poetic dialogue is unabashedly romantic in the sense that love (*bhakti*), which is by no means missing from the *Upanishads,* has become the prime factor in achieving union with God—here represented by the incarnate Krishna. Part of the great war epic describing the struggle for mastery of India, the *Mahābhārata,* also stressed that God is One, and it is possible to be one with Him by following the right path. For the *Gītā,* this is primarily the path of love or devotion, rather than that of knowledge:

"This form of mine which is indeed very hard to see, thou hast seen. Even the gods are ever eager to see this form.

"In the form in which thou hast seen me now, I cannot be seen either by [means of] the Vedas or by any austerities or by gifts or by sacrifices.

"*But by unswerving devotion to me, O Arjuna, I can be thus known, truly seen and entered into . . .*" *(Bhagavad Gītā, 11. 52-54).* Again,

"*Through devotion he comes to know Me, what My measure is and who I am in truth; then, having known me in truth, he forthwith enters into Me*" *(Ibid., 18. 55).*

The love of the soul and God is reciprocal: "*Fix thy mind on Me; be devoted to me; sacrifice to Me; prostrate thyself before Me; so thou shalt come to Me. I promise thee truly, for thou art dear to Me*" *(Ibid., 18. 65).*

Polarities balanced in precarious tension, paradox and the opposition of contraries permeate the Gītā as much or even more than the doctrine of *enantiodromia* characterizes the mysticism of the West. Thus, the Gītā promotes the practices of *yoga*—the art of reconciliation. The Gītā has even been called in this regard "the Gospel of Yoga."

Yoga:
The Reconciliation of Opposites

Since the 18th century, many Westerners have become familiar with the image of the yogi sitting cross-legged in the "lotus position," eyes shut, poised in a state of peaceful contemplation or "*samādhi.*" The image of the physical adept, lying on a bed of spikes, being buried alive for weeks or demonstrating other remarkable feats, is perhaps as indelibly associated with yoga as the other image, although the two styles of life are very different.

Recently, "Western" or Christian Yoga has become popular via books, television and training centers and storefront *ashrams.* Many people are bewildered, amused or concerned about the incursion of such a "pagan" way of life into the West.

Basically, *yoga* comes from the radical *yuj,* which means "to join," and is related to the English word "yoke." Yoga means the unifying or joining of disparate elements into a whole. It is a principle of integration, not a mere set of practices or physical "tactics" for achieving ecstasy.

Originally, Yoga was probably independent of theistic concerns, aiming at self-integration in social withdrawal, what Eliade calls "enstasis" as opposed to the *ekstasis* (ecstasy) of Western theistic mysticism. But throughout its history, Yoga has been adapted easily to theistic traditions, a perhaps inevitable development, if, as most Christians believe, at the center of our inmost spiritual reality God is to be found, the Ground of the Soul.

Yoga doctrines and practical teachings can be found in the *Upanishads,* the *Gītā* and elsewhere. But the great systematization of ancient yogic practices was made by Patañjali, who probably lived in the third century B.C. Fundamentally, Patañjali's monumental *Yoga Sūtras* transformed a mystical, theistic way of life into a *view* of life, a *darśana* or "philosophy." In so doing, he established an alternative system to the nontheistic, cognitive approach to the world known as *Sāmkhya.*

There are many kinds of yoga, the number seven often being taken as a representative, if not inclusive, indicator. Among these are *jñāna-yoga,* the pursuit of unity through scientific and philosophical study; *karma-yoga,* the way of action or works; *bhakti-yoga,* the way to union through devotion and love; *hatha-yoga,* the way to physical-spiritual-mental union through physical exercises; and *raja-yoga,* the "royal" road, which concerns the regulation of consciousness. Tantric yoga includes various symbolic rituals, sexual and magical as well as devotional, which achieve union through "works" (*tantra*). *Mantra-yoga* involves the use of chants, while *yantra-yoga* concentrates on the visual symbolism of *mandalas,* complex designs which focus on the center.

Rather than a variety of practices, however, yoga is more an approach to life with many aspects; one cannot come to the perfection of *raja-yoga* without *hatha-yoga,* as Patañjali says. Full human integration is the objective of all yoga. This is perhaps seen most clearly in the Integral Yoga sponsored by Sri Aurobindo Ghose (1872-1950), the greatest philosophical mystic of modern India.

Bhakti:
The Way of Loving Surrender

In Hinduism, *bhakti* (loving devotion) was not a novel development of the later classical period, but a strand of spirituality present from the earliest times. Already mentioned in the later *Upanishads*, the preeminence of love was explicitly taught in the *Gītā*. Kirshna, the Incarnation of Vishnu (God), tells his disciple, Arjuna, as we have seen, that love is the supreme means as well as the goal of spiritual development: "Having become one with Brahman, and long tranquil in spirit, he neither grieves nor desires. Regarding all being as alike, he attains supreme devotion to Me" (*Bhagavad Gītā*, 18. 54).

The great emphasis on devotional love is characteristic of later Hinduism and survives in many popular movements, of which the "Hare Krishna" Movement and the Divine Light Mission are current examples in the Western forms they have adopted. The development of *bhakti* as a "simple" way beyond all physical and mental disciplines is related to the appearance in India of Tantrism, around 400 A.D., which emphasized, as we have seen, the importance of appropriate method or ritual for attaining union with God by activating the divine potential in human persons.

An important method in tantrism was through sexual union, which provided bhakti movements with romantic symbolism not unlike the imagery of Teresa of Avila and Catherine of Siena. The "right way" of attaining union with God is not by knowledge, but by love, as we have learned from *The Cloud of Unknowing* and other Western classics.

So important was the place of love in later Hinduism that movements or cults such as that of Rādhā-Krishna developed in which, enhanced by tantric influences, union with God was expressed in sexual imagery. Far from being a descent into orgiastic indulgence, this movement parallels the development of "bridal mysticism" in the West, and, like it, also gave rise to an awareness of the feminine, maternal aspect of God.

The differences between East and West in this regard are not merely a matter of degree, however, or of expression; they rest on philosophical underpinnings which warrant further investigation—which, unfortunately, we cannot undertake here. But it is not insignificant to note that while Indian thought has remained largely idealistic in its repudiation of matter, Tantrism being an apparent exception, sexuality has never been the source of deep spiritual conflict it has been for Christianity. Further, if anything, chastity and sexual abstinence have been regarded even more highly in India than in Europe and America.

In hurried retrospective, then, the mysticism of Hinduism, like that of the West, is manifest in the evolution of the fundamental propositions that God is the Supreme Reality, One without a Second; that love is the "better way" of attaining to unity with God; and that in God, all multiplicity is overcome, opposites reconciled. In the first instance, we read in the *Viveka Chudamani* (Crest-Jewel of Discrimination) of the monistic genius, Sankara, the words attributed to God: "I am Brahman, the supreme, all-pervading like the ether, stainless, indivisible, unbounded, unmoved, unchanging. I have neither inside nor outside. I alone am. I am one without a second. What else is there to be known?" But even Sankara admitted that unity with God can be attained by love. In his *Garland of Questions and Answers (Prasnottara Malika)*, we hear "How is one liberated? Through devotion to the Lord."

HINDU MYSTICS

It is hardly possible to do more than mention some of the outstanding representatives of Hindu mysticism; *Patañjali* and

Sankara (ca. 788-820) have left an indelible impact on the history of spirituality throughout the world. *Rāmānuja* (1017-1137) reacted strongly against the monism of Sankara and formulated the devotionalism of Vaishnavism. He stressed the supremacy of love, but denied that all individuality and personality were lost in mystical union; God and the soul remain distinct, if the soul becomes unaware of its separateness. His disciple *Rāmānanda* (1370-1440) greatly influenced Kabīr.

Kabīr (1440-1518) was a gifted poet, influenced by both Hindu and Islamic mysticism, who, like his European contemporaries, wrote in the vernacular rather than in Sanskrit, and whose doctrines influenced the development of Sikhism, a movement founded by *Guru Nanak* (1469-1539) in the district of Punjab. *Caitanya* (ca. 1485-1533) was a Bengali mystic and devotee of Krishna for whom the love of God transcended all religious duties.

In modern times, *Rāmakrishna Paramahamsa* (1834-86) is credited with the revival of authentic Hinduism. Rāmakrishna believed in the essential unity of all religions, and had a profound impact on *Swami Vivekānanda* (1862-1902), who introduced *Vedānta* into the United States in 1893, at the great Columbian Exposition. He believed that a new world order could emerge from a combination of Western science, socialism and Indian spirituality. *Sri Aurobindo Ghose* was a philosopher and mystic, whose Integral Yoga counter-pointed the *Advaita Vedānta* of Sankara. Aurobindo maintained that human transformation was complete only with both inner and outer recreation of the whole person, not just an inner experience of the Divinity. Like orthodox Christian mystics, he also believed that only God could accomplish the final work of mystical perfection, ultimate union with Him, but that human power could prepare the person spiritually for that supreme endowment of grace.

Other outstanding Hindu figures, in addition to the great political and spiritual leader *Mohandas Gandhi,* include *Rabīndranāth Tagore* (1861-1941), mystic poet and philosopher of love, and the contemporary Vivekānanda, the *Maharishi Mahesh Yogi,* whose "Transcendental Meditation" (TM) has affected millions of Western lives in the last fifteen years.

MYSTICAL DEVELOPMENT

Two types of mystical development can be discerned in classical Hinduism: the social growth established as a norm for all within the official caste system, and the more particular forms espoused by those unsatisfied by the ordinary path.

In classical Hindu society, the life span of an ordinary (male) person included four distinct stages culminating in a mystical solitude preparatory for death. These were, first, *brahmacārya*—the student's life, which was characterized by sexual abstinence; second, *gaṛhasthya*—the householder's situation, the period in which a man marries, begets children, and serves the community in appropriate fashion given his state in life; third, *vānaprastha*—the life of the forest-dweller, during which time a man again becomes sexually abstinent and retires into solitude; finally, *samnyāsa*—renunciation, when as a wandering ascetic, perhaps accompanied by his wife, also celibate, he may return to society, but detached from all material possessions and prepared for final liberation.

As a model, this pattern of life has many admirable qualities; in practice, it was followed only with great difficulty by a few in relation to the millions who were barred by fate or lot from attempting it, much as monastic life in the West has traditionally appealed only to a few, even if "all are called." Some of the disenabling factors included widespread poverty, the dislocation of the rural population and rapid urban growth, the gradual erosion of the classical tradition by Western culture, and, perhaps most detrimentally, the inferior role of women in Hindu society and the progressive hardening of the caste system into an oppressive social hierarchy.

As a moral and mystical ideal, however, few if any paradigms of human (or at least masculine) development have aimed higher.

Another, less socially mediated form of personal spiritual growth emerged from the confluence of *yoga, bhakti* and *Advaita* traditions, perhaps in response to the difficulties perceived in the social model. In Patañjali's *Yoga Sūtras,* eight "heads" or stages of development were described, for example. As a path of moral development, these led toward union with God in his life. They included, first, five *yamas* or "restraints"—*āhimsa,* nonviolence or harmlessness to all living creatures; *satya,* total honesty in human affairs; *asteya,* refusal to steal; *brahmacārya,* sexual abstinence or chastity; and *aparigaha,* avoidance of greed or voluntary poverty. Second were the *niyamas* or "disciplines," which included bodily and mental hygienic practices, religious study and complete consecration to the service of God. *Asanas* comprised the third area—the myriad forms of yogi positions only mentioned in passing by Patañjali himself, but developed over centuries of practice. Breathing exercises or *prānāyāmas* are fourth in the series, these exercises based on the belief in the vital energy of *prāna* found in the air.

The last three *yamas* concern the mental life—*pratyahara,* the withdrawal of sense awareness from the world of ordinary perception; *dhārana,* one-pointed concentration; and *dyāna,* meditation proper, but what Western Christians would perhaps call contemplation or objectless, effortless "beholding" in the presence of God. The final stage of development is the achievement of *samādhi,* or union with God in peace and joy, the highest state of consciousness, roughly corresponding in Western terminology to "infused" contemplation.

It is hardly necessary to point out that in terms of mystical development, these *yamas* integrate body, mind and spirit, including social, emotional and moral growth. It is, moreover, instructive to compare these stages with the classical model of Christian spirituality. For instance, it is not difficult to see the elements of the "three ages" of the spiritual life in Hindu mysticism, that is, purgation or renunciation, illumination or enlightenment, and union, expressed in a life of active service for others.

MODERN HINDUISM: TOWARD AN ECUMENICAL MYSTICISM

Many Americans have had their closest encounters with Hindu mysticism in its 20th century forms—*hatha-yoga* as taught by Richard Hittleman or Lilias on television, the "Back to Godhead" movement popularly known as the "Hare Krishna" cult from the mantra chanted by its devotees, the cult of the adolescent "Messiah" figure, "guru" Maharaj Ji, or, in perhaps its most common form, Transcendental Meditation.

While TM might be traced back to the teachings of Sankara, and the Hare Krishna movement perhaps to Caitanya and the *Gītā* itself, these hybridized versions—one more explicitly religious than the other—are somewhat pale reflections of classical Hindu spirituality, despite their authentic mystical aspects. It is much harder to credit the Divine Light Mission with similar mystical depth. As with yoga devoid of its theistic, holistic context, Hindu mysticism is far more than this and must be judged fairly as such.

In its native form, Hinduism can stand with the great mystical traditions of the world's major religions, closer perhaps in spirit and history to Catholic mysticism such as that of the Middle Ages and Renaissance than to any other tradition in the power of its burning devotion to the one God, omnipotent, omniscient, and both intimately personal while also infinitely beyond anything we will ever understand of personality and existence.

But while in some respects Hindu mysticism greatly resembles Catholic and other forms of mystical spirituality in its elements and pattern of development, even its intramural squabbles among rival schools, there are important and fundamental differences in doctrine and practice underlying the similarities.

In terms of beliefs, Hindu doctrine differs from Christianity dramatically (if not wholly) in its basic acceptance of the eternal existence of souls, the doctrine of reincarnation with its connected beliefs in *karma* and the wheel of *samsāra,* the cycle of ebb and flow. Such views have been held at one time or another by various Christians, but have been almost universally regarded as heretical. The Hindu tendency to transcend the material world utterly and to conceive of Ultimate Reality as the impersonal Absolute also distances Hindu thought from Christian, Jewish and Islamic orthodoxy.

It is important to note, however, that the *mystical* strands in Hinduism appear within the rich fabric of that ancient tradition as the farthest removed from a literal interpretation of these doctrines, and it was Gandhi who shot the tubercular cow. In the coming age of serious ecumenical encounter, on the religious as well as the political level, the mystical traditions will probably provide the world with its greatest hope for achievement of a true world community if, indeed, Claude de St. Martin was correct when he reckoned that all mystics come from the same country and speak the same language.

SUGGESTIONS FOR FURTHER READING

S. N. Dasgupta, *Hindu Mysticism,* New York: Frederick Ungar, 1959.

J.-M. Dechanet, *Yoga and God* (trans. by Sarah Fawcett), St. Meinrad, Indiana: Abbey Press, 1975.

Mircea Eliade, *Yoga, Immortality and Freedom* (trans. by Willard Trask), Princeton: Princeton University Press, 1969 ed.

William Ernest Hocking, "History and the Absolute," *Philosophy, Religion and the Coming World Civilization* (ed. by Leroy Rouner), the Hague: Martinus Nijhoff, 1966.

Rayymundo Pannikar, S. J., *The Unknown Christ of Hinduism,* London: Darton, Longman and Todd, 1964.

Sarvepalli Radhakrishnan and Charles A. Moore, eds., *A Sourcebook in Indian Philosophy,* Princeton: Princeton University Press, 1957.

Louis Renou, ed., *Hinduism,* New York: Brazilier, 1962.

Alan Watts and Eliot Elisofon, *Erotic Spirituality: the Vision of Konarak,* New York: Collier Books, 1974.

Chapter 14

BUDDHISM AND MYSTICISM

A monk asked Master Ummon,
'What is the pure body of truth?'
Ummon said, 'A flower in bloom.'
Master: 'A flower in bloom—
what does it mean?'
Answer: 'To add rubbish on top
a pile of garbage.'

from *The Sound of One Hand*
trans. by Yoel Hoffmann

More than 500 million people are called Buddhists—those who follow the *sasāna*, the teachings of the Buddha, the son of an Indian raja who lived over 2,500 years ago. Next to Christianity and Islam, it is the largest religion in the world in terms of numbers of adherents, and next to Hinduism and Judaism among the major faiths, the oldest. Yet Buddhism has been known in the West only since the 19th century.

When it was first "discovered" by Western scholars, it was not certain that Buddhism was a religion at all, much less a mystical one. Part of the problem stemmed from the curious character of the Buddhist perspective. Contrary to some opinions, Buddhism is not atheistic—in some forms of Buddhism, the pantheon is as full as that of Hinduism. The Buddha never denied the existence of the gods (it is not clear, however, whether he was a monotheist), and popular devotion, prayers and temple offerings are common practice in all Buddhist traditions to this time.

It is the relative inability of the gods to *save* or *enlighten* their devotees that characterizes Buddhist "theology" and has caused much misunderstanding among non-Buddhists.

Salvation in Buddhist theology, much like that of its parent, Hinduism, means deliverance from the wheel of *samsāra*—the cycle of rebirth, by the attainment of Enlightenment (*bodhi*), which, combined with right action, leads to eventual "cessation" or extinction (*nirvāna*). Enlightenment "comes" as a result of arduous self-discipline—the purification of the mind, body and spirit. It is not, however, an effect of asceticism or a divine gift unmerited.

The mystical aspect of Buddhism resides in the belief in (and practice of) the attainment of total human integration by achieving harmony with ultimate Reality—conceived not in personal, theistic terms, but as the whole, that which *is*. The "path" to this state of endless unity and everlasting peace (*nirvāna* is not thought of as annihilation) comprises a lifestyle of renunciation, contemplation and compassionate action, supremely but not exclusively embodied in the life of the monk or nun. It is not beyond the capacity of lay persons.

THE THREE JEWELS

Buddhism is a complex religious system consisting of many schools, traditions, languages and interpretations. Its historical development is no less complicated. As a whole, however, Buddhism rests on several fundamental components, which are both factual as well as the objects of deepest faith. The most basic of all is called the Three Jewels or Gems, in Sanskrit, *Tri-ratna*: the *Buddha*, the *Dharma* or Teachings and the *Saṅgha* or monastic community. One of the most sacred of Buddhist rituals is "taking refuge" in the *Tri-ratna*, a ceremony called the *Tri-sarana-garana*. (Buddhist beliefs and practices are generally referred to in Sanskrit, although Pāli became the canonical scriptural language very early, and it is preferred among scholars. Pāli usage is, however, less familiar to Americans than Sanskrit.)

THE BUDDHA

The Buddha's place in Buddhism resembles that of Christ in

Christianity; the historical figure is visible largely through the lens of subsequent belief and legend, the development of the "divine" being.

In historical fact, Siddhartha Gautama, sometimes called Shākyamuni, was born near Kapilavastu, capital of the Sākyan republic, now modern Nepal. Various dates are assigned to his life in different traditions. Theravādins give either 623–543 B.C. or 624–544 B.C., while the Mahayana tradition and western scholars place him between 566–486 B.C. At any rate, it is agreed that he lived to be quite old, at least 80, and died venerated as a saint near Kusinārā.

Physical descriptions of Gautama are lacking; indirect references in early literature suggest that he was fair, with blue eyes and possibly had a mole between his eyebrows.

The son of a district ruler (*raja*), Siddhartha Gautama was rich, well-born and able. But at the age of 29, he became disillusioned by the sorrows, suffering and transience of life. He renounced his position and wealth, left his wife and child, and undertook a life of austere asceticism, particularly the practice of Yoga. For six years he wandered and questioned until, unsatisfied, he abandoned traditional schools and methods. According to legend, he sat beneath a tree on the bank of the river Neranjarā and vowed to remain there in silent meditation until he had achieved enlightenment (*bodhi*).

However that may be, at the age of 35, Siddhartha was enlightened. He ended his silence by delivering his first sermon on the Wheel of Dharma (Truth) to five former associates at the Deer Park at Isapatana, near Benares.

Until his death forty-five years later, Siddhartha Gautama, Shākyamuni ("the Sage of the Sākyas"), now the Buddha ("the Enlightened One") wandered, preached, taught and gathered around him thousands of disciples. As with the Gospel of Jesus, the Buddha's teachings were first "transmitted orally (as still emphasized by the Chinese Ch'an Buddhists and Japanese Zen Buddhists) . . ." (Gard, *Buddhism*, p. 44). Gradually, these vernacular teachings, taken to various parts of India and Southeast Asia, Tibet, China and Japan, were collected by monks and written down. Final canonization of the Buddhist scriptures has never taken place, and separate Pāli, Sanskrit and Hybrid Sanskrit traditions exist, as well as Tibetan, Ceylonese, Chinese, Korean, Vietnamese and others.

Within twenty years of his death, the Buddha, who had never claimed to be anything more than a simple mortal, was venerated and eventually "canonized," if not beatified, by his followers. Legends replete with miracles and divine attestations developed. Homage to the Buddha in the *Tri-sarana-garana* was established. Flowers and gifts were left before images and shrines were built to house his relics and personal utensils which became objects of pilgrimage. This "worship" of the Buddha survives even in the otherwise more austere Theravādan tradition, where he is often referred to as *Tathāgata*—"he who has arrived."

Unlike Jesus, the Christ of Christianity, the Buddha was unique only in a qualified sense in Theravādan tradition. According to his teaching, anyone could become Enlightened, a Buddha, and may have. Illustrious buddhas or *bodhisattvas* are known in every tradition, and many of them have also been duly canonized. But Siddhartha Gautama will remain *the* Buddha as long as memory survives. (As in Christianity, however, many Buddhists believe in the Maitreya Buddha—the Buddha who is still to come.)

THE DHARMA: THE TEACHINGS OF THE BUDDHA

Three months after the Buddha's death, his "entry into *parinirvāna*," a great council was called to establish the content of the teachings, discourses and rules which characterized the *sasāna*. These are known as the Triple Canon, the Three Collections or "baskets"—the *Tripitaka*. The first written versions of the teachings date from the first century B.C. Up to that time, all transmission was oral and in many vernacular forms.

The first and most important *Pitaka*, the *Sutra-pitaka*, represents the actual teachings of the Buddha as remembered by his disciples. These are arranged in five *Nikāyas* or groups. The *Vinaya-pitaka* constitutes a kind of canon-law introduction to the *dharma*, consisting of disciplinary rules, primarily for monasteries. The *Abhidharma-pitaka* is a body of instructions in higher *dharma*, something like Christian mystical theology.

The fundamental teaching on which the rest of Buddhist theology stands has been called "The Four Noble Truths," although *principles* might be more accurate. First is *Duhkha-satya*, "the nature of imperfect existence." From the Buddha's perspective, all life is characterized by anguish, craving, suffering and impermanence, a radical discontent.

Second is *Duhkha-samudaya-satya*—"the nature of causation of imperfect existence." This, simply, is *desire*, the craving to be, to have, to do, the "thirst" for existence that sets the wheel of manifold existence (*samsāra*) in motion. Thirst, *tṛṣṇā*, is in the psychological and spiritual order on the same level as the Christian notion of concupisence.

The third Noble Principle is *Nirodha-satya*, "the stopping of the wheel of existence by removing the causes." Positively stated, this is the realization of perfect existence in ultimate freedom or *nirvāna*, final liberation. Last is *Mārga-satya*—concerning "the ways to know and accomplish the achievement of *nirvāna*." The content of the fourth Principle is in fact the Eightfold Noble Way, the *Arya-astingika-marga*.

The Eightfold Path is an elaboration of the Buddha's practice and teaching of "the Middle Path," *madhyama-pratipad*. Having labored for six years to master the ascetical methods of Yoga and other forms of Hindu spirituality, Siddhartha had ultimately come to realize that the true "way" to liberation lay *between* the extremes of worldly indulgence (his former life as the son of a raja) and the severe austerities of the ascetic. The "middle path" lay through other extremes—the philosophical extremes of materialism and idealism, of pluralism and monism, of existence and non-existence. Here, indeed, the mystical, paradoxical aspect of the Buddha's teaching is manifest. It is even more apparent in the primarily practical nature of his teaching.

The eight items of life constituting the Middle Path are Right Understanding, Right Thought, Right Speech, Right Action, Right Livelihood, Right Effort, Right Mindfulness and Right Concentration. The whole of these make up a plan of life that encompasses both moral and spiritual progress, consisting of both negative and positive "advice" (not "commandments") highly evocative of Jesus' ethical and spiritual teaching and that of St. Paul.

ANĀTMAN AND NIRVĀNA: SELFLESSNESS AND BEATITUDE

Two basic notions not only characterize the Buddhist attitude toward life, but are the occasion of considerable misunderstanding and difficulty to Westerners, who blanch at the idea of denying the existence of the soul (despite Skinner and the behavioralists) and of the "extinction" of individual, particular identity as the meaning of liberation. It is impossible even to begin to explain these doctrines in so short a description. But the importance of these notions demands some attention, even if inadequate.

The denial of the ego or self is undoubtedly one of the Buddha's original tenets. From the viewpoint of Western Mysticism, it seems to strike hard at what Underhill called a fundamental principle: the existence of a self capable of communion with God.

Basically, *anātman* ("no-*ātman*," "no-self"—in Pāli, *anatta*) means that there is no permanent, unchanging substance "behind" the fluctuations of our ordinary ego-states, themselves conditioned by events outside us. An *empirical* ego, a "momentary" self, does indeed exist from moment to moment, but only as a transient construction of the interaction of sense experience and mental awareness. The continuity of experience is an illusion produced by the succession of sensations and events, much like a motion picture is produced by a rapid sequence of still projections. The "self" is only one of fifty-two constructions of the mind in Buddhist psychology.

The Buddha's conviction of the unreality of the "transcendental ego" stands in sharp contrast to the Hindu belief in its reality, which provides fundamental reason for belief in the transmigration of souls, or rebirth. However, even in Hindu mysticism, as we have seen, not only is the self the same as Brahman (God) in its highest manifestation ("That art Thou"), it is also the goal of ultimate liberation (*moksa*) for the cycle of rebirth, which entails reabsorption into Brahman. Thus the appearance of individual existence is overcome in the reality of undifferentiated and blissful awareness.

Nevertheless, despite its retention of the notion of rebirth, Buddhism denies that there is any *ātman* (in the substantial or transcendental sense) to be reabsorbed into Brahman. All notion of a distinct self must be surrendered in order to attain freedom from *duhkha*—anxiety. It should be observed, however, that the denial of the self does not inevitably mean the denial of Selfhood in all Buddhist traditions. D. T. Suzuki, perhaps the foremost recent interpreter of Zen Buddhism, noted that "the denial of *Atman* as maintained by earlier Buddhists refers to *Atman* as the relative ego and not to the absolute ego, the ego after enlightenment-experience" (*Mysticism Christian and Buddhist*, p. 51). But what is the "absolute ego" after enlightenment?

Here we have a riddle, perhaps a *koan* as perplexing as Jesus' dictum that one who seeks to save his or her soul will lose it, but the one who loses it for Jesus' sake, and the gospel's, will save it forever. (See Mk. 8:35, Mt. 10:39, 16:25; Lk. 9:24, 17:33 and Jn. 12:25. It should be noted that *all* the Gospels cite this text, arguing for its independent validity and that, further, the word often translated "life" in modern versions is, in Greek, *psyche*, which means "soul" or "mind.") Selflessness is not unique to Buddhism.

To grasp the practical as well as theoretical significance of *anatta*, it is also well to bear in mind Eckhart's teaching on the "no-thingness" of God and the human soul, the "self-naughting" of the English mystical tradition, the revelation to Catherine of Siena, "I am He who is, and you are she who is not." We are here in the realm of experienced *fact*, which also functions as an ideal or *objective* of practical conduct, both East and West. The path to Unity lies through the destruction of the self-concept and quite literally of the self as a grasping, anxious, self-centered focus of concern.

Nirvāna is the logical and mystical correlative of *anātman* in Buddhism, just as the beatific vision is of Christian selflessness. *Nirvāna* does not mean annihilation, but extinction—extinction of desire, craving, lusting after existence. *Nirvāna* in this sense *is*—and it alone is, "after" perfect Enlightenment.

Perhaps the best way for a Christian to grasp something of the *positive* meaning of *nirvāna* as the goal of Buddhist spirituality, or, rather, its culmination, is to meditate on the meaning of the beatific vision in Christian theology—an apt parable about which is Andersen's story of "The Little Match Girl." If Buddhism is psychologically and philosophically akin to Sartre's existentialism, it is spiritually akin to the high mysticism of the 14th century. And more like the joyful self-naughting of Francis of Assisi and Catherine of Siena than the bleak perspective of Sartre, Buddhism is a way of life characterized by serenity, happiness and a highly positive outlook on things. It is as well supremely respectful of life in all its forms, valuing highly the place of *karunā*—which is sometimes translated as "love, compassion" and sometimes as "grace."

THE SAÑGHA: BUDDHIST MONASTICISM

The third jewel of the *Tri-ratna* is Community—the Order,

Brotherhood or Assembly. Basically, the *sangha* is the authoritative group, generally of monks, which studies, experiences and expounds the *dharma* in the various traditions of Buddhism. There is no single or supreme *sangha*, and its importance varies from country to country, but it is everywhere observed with great reverence as the corporate embodiment of the Teacher.

From the earliest times, the Buddha, like St. Benedict, gathered his disciples into monasteries, or *wats* as they are often called. (In Srī Lanka, they are also known as *Vihāras* or *Saṅghārāmas.)*

The *sangha* as a monastic community is somewhat like the Christian monastic community, including lay members, but it lacks the ascetical rigor of, for instance, compulsory life-long vows; some members will stay in the monastery only for three months of their lives and are, in fact, expected to do so. Dedication may also be life-long.

Monks are generally called *bhiksus*, while nuns are *bhiksunīs*. Disciples are known as *srāvakas*; male novices are *srāmaneras* and female novices are *srāmanerīs*. The non-clerical or lay devotees are called either *upāsakas* or *upāsikās* as male or female members. While monks and nuns can leave at will, automatic expulsion also exists and is prescribed for an infraction of a variety of rules. As noted before, while monastic observance represents the ideal life for a Buddhist, a lay person is by no means barred from attaining Enlightenment. The Buddha himself testfied to having known many advanced disciples who were not in vows.

It should perhaps be noted here that, as Evelyn Underhill reminded us in *The Essentials of Mysticism*, Western monasticism was founded no less than the Eastern variety to provide an environment conducive for following the mystical life.

THE DEVELOPMENT OF BUDDHIST TRADITION

The spread of Buddhist teaching and the use of vernacular

long before a written canon was developed, inexorably destined the rise of various, even competing traditions of interpretation. Four major traditions should be noted, but by no means exhaust the varieties of Buddhist spirituality.

The oldest and most conservative tradition is called *Theravāda*, "the way of the Elders (*Theras*)." It is found primarily in Southeast Asia—Thailand, Burma, Srī Lanka, Laos and Cambodia. *Mahāyāna* Buddhism, "the Great Way" probably represents the majority of the world's Buddhists in India, China, Japan, Korea, Nepal and parts of Tibet and Srī Lanka. Although possessing traditions as ancient as those of the Theravāda, Mahāyāna Buddhism is considered to be more "liberal" in its acceptance of beliefs and practice at variance with the more austere way of life of the Southern Buddhists.

Vajrayāna ("the way of the Vajra") developed in Northern India and Tibet under the influence of Mahāyāna and Tantric doctrines, and is characterized by a greater emphasis on esoteric teachings. The fourth major tradition, although not numerically as large as the preceding schools, is called *Ch'an-tsung* in China and *Zen-shu* in Japan—more familiar as Zen Buddhism. Having achieved immense popularity in the United States, especially for its mystical aspects, special attention will be given Zen below. It is well to bear in mind that many other forms of Buddhism exist in addition to these, however, both historically and at the present time. The so-called Hīnayāna movement numbered eighteen traditions, including Theravāda; the Mahāyāna movement more than five major traditions, and many minor ones.

THE PATHS TO NIRVĀNA

Despite the plethora of traditions (*yānas* and *vādas*), there is held to be only one Way or path as taught by the Buddha—the Middle Path. However, even that has developed into five major variations and a number of minor ones. As in Hinduism, the influence of which is evident in the paths (*margas*), the varieties are determined by a relative predominance of knowledge, love or another human function. The first four *margas* are found in both Theravādan, Mahāyānan and Vajrayanan traditions; the fifth almost exclusively in the former two.

The first *marga* is *sīla-marga*, training in discipline and virtuous conduct. *Dhyana-marga* emphasizes meditative concentration, *prajñā-marga* universal compassion and wisdom leading to Enlightenment, and the fourth, *bhakti-marga*, devotional practice, especially the veneration of the Buddha. The fifth major form is *Buddhanusmrti-marga*, complete reliance on *karunā*, or "saving grace."

These paths are part of the overall training, called *Tri-śiksā* in Sanskrit ("the Threefold Training"): *Adhisīla*—the higher morality, as found particular in the third, fourth and fifth paths of the Eightfold Noble Path; *adhicitta*, training in "higher thought" or *samādhi*, which corresponds to the sixth, seventh and eighth paths of the Eightfold Path; and *adhiprajñā*, training in wisdom in order to attain *bodhi* (Enlightenment), reflected in the first and second parts of the Eightfold Path.

Many ramifications of these three areas of development are found in the traditions, especially in their monastic form. All of them indicate the importance of *development* in Buddhism, and it should not be overlooked that the *Tri-śiksā* bears a strong resemblance to the Three Ages of the Spiritual Life in Christian spirituality.

DEVELOPMENTAL STAGES

From earliest times, the progression of a follower of the Buddha toward Enlightenment and *Nirvāna* was structured in four stages, given poetic titles referring to liberation from the cycle of rebirths. The beginner was the *Satapannā*, the stream-entrant just having turned onto the Way. The once-returner had achieved virtual perfection, being proficient in development: *Sakadāgāmin*. One who would never return to this life, although not completely perfected, was called *Anāgāmin,* the never-returner. Finally, one who had achieved spiritual perfection was known as an *Arhat,* one who has attained *Nirvāna.*

The complete Enlightenment of the *Arhat* entitles one to the appellation *"buddha,"* which, as noted previously, is not reserved for Siddhartha Gautama except by Theravādins. However, from early times, and especially in the development of the Mahāyāna, the doctrine of the *bodhisattva* was a subtle variation. Originally, *bodhisattva* meant something like "buddha-candidate," but later acquired the meaning of "one who postpones supreme enlightenment"—precisely out of compassion for others, to whom the *bodhisattva* returns in order to help them attain Enlightenment as well. The emerging sense of altruism in later Buddhism was a result of the development of the basic teachings regarding compassion *(karunā)* and Right Action, and should be compared with the parallel development in Christian and Hindu spirituality.

Individual development and its correlative corporate development occupy a vast amount of Buddhist teaching, which delights even more than Christian thought in charting progress by means of categories of growth toward perfection. At least four different schemas exist in the major traditions outlining the passage through various *bhūmis* or stages of development—there being either 7, 10 or thirteen, depending on which tradition one follows. What is clear in Buddhist spirituality, as in the other great mystical traditions, is that progress toward perfect human development is gradual for the most part and involves the integral growth of the *whole* person. By implication at least, the varieties of classification indicate that these stages are not always a matter of exact sequences, but refer to *idealized* stages of human growth, much like Erikson's psychological structures or Kohlberg's stages of moral growth. Stages are not simply states through which one must pass on the way somewhere else; the stages, the entire journey, constitute an integrated passage toward human wholeness.

ZEN BUDDHISM

Of all forms of Buddhism, Zen is undoubtedly the most familiar to Americans, but perhaps the most misunderstood, mainly because of distorted "beat" and "square" interpretations common in the halcyon era of the late fifties and early sixties among San Franciscan and Greenwich Village poets and their coffeehouse devotees.

For a variety of reasons, Zen Buddhism appeals to many Western spiritual writers as the most mystical form of Buddhism in terms of Christian belief and practice. The Japanese form of Chinese Ch'an Buddhism, Zen is a movement within the Mahāyāna tradition deeply influenced by Taoism—the ancient religion of China, itself mystical, which originated perhaps as early as the sixth century B.C. A Chinese monk, Tao-Sheng (ca. 360-434 AD) is credited as the originator of Zen by combining Taoism and Buddhism. His teaching emphasized sudden enlightenment, which, as *satori,* has been a characteristic feature of Zen ever since.

The sixth century monk, Bodhidharma, is generally considered the first Zen Patriarch, however. In Japan, his Ch'an Buddhism was developed as Zen-shu in the twelfth century A.D., eventually dividing into various schools, the chief of which are Rinzai and Soto. More austere than other Mahāyāna forms, Zen Buddhism relies primarily on the oral transmission of doctrine and the master-disciple relationship. Art and sport are particularly important as experiential means leading toward *satori;* swordsmanship, archery, painting and poetry, particularly the exquisite seventeen-syllable *haiku,* are integral to spiritual development, as are the *koan* or "riddle" and *zazen,* sitting meditation. All develop the non-rational, "right-brained" aspect of consciousness, which too great a focus on reason can inhibit and thus prevent full wholeness.

Among the famous Zen Masters, perhaps Dogen (1200-1253) and Hakuin (1685-1768) are best known in the West. From

Hakuin comes the famous *koan* "What is the sound of one hand clapping?" Both were gifted poets, teachers and artists.

IS BUDDHISM MYSTICAL?

Today, Buddhism is widely accepted by scholars as a true religion, despite its rather idiosyncratic attitude toward both the self and God (or the gods). While the background of oriental polytheism provides some explanation of the theological stance of Buddhism, and Hindu *ātman* doctrine a reason for its psychology, it is perhaps its *mystical* quality as a whole that has determined the character of Buddhism. For, despite their volubility, it is a commonplace among all mystics that the culminating moment of their mystical experience, their union with God, is ineffable. Buddhism takes ineffability into a different but related area of concern.

Similarly, as we have seen, the Buddhist denial of the permanence and centricity of the self is at least similar to the selflessness preached by Jesus and a bedrock doctrine in all Christian mysticism. Developmental aspects of Buddhist spirituality also argue for its mystical character, especially its emphasis on purification, enlightenment and ultimate liberation. And if the conversion to action is a hallmark of authentic mysticism, here, too, Buddhism is remarkably close to Christian mystical theology.

As we have seen, two *kinds* of Buddha are generally acknowledged; the *Arhat* (or, in Pāli, the *pacceka-buddha*), who attains enlightenment but does not preach the way of salvation to others, and the *bodhisattva* (or *sammāsambuddha*)—all-knowing, all-powerful, all-compassionate, who preaches salvation to all sentient creatures.

The existence of monasteries for men and women has been taken as evidence, as in Catholicism, of an un-social, withdrawn spirituality, of no service to the world at large. But Buddhist monasticism exists as a "refuge" only in the sense that there, the essential practices and teachings of Buddhism may be pursued unhindered. One need not be a monk or nun to become a *bodhisattva,* however.

As in Christian monasticism, it is important to grasp that it is not the environment that produces Enlightenment, but the attitude and readiness of the individual. As Rāhula wisely observes, ". . . if a man lives all his life in solitude, thinking only of his own happiness and 'salvation,' without caring for his fellows, this surely is not in keeping with the Buddha's teaching which is based on love, compassion and service to others" (*What the Buddha Taught,* p. 77).

The Buddha and Buddhist tradition are exacting about the mutual obligations and duties of parents and children, pupils and teachers, husbands and wives, friends, relatives and neighbors, masters and servants, owners and workers, religious and lay persons. And, while relatively unknown in the West, the Buddha's social teachings were definite concerning the elimination of crime by eliminating poverty rather than by punishment, the appropriate promotion of commerce and industry, the obligation of honest labor, just wages, and peace among persons and nations. (See Rāhula, pp. 81-83).

Does Buddhist contemplation, especially perhaps Zen meditation, provide a true mystical experience in the sense in which we have been considering—a direct and immediate experience of the presence of God, culminating in union? The relative silence of the Buddha and the tradition on crucial Western theological issues renders both a simple affirmation and a simple negation equally open to doubt.

But Suzuki certainly notes a strong resemblance between Zen experience and that described by Eckhart and other Christian mystics, which argues in favor of a true mystical awareness of the divine ground of being. Is such consciousness unitive? Excepting the likely possibility of the action of grace—which Christian teaching affirms is not a Christian monopoly!—it has been proposed by the great Catholic theologian, Jacques Maritain, as well as by Aelred Graham, William Johnston and others, that the contemplative experience of "emptying" (*sūnyatā*) in Buddhism, as in Hinduism, gives a true "natural" mystical experience, unlike "merely" analogous philosophical and artistic experiences.

But then, why should we preclude the operation of grace? For, as Bernanos' hero in *The Diary of a Country Priest* died confessing, *"Toute est grâce"*—All is grace.

SUGGESTIONS FOR FURTHER READING

Edward Conze, *Buddhism: Its Essence and Development,* New York: Harper Torchbooks, 1959.

Richard A. Gard, *Buddhism,* New York: George Brazilier, 1961.

Dom Aelred Graham, *Zen Catholicism,* New York: Harcourt, Brace and World, 1963.

William Johnston, *Silent Music,* New York: Harper and Row, 1974.

________________, *The Still Point,* New York: Fordham University Press, 1970.

Walpola Rāhula, *What the Buddha Taught,* New York: Grove Press, 1974 ed.

D. T. Suzuki, *Mysticism, Christian and Buddhist,* New York: Harper and Row, Perennial Library ed., 1971.

Chapter 15

JEWISH MYSTICISM

A person should be so absorbed in prayer
that he is no longer aware of his own self.
There is nothing for him but the flow of Life;
all his thoughts are with God.
He who knows how intensely he is praying
has not yet overcome the bonds of self.

Or-Ha-Emet
Your Word is Fire

As it is known today, Judaism has had a continuous history for over 3500 years. Its origins among the ancient Semitic tribes of Mesopotamia extend that story at least another 500 years. It is the oldest monotheistic religion in the world and the parent of Christianity and Islam, with whom Judaism constitutes "the religions of the Book"—that is, *the* Book, the Bible.

The mystical aspect of Judaism has been recognized to have been manifest from the post-exilic period unto the present, especially in medieval Kabbalism and 18th century Hasidism. Whether mystical elements can be found in earlier Hebrew religion is disputed, however. Much depends on how mysticism is conceived and what criteria are employed to judge its presence.

Given our general notion of mysticism as the practice of the presence of God, together with the theory of that practice (Hocking), I believe that Hebrew religion was mystical from its historical inception. Whether among the patriarchs, the prophets or sages, the dominant characteristic of Jewish spirituality has centered implicitly or explicitly, as it does today, on the presence of God, once called the *Shekinah*.

To grasp the essential fact of this biblical mysticism, it is necessary to explore Judaism from its earliest appearance. We should remember as we do, however, that important and even essential aspects of Judaism, like those of Christianity and Islam, are not mystical, such as the sacrificial practices, the legal ethicalism and the political-theocratic structure and function of the state. But the heart of early Judaism as well as the more explicit mysticism of later centuries, including the prophetic element, was the active presence of God in all human experience, supremely realized in a *moral* union of *wills,* not an ontological melding of identity.

ABRAHAM AND THE PATRIARCHS

The Jewish faith began in ancient Sumeria, or, as it was once called, Chaldea, where, in the 20th century before Christ, the Elamites overran the city of Ur, capital of the Sumerian Empire. Among the fugitives was the family of a man called Terah. Intending to move farther to the northwest to escape both Elamites and Amorites, they paused at their ancestral home, Haran, where Terah died. His eldest son, Abram, now head of the family, decided to press ahead toward Canaan, having been moved to do so by an experience of his God.

Unlike his contemporaries and even his family, Abram was a monotheist, or at least a "henotheist"—worshipping one supreme divinity, "Yahweh," who, unlike other gods of ancient Mesopotamia, was neither a nature-god nor a territorial god. The Jewish historian Isodore Epstein suggests that Abram may have arrived at his unusual conception by reason, by attribution of his own high ethical qualities to God, or—which I believe the more likely case in view of the biblical tradition—"by means of some inner illumination, a mystical experience, a revelation" (p. 13).

Several such experiences are recorded in Genesis—such as Abram's vision and the great promise made under the starry desert sky, followed by the mysterious "cutting" of a covenant by the firebrand so evocative of the later theophany to Moses (Gen. 15:1-21). At first, God promises Abram to bless him and make his descendants a great nation. He promises Abram the land of

Canaan; he will be his shield in battle. He will give him an heir to fulfill the promise. But the climax of God's promised covenant is reached when, according to the Priestly tradition, God appears to Abram at the age of 99. "Bear yourself blameless in my presence," he is told. Then his name is changed to Abraham—"Father of a multitude". The apparition at Mamre and the destruction of Sodom and Gomorrah, Isaac's birth and "sacrifice" are similar experiences in which God becomes manifest and alters the course of Abraham's life and with it, that of the human race (see Gen. 12:2; 13:14-15; 15:1, 5; 17:7).

ISAAC AND JACOB

The presence of God, mentioned once in the story of Abraham, becomes increasingly important as the saga of the patriarchs unfolds. One of the great mystical experiences in Genesis is Jacob's vision at the rock of Bethel (Gen. 28:11-22). His father Isaac also experienced the presence of God in a dream in which he heard the Lord say "I am the God of Abraham your father. Do not be afraid, for I am with you" (Gen. 26:24). To Jacob, similarly, God says, "I am Yahweh, the God of Abraham your father, and the God of Isaac. . . . Be sure that I am with you" (Gen. 28:13, 15).

Jacob sees God again at the famous "wrestling match" at the ford of the Jabbok. Having been blessed as well as crippled by the encounter, Jacob renames the place *Peniel* (the face of God) ". . . because I have seen God face to face and I have survived" (Gen. 32:30). At this time, Jacob's name, too, is changed—to *Israel,* "may God show his strength," or "he has been strong against God."

Folklore and later theological redaction have undoubtedly influenced these ancient accounts, but the clear intent remains the fact that God directed the destiny of the patriarchs by personal encounters in which his will *and* his presence were made known. Not only will Abraham, Isaac and Jacob-Israel be the ancestors of many nations, but *"I will be with you."* Such is the promise.

The great theophanies cease for a time—no more are recorded in the lives of the later patriarchs, whose destinies take them and their clans into Egypt to escape famine and the incessant hostility of Canaanite tribes and towns. For hundreds of years, the "Hebrews" remain in the land of the Pharaohs, eventually becoming enslaved as despised outsiders. At this time, God's promise to be present to his people is renewed in the great theophanies and interventions of the Exodus, as God reveals himself in the personal experience of the greatest mystic of the Bible, perhaps of all time, a man called Moses.

MOSES AND THE EXODUS

While it is certain that as law-giver and leader, Moses ranks among humanity's giants, it is perhaps less evident that he was a mystic or that, in fact, his mystical sensitivity was the core of genius about which his other skills were grouped and from which they drew their strength. But if the mystic is one who has seen God in the immediacy of his experience, then Moses must be listed among the supreme mystics of all time.

The record has grown familiar over the centuries, but it is still clear for those who can read. Moses, a fugitive in the land of Midian, encounters the living God in a mysterious bush, burning but not consumed (Ex. 3:2-6). Moses inquires of God, "Who am I to go to Pharaoh and bring the sons of Israel out of Egypt?" But God said "I shall be with you" (Ex. 3:11-12). Again and again, God speaks to Moses, guiding and strengthening him to accomplish the wonder of the Exodus, the pivotal event of Jewish history.

In the desert, encamped at the foot of Mt. Sinai, the Hebrews made their covenant with the Lord in one of the greatest theophanies ever described (see Ex. 19 to 31). Not only Moses, but others experienced God directly: "Then Moses and Aaron,

Nadab and Abihu, and seventy of the Elders of Israel went up, and they saw the God of Israel; and there was under his feet as it were a pavement of sapphire stone, like the very heaven for clearness. And he did not lay his hand on the chief men of the people of Israel; they beheld God, and ate and drank" (Ex. 24:9-11).

Moses, however, is led to venture farther alone, into a dark cloud obscuring the top of the mountain. "The glory of the Lord settled on Mount Sinai, and the cloud covered it for six days; and on the seventh day he called to Moses out of the midst of the cloud. Now the appearance of the glory of the Lord was like a devouring fire on the top of the mountain in the sight of the people of Israel. And Moses entered the cloud, and went up on the mountain. And Moses was on the mountain forty days and forty nights" (Ex. 24:16-18).

After the apostasy and repentance of the Hebrews during Moses' prolonged sojourn on the mountain, God appeared again to him in his tent. "Thus the Lord used to speak to Moses face to face, as a man speaks to his friend" (Ex. 33:11). Yet Moses had not seen God's face fully, "for man shall not see me and live" (Ex. 33:20). The Lord protects Moses in a cleft of rock and covers him with his hand until his glory has passed.

The images of Exodus—the ascent of the mountain, the cloud and darkness, the hidden God, the unspeakable glory—provided both later Jewish and Christian mystical writers such as Philo, St. Gregory of Nyssa and the author of the *Cloud of Unknowing* with the mystical metaphors by which they described the growth of spiritual awareness. For them all, Moses himself epitomized the mystic and of whom it was written at the conclusion of the Pentateuch, "And there has not arisen a prophet since in Israel like Moses, whom the Lord knew face to face . . ." (Dt. 34:10).

JUDGES AND KINGS

After Moses' death, Joshua led the Hebrews into the promised land, beginning the long struggle against the resident tribes and fortified towns. Although a period of bloodshed and war, the Conquest was also a time of spiritual purgation, and the presence of God dwelled among his people. Theophanies are rare but not absent (see Joshua 5:13-15, 7:10-15, 8:1-2).

Following Joshua's death, a series of heroes helped the Hebrews settle the conquered territories, leading them in battle, judging them in peace. Of these, Gideon, like the patriarchs, "saw the angel of Yahweh face to face." Yahweh answered his fear, "Peace be with you. Have no fear—you will not die" (Judges 6:22-23). Manoah and his wife, the parents of Samson, were foretold of their son's birth by a visitation of God. "We are certain to die because we have seen God." But his wife allays Manoah's fear: "If Yahweh meant to kill us, . . . he would not have told us these things" (Judges 13:8-25).

Prophets of God were also active at this time, including the redoubtable Deborah (Judges 4-5). The greatest of them was Samuel, to whom God called in his youth. "And Yahweh was with him and let no word of his fall to the ground" (1 Sam. 3:19).

Under Samuel's reluctant tutelage the monarchy was established in Israel with the selection of Saul. His successor, David, a consummate politician, military leader and poet, was no less a mystic, judging from the great psalms he wrote. "The presence of the Lord" echoes repeatedly in his prayers; he longs for the feeling of God at his side (see Psalms 11:7, 13:1, 16:8-11, 17:15, 24:6, 27:8, 105:4 etc.).

God appears twice to Solomon, David's son and successor (1 Kings 3:5-15, 9:1-9). His presence comes to fill the Temple Solomon has built (1 Kings 8:10) and he promises to dwell there forever if Israel remains true: "I consecrate this house you have built: I place my name there forever; my eyes and my heart shall be always there. . . . But if you turn away from me, you or your sons, . . . then I will cut Israel off from the land I have given them and I will cast out from my presence this Temple which I have consecrated to my name . . ." (1 Kings 9:3, 6-7).

Solomon himself fell into idolatry, and the tragic schism between the Northern and Southern Kingdoms ensued. Solomon's sons likewise failed to remain true. Ultimately, the priest-prophet Ezekiel sees the Shekinah leave the Temple at the onset of the Babylonian captivity (Ez. 10:18).

PROPHETS AND POETS

The prophetic tradition in Israel began with the history of that land and its people. But those we consider "the" prophets were mainly sixteen men who foretold the fall of the Northern and Southern Kingdoms or who strengthened the captives during the ordeal of the Exile. In an earlier chapter, we observed that the experience of the presence of God shared by the prophets could only be considered a mystical awareness.

The great prophets are perhaps the supreme embodiment of Jewish spirituality, and their experiences of God become the paradigm of later Jewish mysticism (see 1 Kings 19:11, Isaiah 6:1-13, Jeremiah 1:4-19 and Ezekiel 1:1-15). Similarly, the great psalms, as we have already observed, express the prophetic zeal and longing for God's presence in time of distress and exile as well as in prosperity. "These compositions, each of which is the product of a vivid personal experience of God, are gathered in the Book of Psalms, in which Israel's genius for religion finds its highest expression" (Epstein, *Judaism,* p. 66).

WISE MEN AND RABBIS

With the death of the last "minor" prophets, Joel and Malachy, the age of the Hebrew prophets ended, although the spirit of prophecy remained with the Chosen People as a whole. During the Exile, especially after the destruction of the Temple, the role of the teachers and scribes, the *hakamim* and *soferim,* became greater in preserving the faith of the Jews.

The writings of the sages were no less mystical than the great literature of the past, although the theophanies and calamities were replaced by an emphasis on the inner awareness of God's guidance. Walking in the presence of the Lord epitomized true wisdom. The Book of Job characterizes this attitude well: "I heard of thee by the hearing of the ear, but now mine eye seeth thee; wherefore I abhor my words and repent, seeing that I am dust and ashes" (Job 42:5-6).

After the conquests of Alexander the Great had brought a kind of cultural unity to the Near East, many Jews migrated to Alexandria in Egypt, encouraged by the liberal policies of King Ptolemy and his successors. Gradually, the Alexandrian Jews assimilated the culture of the city, although they remained faithful to their religious beliefs and practices. A Greek translation of the Bible, the Septuagint, was commissioned for them about 280 B.C.

Exposed to the mystery religions of the Egyptians and Greeks, the Jews, rather than imitating their pagan neighbors, emphasized the mystical element in their own tradition, especially in the teaching and writings of the greatest of their scholars, Philo (c. 25 B.C.-50 A.D.). Philo in fact asserted the superiority of Jewish "mysticism," developing the technique of allegorical interpretation of scripture which would figure so prominently in both later Jewish and Christian mystical theology.

From Philo, as well as from his Romanizing contemporary, Josephus, we also learn of mystical sects, primarily the Essenes and the Therapeutae, who had retired into the desert to live according to their apocalyptic or contemplative beliefs regarding the coming of the Messiah. Philo's description of the gentle Therapeutae in the Egyptian desert so impressed the Christian historian Eusebius three hundred years later that he mistook them for early Christian monks.

The literary remains of the Essenes are scant, the Qumran scrolls being an apparent example. Of the Therapeutae, none remain. But the mystical tradition of both continued its influence down through the ages in other forms. Meanwhile, the Christian school of Alexandria succeeded the Jewish Wisdom school, and Philo's allegorical method of interpretation was adopted by Clement, Origen and the great Cappadocian Fathers. Of particular importance was Philo's use of the Mosaic themes of the cloud and darkness of Sinai, the hiddenness and inconceivability of God, which formed the "apophatic" or "negative" theology of Christian mysticism that endured until well into the late Middle Ages in writers such as Meister Eckhart.

TRADITION: THE KABBALAH

By this time, the Torah was acknowledged to have both a written and unwritten aspect. The unwritten Torah, which was transmitted by oral teaching, was further divided into *midrash* and *mishnah*. Midrash means "investigate" or "expose," and consists of sometimes greatly detailed commentaries on scripture—either *midrash hallachah,* "walking" midrash, which dealt with specific legal and doctrinal issues, or *midrash aggadah,* "talking" midrash, which was concerned with devotional, historical and literary issues. The mishnah, on the other hand, "repetition," was commentary without explicit reference to a written text. The Babylonian and Palestinian Talmuds consist primarily of mishnah with the addition of the *gemara* or "completions," which served to deal with issues not covered by mishnaic commentary.

The halachic and aggadic elements of both midrash and mishnah, when considered apart from the written Torah, constitute what could simply be called "tradition," or *kabbalah.* Over the centuries, however, *kabbalah* acquired a more specifically aggadic significance, referring to the "hidden" aspects of Torah. By the 10th century and thereafter, as Louis Jacobs explains, "the Torah was thought of as having two elements—the esoteric (*nigleh,* 'revealed'), consisting of the Bible, Talmud, religious philosophy and the legal Codes; and the esoteric (*nistar,* 'hidden'), consisting of the Zohar and the other kabbalistic works.

The usual name for the Kabbalah is, in fact, *hochmah nistarah,* 'the hidden science' " (*Jewish Mystical Testimonies,* p. 2).

The Kabbalah, or Jewish mystical tradition, could thus have both or either a hallachic or aggadic character, and it is the attitude to these that, according to Gershom Scholem, perhaps the greatest recent authority on Jewish mysticism, differentiates various forms of that tradition. It is the intensity with which the mystic approaches these elements as means for attaining communion with God that distinguishes him from other devout Jews—not in kind, that is, but in degree of devotion.

Four general types of Jewish mysticism can be discerned in terms of reliance on various aspects of the biblical tradition. First is a *creation-centered* mysticism, based on the *Maaseh Bereshith* (Work of Creation) theme of the Talmud. Cosmological in character, it emphasizes the emanation of all things from God and their return to him in the great restoration or *tikkun.* The oldest work of speculative mysticism, the *Sefer Yetzirah* (ca. 225 A.D.) belongs to this tradition. The second type is known as *"Throne mysticism,"* taking as its motif the vision of God's throne in Isaiah. Through a long sequence of bodily, mental and spiritual purifications, the mystic gradually ascends to the vision of God's throne, but not of God himself, whom no man can behold and live.

Ezekiel's vision of the throne mounted on God's mystical chariot provides the dominant image of the third type of kabbalistic mysticism, *Merkabah* or *"chariot" mysticism,* based on the Talmudic *Maaseh Merkabah.* Again, by a series of "ascents," the prepared soul gradually mounts to a vision of God, represented by the "riders" of the chariot. Consisting of the *hekaloth* literature, this tradition concentrates speculatively on the mysteries and attributes of the Godhead. Finally, a lesser tradition was based on the *apocalyptic visions* of the Book of Daniel, concentrating on God as the Ancient of Days, and emphasizing various eschatological elements, found in its earliest forms in apocryphal works such as IV Ezra, the Book of Jubilees and Enoch, which dates from as early as 200 B.C.

Kabbalistic mysticism was both speculative and practical. In the ninth and tenth centuries, both forms were introduced into Western Europe by Jewish emigres from Babylon and Palestine—the first group migrating particularly to France and the Iberian peninsula, the second to Germany, although contacts between these groups continued unabated, often with controversy in their wake.

Speculative mysticism reached its acme in Spain by the 14th century, its great leaders being Issac the Blind and his disciples Azriel ben Menachem and Moses Nachmanides in the 12th and 13th centuries. Around the year 1300, the *Zohar* or "Splendor" was compiled from ancient sources by Moses de Leon of Granada. This famous mystical work influenced both Catholic and Protestant writers of the Renaissance, and is for all purposes the chief work of Kabbalistic mysticism. Its chief proponents were Moses Cordevero (1522-76) and Isaac Luria, or "Ari" (1514-72).

Central to the teaching of the Zohar are the ten *sefiroth* or "rays" by which God structured his self-communication to the world of creation. These creative agencies are also the means by which restoration is achieved—the reconciliation of the *shekinah* in exile with God as *En Sōf*, the Endless. Thus, in addition to providing a cosmological structure for interpreting the universe, the sefiroth also constitute a practical structure for the ascent to God.

Germanic Jews, the Ashkenazim, maintained a less speculative tradition of ecstatic, devotional mysticism, which, although influenced by the kabbalism of the Zohar, gave rise to a new—and the last—form of Jewish mystical spirituality in the 17th and 18th century, *Hasidism*.

THE HASIDIC TRADITION

After the Cossack persecutions of 1648, and in the wake of

Messianic expectations doomed to quick disillusionment, Hasidism developed as a popular movement which extended the esotericism of kabbalistic Judaism to all. Developed mainly by the immortal Israel Ba'al Shem Tov, called "Besht" from his initials, Hasidism directed its appeal to the emotions rather than the intellect, although it was based on the theoretical kabbalism of Isaac Luria. "Central to the teachings of Besht was the love and concern for the uneducated man, commonly described as *Am-haaretz* (people of the soil)" (Epstein, *Judaism,* p. 271). Instead of emphasizing visions of an apocalyptic future messiah, Hasidism "directs the mind to the redemptive power of God in the present and in the context of everyday life" (Ibid., p. 272).

Beginning in a small corner of the Ukraine, Hasidism spread over Europe and eventually reached the United States. A band of 300 Hasids migrated to Palestine under Mendel of Vitebsk in 1777, laying the foundation for the future state of Israel almost 200 years later. While by no means unopposed, Hasidism attracted thousands of adherents. Besides Besht, its outstanding representatives include Dov Baer of Meseritz (1710-72)—the Great Preacher or *Maggid,* Nahman of Bratzslav (1772-1811) and Shneur Zalman of Ladi (1746-1813). Contemporary representatives include the Lubavicher School of New York, founded by Rabbi Menachem Mendel, and the great philosopher and mystic, Martin Buber (1878-1965).

THE MODERN PERIOD

In the wake of the Holocaust in the countries of the Nazi "Third Reich," in which a third of the world's Jews lost their lives—the single most devastating experience in the long history of Judaism—many developments have occurred which bear on mysticism, including the foundation of the State of Israel in 1948. Many Jews have relinquished belief in God's presence or providence. On the other hand, a more militant kind of prophetic, even patriarchal, spirituality, which Rabbi Richard Rubenstein calls "neo-archaism", has arisen in response to anti-Jewish oppression.

The writings of Martin Buber, Chaim Potok and others have increased interest in Hasidism, while the books and lectures of Elie Wiesel and Abraham Heschel have brought many to a new realization of God's active presence in their lives. The teachings of Jewish mystics from earlier times, such as the Ba'al Shem Tov, Nahman of Bratzslav and Abraham Kook have found new audiences among Christians as well as Jews. Even kabbalistic practices have been taken up by a new generation of adepts of the mystic arts.

The mystical traditions of Judaism, far from having spent their force in the 18th and 19th centuries, seem about to enter the 21st century in the vanguard of a revived, strengthened and resolute Jewish spirituality.

SEEING GOD

Denying the mystical character of the experiences of the Patriarchs, of Moses and of the prophets in favor of a notion of mysticism as a wholly "interior" event, i.e., a merely subjective state of consciousness, stems from a failure to grasp the nature of experience and the meaning of mysticism. To behold God, to experience the Presence immediately and directly, "face to face," is not an "external" and therefore objective event, unlike the supposedly "inner" awareness attributed to the mystics by Ninian Smart and other scholars of religion. Rather, the experience of God, is, like all experience, *transactional* and *unitary*.

Merely "seeing" God without a profound inner transformation means sure death to the body in Jewish spirituality, because the spirit is already dead. Human experience is the correlation of subjective and objective events, an engagement with reality unified not only by the wholeness of the human person, but by the *social* dimension of our existence.

Jacob, Moses and Elijah saw God and lived; they heard his voice, felt his presence, and lived in the awareness of his glory. So also did Peter, James, John and Paul, and it is not by accident that as the glory of God fell upon Jesus on his mount of transfiguration, it was Moses and Elijah who appeared at his side. In a note to the Jerusalem Bible we read, ". . . in Christian tradition Moses and Elijah (together with St. Paul, 2 Cor. 12:1f) are the three pre-eminent mystics" (1966 ed., p. 121).

The presence of God is not confined to the fluctuating chambers of human consciousness; it charges the world, "flaming out like shining from shook foil." To *live* in that all-enveloping, penetrating presence in all its manifestations is the message and meaning of Jewish mysticism. To grow from fear of the Lord to the perfect wisdom of love marks the path of development in the ancient traditions and in the Zohar, where in terms of reconciliation of opposites, we read "Love unites the highest and the lowest stages and lifts everything to the stage where all must be one" (III, 288a).

The vision of Jewish mysticism is one of universal reconciliation, the sharing of all human persons in the everlasting peace of God's presence. But in the pure and lofty monotheism of the Jewish faith, an achievement of many centuries of struggle and purification in the crucible of God's love, the only mystical union conceivable is that of communion, never of absorption. God remains God, the One, undivided, without a second, and we, as sparks of divine fire cast to the far reaches of the universe, are called to *return* to our source, not to *become* our source. The prophetic impetus of Jewish (and Christian and Moslem) mysticism finds the path of that journey lying through the complex and often baffling obstacles of the public world, however, wherein there is no niche or corner that God's presence cannot reach.

MYSTERION

SUGGESTIONS FOR FURTHER READING

Isodore Epstein, *Judaism,* New York: Penguin Books, 1959.

Arthur Green and Barry Holtz, ed. and trans., *Your Word is Fire: The Hasidic Masters on Contemplative Prayer,* New York: Paulist Press, 1977.

Louis Jacobs, *Jewish Mystical Testimonies,* Jerusalem: Keter Books, 1976.

Roger LeDeaut et al., *The Spirituality of Judaism,* trans. by Paul Barrett, O.F.M. Cap., St. Meinrad, Ind.: Abbey Press, 1977.

Nahman of Bratslav, *The Tales,* trans., intro. and commentaries by Arnold J. Band, New York: Paulist Press, 1978.

Gershom Scholem, *Major Trends in Jewish Mysticism,* New York: Schocken, 1961 ed.

Chapter 16

CHRISTIAN MYSTICISM: AN OVERVIEW

A true Christian may almost be defined as one who has a sense of God's presence within him.
Cardinal Newman

Despite the common elements Christian mysticism shares with other traditions, from its inception it had several distinctive components retained by all its schools and orders. Chief among these and most representative, the ultimate factor in the rupture between the early Christians and their Jewish predecessors as well as their Muslim successors, is the place of Jesus as Messiah and Lord—the incarnate Presence among us, or, as William Ernest Hocking was perhaps first to call him, "the human face of God."

JESUS AND THE CHRISTIAN SCRIPTURES

Earlier, we explored the essential teachings of all Christian mysticism as found in the life and message of Jesus—the lives and teaching of the mystics being but the continuation of that power and vision. For some of his contemporaries, Jesus realized the presence of God in a true *mysterion* that was for others a *skandalon,* a stumbling block, for he claimed—and died for his claim—that he and God, "the Father," were *one* (see especially John 10:15, 30, 38; 14:10; 15:23; 17:11, 21, 23 etc.). Union with God through him becomes the Way of his disciples, a way that clearly lies through purgation and enlightenment, but, as Paul most eloquently preached, is the achievement of God's favor and assistance, his *grace.*

As reflected in the earliest writings, the unity of Jesus' followers in himself and thus in God was a favorite theme of the early church (Cf. Matt. 18:15, 20; 25:40; John 14:20; 17:21-23, Eph. 4:6 etc.). *Love* is the bond and basis of that unity (John 13:34-5; 14:21; 15:9-10, 12, 17; 1 John 2:5-6; 3:10-11, 14; 4:16, etc.). Through his life, passion and resurrection, that is, through his love and that of his Father which it revealed, Jesus is the reconciliation of opposites, uniting humankind to the One from Whom it had estranged itself: "But now in Christ Jesus you who once were far off have been brought near in the blood of Christ. For he is our peace, who has made us both one, and has broken down the dividing wall of hostility, by abolishing in his flesh the law of commandments and ordinances, that he might create in himself one new man in place of the two, so making peace, and might reconcile us both to God in one body through the cross, thereby bringing the hostility to an end" (Eph. 2: 13-16. See also Rom. 5:10-11; 11:15; 2 Cor. 5:18-19; Col. 1:19-22).

Having been reconciled, Jesus' disciples are in turn to actualize that reconciliation among others, thus by their love bringing all things to unity in God. God's reconciliation by Christ is *realized* in human reconciliation (see Matt. 5:24; 1 Cor. 7:11, 2 Cor. 5:20-21 and especially John 17: 22-23).

THE APOSTOLIC AGE

No attempt is made in the Christian scriptures to provide a systematic mystical theology, nor would there be for centuries. But the reality is there. The essential *mysterion* had been revealed: in Christ Jesus, all had been called to become one in God, being saved from the alienation wrought by universal sin. Even the "natural" separation between Creator and creature had been bridged in the "hypostatic" union of the divine and human natures of Jesus, as later theologians would describe it, following St. Cyril of Alexandria.

As sharers in his human nature, all human persons share Christ's divine nature by participation. Such a process of realization of the divinity of humanity, or "divinization" *(theosis)* is the dynamic of Christian mystical development. Thus St. Irenaeus (130-200) could rightfully proclaim, "The glory of God is humanity fully alive!" following John's gospel, "I came that they might have life, and have it in abundance" (John 10:10). (Compare Rabbi Heschel's statement, "Just to live is holy."). The whole mystical theology of the New Testament is aptly summarized, however, in John's simple, brilliant formula, "God is love, and he who abides in love abides in God, and God abides in him . . ." (1 John 4:16).

Mystical elements that derive from the original Christian testimonies include the hidden presence of God in the "mysteries" of Scripture, in baptism and the eucharist, in the events of daily life, prayer, almsgiving, service, marriage (see Eph. 5:32-33) and, in those days, martyrdom. The basis of the doctrine of the "mystical body of Christ" is clearly present in the theologies of John and Paul and serves to synthesize many other themes. Similarly, the unity of all in Christ is summarized in the "communion of saints."

During the later apostolic era, these mystical currents flow subtly but definitely in the pastoral and liturgical writings such as *The Shepherd of Hermas,* the letters of Sts. Ignatius and Polycarp and the works of Justin Martyr. The theme is constant—progress toward union with God in Christ, expressed and realized by renunciation of self and in loving service to others.

The lack of systematic articulation in the New Testament has the advantage of allowing for further but never quite definitive articulation in terms of the opportunities and needs of various cultures and epochs. It is therefore not surprising that, as Christianity spread over the Western world in the next fifteen centuries, its mystical spirit found engaging expression in the language of the times, as is still happening today. Three major periods of development can be discerned in this process, those of the Fathers, the Medievals and the Reformers.

Richard Woods

THE EARLY CENTURIES: GREEK MYSTICAL THEOLOGY

At Alexandria, as we have seen, the currents of humanistic Platonism, the Jewish Wisdom tradition culminating in Philo's mystical hermeneutics and social criticism, and the Christian gospel of Mark flowed together to create a stream of theology, spirituality and scriptural exegesis that would influence the Christian world for centuries. One of its first achievements was the great catechetical school or Didascalion founded by Pantaenus in the second century. His successor, Clement of Alexandria and Clement's brilliant pupil, Origen, were the first and brightest flowers of this first period of Christian culture. Clement first proposed the doctrine of *theosis* or "divinization," and he coined the term "synergy" to describe the operation of the mystical union of divine and human wills.

As the first true mystical theologian, Clement provides a link between the Jewish mysticism of Philo, the primitive church and the developed theology of the Cappadocian Fathers of the fourth century—Sts. Gregory of Nyssa (330-95) and his brother, Basil the Great (330-379), and Gregory of Nazianzus (329-89). St. Athanasius, too, (296-373) must be reckoned among the great mystical theologians—one of the first Christian authors to develop the ancient themes of the divine "darkness" and the unknowability of God—the "apophatic" or paradoxical "negative" theology which would dominate the further history of mysticism in both East and West.

Evagrius Ponticus (346-99), while in the "noetic" contemplative tradition, stressed and indeed inaugurated the psychology of mysticism by drawing attention to stages of development in mystical life. These he called the way of the *praktiki*, the *physiki* and the *theologi*—the life of action or works, the contemplation of God in the world of creation and the contemplation of God alone. Evagrius based his division most probably on the ancient

Greek distinction of life and science into active and contemplative phases.

The homilies attributed to St. Macarius of Egypt (d. 390), on the other hand, emphasized experience, *aisthesis,* not *noesis.* More simple and direct than the speculations of Evagrius, the Macarian Homilies, which found great favor among evangelical Christians in later centuries, most likely reflect the spirit of the monks of the Syrian desert rather than Egypt—the same area out of which would one day come the most influential of all mystical writings.

The Macarian approach extolled feeling in the life of prayer, a needed corrective among the heady Christians of Alexandria and Constantinople. Later, the "Byzantine Synthesis" of Diadokos of Photike (c. 450) and St. Maximus the Confessor (580-662) joined the head and the heart of Eastern mysticism into a lasting unity which has remained central to Orthodox spirituality to the present.

THE DESERT FATHERS

In contrast to the urbane traditions of Alexandrian and "metropolitan" spirituality in general, there also arose at the same time the Christian eremitical tradition. At the end of the third century, Christian hermits began to appear in the deserts of Egypt (and later, of Syria)—near where Philo had found the mysterious Therapeutae two centuries before. Seeking to "confess" their faith before an incredulous world, but deprived of martyrdom by increasing Roman toleration, these men (and women) sought union with God in a life of prayer, solitude and austerity apart from the bustle and decadence of the flourishing cities of the Empire.

St. Antony (c. 251-356) was perhaps the most famous, along with St. Pachomius (290-346). Both founded communities which greatly influenced the later development of both Eastern and Western monasticism. For centuries, "the contemplative life" was virtually—if inaccurately—synonymous with the desert hermitage.

It was through the monk John Cassian's writings (360-435), which reflect his early years among the great hermits of the East before migrating to the West, that the spirit of desert monasticism entered Europe, particularly because of the work of St. Benedict (480-550). Cassian himself founded at least two monasteries in France. Thus, the monastic tradition was established in both the East and West to provide a suitable environment for the cultivation of the mystical life. It was not by accident that Bruno, Bernard and many other great Western mystics, as well as Gregory Palamas in the East, were the fruit of that flowering.

St. Augustine (354-430) and St. Jerome (342-420), as well as Pope St. Gregory I, "the Great" (540-604), also shared in and shaped this monastic tradition. Augustine in particular contributed to the growth of Western mysticism by the force of his example and writings as well as his rule. His doctrine of the "inner light" would influence generations of mystics, down to George Fox and John Henry Newman. A profound psychologist, he was one of the first to trace the stages of mystical development as a gradual process from conversion to union. His own mystical experiences are recorded in his immortal *Confessions*.

Of all the mystical sources of late antiquity, however, none can rival the influence of the writings of the pseudonymous Syrian monk of the late fifth and early sixth centuries; who styled himself "Dionysius the Areopagite"—a pious fraud which not only obscured his identity but lent his works a spurious but probably unintentional apostolic authority. "Denis" (as he was known in the West) was as near a spiritual and theological genius as any writer of the period, and his works are still studied and admired as they were in the sixth, thirteenth and nineteenth centuries.

The structure of Denis' thought is largely provided by the dominant Neoplatonic philosophy of the day, that of Proclus, but the content is far more indebted to the Bible, Philo, Gregory of Nyssa and the other Greek fathers. His "negative" or apophatic theology, affirming the utter unknowability of God, brilliantly brought the tradition of Athanasius and the Cappadocians into focus, but was balanced by a more comprehensive "positive" theology.

To Denis we also owe the explicit formulation of the second schema of mystical development, one which, however, also had its roots in earlier Jewish mysticism. He called the three stages *katharsis, erlampsis* and *henosis:* purgation, illumination and union.

Also during the Patristic period, St. John of Damascus (675-749), the great Syrian theologian, mystic and Doctor of the Church, harmonized the writings of his predecessors from the Cappadocians to St. Maximus the Confessor. But among the Byzantine mystics, none was reckoned more highly in the Eastern Church than St. Simeon "the New Theologian" (949-1022), one of the three "Theologians" of Greek Christianity with St. John the Evangelist and St. Gregory Nazianzen. The greatest of the Byzantine mystical theologians, he synthesized the teachings of St. Basil and Isaac of Nineveh and contributed to the development of the Hesychast movement.

"Hesychasm" comes from the Greek *hesychia,* "quiet." Long associated with the spirituality of Mt. Athos (founded 962), a monastic community at the tip of a peninsula extending from the Macedonian coast into the Aegean sea, this tradition constitutes one of the oldest mystical practices of oriental Christianity. Its origins lie in the teachings of St. Gregory of Nyssa, Evagrius Ponticus and the Macarian Homilies. It was furthered by the teachings of St. John Climacus and Maximus the Confessor, but reached its full development in the life and teachings of St. Simeon and St. Gregory Palamas.

The heart of hesychasm is the "Jesus prayer"—the repetition of the words "Lord Jesus Christ, Son of God, have mercy on me, a sinner," although variations are sometimes used. To facilitate the prayer, a "rosary" of ninety-nine beads or knots is often used, called a *komboschinion* or, in Slavonic, *tchotki.* True hesychasm, however, includes other elements, some of which may have been influenced by Hindu or Buddhist tradition. These were, first, the achievement of a state of deep tranquillity or quiet, the stilling of the discursive mind. The second element involves various acts of concentration, especially attention to and control of breathing, which can be synchronized to the rhythm of the Jesus prayer. Third is the awareness of inner warmth and the "divine light" of Tabor.

These attendant practices are not widely found today, although in the fourteenth century they occasioned years of bitter controversy. But the Jesus prayer has continued to be a vital part of Orthodox spirituality, the practice of which has been the focus of centuries of exposition. In the eighteenth and nineteenth centuries, the major writings on this "Prayer of the Heart" were collected into the *"Philokalia"* ("Love of Good"), portions of which have been translated into English.

We now reach the "Middle Ages" in both Byzantium and then Europe, and with that, a new mystical era.

THE GOLDEN AGE OF THE WEST: MEDIEVAL MYSTICISM

At the dawn of the period called "Middle" by later classicists in the West, the tragic political and theological dialectic originating in previous centuries of tension between Rome and Constantinople escalated into formal schism. The break is usually dated 1054. At that time, Muslim armies already imperiled the Byzantine Empire, having overrun all of Northern Africa and Palestine, ending with the conquest of the ancient Christian cultures of Egypt and Syria. Byzantium was now at the height of its glory, if not its power. But ultimate defeat already lurked in its progressive encirclement by Islamic forces. The break with the West only assured the fall of the East, which became final and irreversible in 1453.

In the Latin West, civilization was emerging from the decline caused by centuries of barbarian invasion and the collapse of the

Roman Empire, the so-called "Dark Ages." The medieval mystical renaissance could be dated with the Latin translation of Denis' *Mystical Theology* in the ninth century by a brilliant Irish monk at the French court, John Scotus Erigena, who also translated works by St. Gregory of Nyssa and Maximus the Confessor. But the true beginnings of medieval mysticism occurred with the writings and preaching of the Cistercian reformer, poet and saint, Bernard of Clairvaux (1090-1153), declared a Doctor of the Church in 1830.

Bernard's classic *De Diligendo Deo* (On Loving God), his sermons and biblical commentaries greatly advanced the development of Western mystical spirituality. In particular, his commentary on the Song of Songs reintroduced the bridal imagery of ancient Judaism and set the stage for the later development of Christian *brautmystik* by Eckhart, the Rhineland mystics, Catherine of Siena and the great Spanish Carmelites of the sixteenth century.

Like the Greek Fathers, Bernard's spirituality rests on the conviction that through a purifying process of self-emptying and ecstatic love, it is possible by God's grace to become one with him. Also like his Orthodox predecessors, Bernard knew from experience that authentic Christian mysticism naturally tended to express itself in action.

In the twelfth and thirteenth centuries, the mystical element in medieval Christianity flourished and spread. Hugh and especially Richard of St. Victor's Abbey in Paris wrote profoundly and beautifully of the contemplative life. St. Hildegaard (1098-1179) was only one of a host of outstanding women mystics at this time. Others were St. Mechtilde (1210-1280) and Gertrude the Great (1256-1302).

With St. Francis of Assisi (1181-1226), a simpler and more creation-centered spirituality arose in the West, similar in spirit to the Macarian Homilies. Several early Franciscans became famous for their mystical poetry and theology as well as their involvement in controversies of the age: St. Bonaventure

(1217-74), Bl. Angela de Foligno (1248-1309) and the outstanding lyrical poet, Jacopone da Todi (1230-1306). The other great mendicant patriarch, St. Dominic Guzman (1170-1221), himself a mystic, inaugurated a tradition of service-oriented spirituality centered on study and contemplation. His order found outstanding representatives in Sts. Albert the Great and Thomas Aquinas and the prince of medieval mystics, Meister Eckhart.

Strong opposition met the message of the medieval mystics. Jacopone was imprisoned during the suppression of the Spiritual Franciscans; Bonaventure and Thomas, both Doctors of the Church, were hounded and persecuted, even in Thomas' case, to the point of condemnation. Eckhart, like his master, was condemned after his death. His followers, Bl. Heinrich Suso and Johann Tauler were targeted for official displeasure and inquisition.

But the mystical currents loosed in the monasteries and priories of the previous centuries could not be easily dammed by established conservatism or reaction, and fortunately so. For in the fourteenth century, as the institutional church tottered and swayed in the luxury and tumult of the Avignon "Captivity" of the Papacy and the Great Western Schism, which, together with the Black Plague and the Hundred Years' War turned the period into an era of strife and calamity, the people of Western Europe sought desperately for spiritual support and meaning. As the mystical movement spread from cloister into the towns and cities, they found what they were seeking.

Thus, the fourteenth century, an age born to woe, as Barbara Tuchman recalls, was also the era in which occurred what the Quaker historian (and mystic) Rufus Jones called "the flowering of mysticism."

THE REMARKABLE FOURTEENTH CENTURY

It is impossible to adequately describe in so brief a report the mystical developments and figures of this astounding period.

Throughout Europe, as well as in Byzantium, a mystical ferment arose, bringing about flights of the human spirit, social reform and also manic excesses on a scale never seen before or since.

In Germany, besides St. Gertrude, and Suso and Tauler, the Rhineland mystics following Eckhart, we find the *Gottesfreunde*, the "Friends of God," and the great lay mystic and businessman, Rulwin Merswin (1307-82). In Italy, Angela de Foligno, Jacopone da Todi, Dante (1265-1321), Sts. Bridget of Sweden (1303-73), Catherine of Siena (1347-80) and Bernardino of Siena (1380-1440) span a century of strife with their love and devotion.

In England, a profound eremitical and pastoral tradition matured alongside the radical evangelism of Wyclif and the Lollards with Richard Rolle (c. 1300-1349), the author of the *Cloud of Unknowing* (c. 1380), Walter Hilton (d. 1396), Dame Julian of Norwich (c. 1342-1420), William Langland (1332-1390) and the *Pearl* Poet. In the Netherlands, where the Beguines were so often found, lived Bl. Jan van Ruysbroeck (1293-1381), and his disciple Geert de Groote (1340-84), founder of the Brethren of the Common Life, whose most famous member was Thomas à Kempis (1380-1471). St. Vincent Ferrer preached throughout Spain (1350-1419), where the Catalan mystic and lawyer Ramon Lull (c. 1233-c. 1315) had labored long and lovingly to convert the Arabs. In the Eastern Church, one of the greatest mystics of any age lived amidst ecumenical controversy and open conflict—St. Gregory Palamas (1296-1359).

This was the golden age of Christian mysticism, a robust, outgoing, Christological spirituality anchored in the great Fathers of the East, but already part of a new world. That would be a world of even greater conflict and dissension, as the Turks swept over Byzantium and into Eastern Europe, while the Reformation and incipient nationalism further fragmented Western Christendom. Spiritually, the fourteenth century is the bridge of a renaissance, a time when the gospel had to become increasingly internalized and lived without the assured support of church or state, or else wither in the fire of continual catastrophes. In all, a time much like our own.

THE THIRD AGE OF CHRISTIAN MYSTICISM: REFORMERS

While Spain had not missed the upsurge of mysticism in the late medieval period, *the* Spanish mystics familiar to all, both West and East, lived at the time of the Protestant Reformation—although in Catholic Spain, they seem more the last blossom of a waning medieval mysticism than children of the Renaissance. Romantic, passionate, idealistic, tireless and controversial, these saints epitomize the light and fire of Catholic mysticism at its best: Ignatius of Loyola (1491/5-1556) and the two Carmelite doctors, Teresa of Avila (1515-82) and John of the Cross (1542-91).

Other great Catholic mystics lived at this time, but again the last medievals rather than harbingers of a new era: Nicholas of Cusa (1401-64), Denis the Carthusian (1402-71), St. Catherine of Genoa (1447-1510), the Dominicans St. Luis of Granada (1544-88) and St. Catherine de Ricci (1522-90) and the Carmelite St. John of Avila (1500-69), one of St. Teresa's advisors. But by now, Catholicism was no longer the sole heritage of Western Christian mysticism.

PROTESTANT MYSTICS

The schism of the eleventh century was amplified by a further rending of the Western Church in the sixteenth, a tragedy which words such as "heresy" and "reform" almost mock. Mysticism at this time was largely associated with late medieval spirituality, much of which was mystical in name only. And for this reason, many of the Protestant reformers repudiated mysticism as a contamination of the apostolic purity of the Christian faith. This bias has continued to the present in many denominations. W.T.

Stace, himself a Protestant, somewhere wrote, "there are *no* Protestant mystics."

Nonetheless, history seems to defy so categorical a denial. Although the Calvinist tradition has generally suppressed the mystical element, it has survived there and elsewhere, if not without opposition. This should not be surprising if, as I believe, mysticism touches upon the essence of the Christian faith.

Luther himself (1483-1546) was something of a mystic, holding the *Theologia Germanica,* a mystical classic, in high regard. Likewise, the sermons of Eckhart had influenced him profoundly. In many respects, Luther continued Eckhart's mission, especially by his espousal of the vernacular. Not the least of his accomplishments was the translation of the Bible into German while at Wartburg Castle.

Other Lutheran mystics have achieved widespread acclaim, chief among them Jakob Boehme (1575-1624). Over the years, many names were added to his, including Kelpius, Swedenborg, Tersteegen, Goethe and Hölderlin the poets, Novalis and perhaps Kierkegaard. Despite the Calvinist antagonism, based firmly on an overmastering sense of God's transcendent otherness, it is possible to mention Komensky, Rutherford, Pierre Poiret, Jonathan Edwards, David Brainerd and the artist, Vincent van Gogh.

The Anglican tradition has produced a long line of mystics among the clergy and laity, including artists and poets: John Donne, George Herbert, Jeremy Taylor, Henry Vaughan, Thomas Traherne, William Law, John Wesley, William Blake, Wordsworth, Keats, Tennyson, Emily Brontë, Yeats and AE (George Russell). The founder of the Quakers, George Fox, (1624-91), was the son of Puritans. Among his followers, Isaac Pennington, Charles Marshall, John Woolman and Anne Hutchinson should be mentioned. John Bunyan and Jacob Bower were Baptists.

To this brief list should be added the names of R. W. Emerson,

Henry Thoreau, Walt Whitman and Emily Dickinson, the 19th century American poets.

It is not a contradiction to speak of Protestant mystics. Without an overarching tradition, however, it is difficult to characterize them, except in terms of their teachings, which differ sometimes greatly, sometimes not at all, from their Catholic and Orthodox contemporaries. Perhaps their most distinguishing character is their very protestantism, their religious individualism. Anne Fremantle thus observed: "For the mystic who happens to be a Protestant, although he is not more isolated than the Catholic—the flight is always, as Plotinus called it, from the alone to the Alone—the fellow climbers are not roped. For the Catholic there are 'recognitions' everywhere. But for Jakob Boehme the sixteenth century shoemaker, or John Wesley the founder of Methodism, or George Fox the Quaker, or Emanuel Swedenborg, there was no benefit of clergy, no scaffolding to hang onto, few guidebooks, and little in history to help" (*The Protestant Mystics,* pp. 11-12).

In 1944, William Ernest Hocking, himself a Protestant and a mystic, accurately described the character of Protestant mysticism—or, rather, the Protestant character of mysticism: "The historic Church took the view that the life of God must be brought to individual men through the channels of revelation and the spiritual body of the Church. The Protestant view was that the life of God is already in the souls of men, and that this must be their guide in recognizing any outer authority" ("The Mystical Spirit and Protestantism," p. 198).

But since both views are true, if partial aspects of the whole, "a fully understood mysticism may hold together what the accidents of Church history in the fifteenth and sixteenth century put asunder" (Ibid.). For Hocking, the Protestant mystical tradition involves three corollaries: "the actuality of certitude, the possibility of new religious insight, and the importance of a stable corpus of faith" (Ibid., p. 199).

TOWARD THE MODERN ERA

Both Catholic and Protestant reaction to the excesses of enthusiasm and Quietism led to a virtual suppression of the mystical spirit in the seventeenth and eighteenth centuries, creating a bias which endured until the turn of the twentieth century, as recounted elsewhere in this book. But there were always mystics here and there who failed to heed the censure or were unaware of the fact that they had been relegated to the periphery of theological seriousness.

Catholicism continued to shape mystics in the womb of monastic silence and in the marketplace—space allows us only to mention Bro. Lawrence of the Resurrection (1605-91), Angelus Silesius (1624-77), St. Grignion de Montfort (1673-1716), J.-P. de Caussade the Jesuit (1675-1751), Gerard Manley Hopkins the Jesuit poet (1844-89), Charles de Foucauld (1858-1916), Francis Thompson the poet (1859-1907), St. Gemma Galgani (1878-1903) and St. Therese of Lisieux, co-patroness of France (1878-97).

We have already noted many Protestant mystics of the Renaissance and the Enlightenment. To this number, we should no doubt add the names of William Booth, founder of the Salvation Army (1829-1912), George Macdonald the writer (1824-1905) and many others. But here we are already past the verge of a new era which we shall consider separately.

In the Eastern Church, after the fall of Constantinople, the mystical tradition fell into a desuetude similar to that of the West after the Reformation and the Wars of Religion. During the late nineteenth century, however, Orthodox spirituality began to undergo a revival much like that about to reinvigorate Western mysticism. This was partly due to the translations of the *Philokalia* and the revitalization of monasticism. It also sprang from a literary renaissance which had among its brightest stars writers of true spiritual genius, Tolstoi and Dostoevski only the most brilliant among them. The collapse of Czarist Russia in the revolution of

1917 brought the renewal to a halt, but also brought about a new interest in Orthodoxy in the West and a new era of spirituality.

TRANSITION

At the beginning of the present century, then, Christian mysticism, indeed Christianity itself, began a profound and rapid sequence of change, and the effects of that change will be considered in another chapter. We break off thus after nineteen centuries of development, during which the essential message of Christian mysticism varied remarkably little in essentials. Overall, its meaning and message still hold that any man or woman who sincerely desires it may come to closer union with God, that the way to union is not a matter of knowledge or position but of love expressed in service, and that such love eventually reconciles all opposition.

The path to union lies through a gradual and progressive series of developmental stages through which a person's whole existence is reshaped and which eventuates in active involvement in the world, not retreat from it. Ultimately, the mystical life in its alternating currents of action and contemplation must be accepted with childlike freedom, for it remains the achievement of God's grace, a gift. But it is a gift offered to all, if all do not in fact accept it. And the first fruit and guarantor of the transformation promised within human experience, which in the end overpowers even death, remains the God-man, the mystical bridge and mediator of all, Jesus the Christ.

SUGGESTIONS FOR FURTHER READING

Paul de Jaegher, ed., *An Anthology of Christian Mysticism*, Springfield, Ill.: Templegate, 1977.

David Fleming, ed., *The Fire and the Cloud: An Anthology of Catholic Spirituality*, New York: Paulist Press, 1978.

MYSTERION

Anne Fremantle, ed., *The Protestant Mystics,* New York: New American Library, 1965.

Georgia Harkness, *Mysticism: Its Meaning and Message,* Nashville: Abingdon Press, 1973.

William Ernest Hocking, "The Mystical Spirit and Protestantism," in Richard Woods, ed., *Understanding Mysticism,* Garden City, New York: Doubleday Image Books, 1980.

Kadloubovsky and Palmer, trans., *Early Fathers from the Philokalia,* London: Faber and Faber, Ltd., 1954.

Vladimir Lossky, *The Vision of God,* Bedfordshire, England: Faith Press (American Orthodox Book Service), 1973 ed.

Orthodox Spirituality, by a Monk of the Eastern Church, London: S.P.C.K., 1974.

Chapter 17

ISLAMIC MYSTICISM

> *A horse once met a frog. The horse said, "Take this message to a snake for me and you can have all the flies which surround me."*
>
> *The frog answered: "I like the pay, but I cannot say that I can complete the work."*
>
> from *The Way of the Sūfī*
> Idries Shah

Recent political crises in Iran, Saudi Arabia and Afghanistan have focused attention sharply on the youngest of the world's major religions—Islam. The tension between minority Shi'ites and the majority Sunnites, the odd-sounding titles "ayatollah," "mullah," and "imam," the practices of penitence and prayer, even *Time's* portrayal of the Ayatollah Khomeini as "the mystic who lit the fires of hatred" while naming him "Man of the Year," have all been "news" to most Western listeners. Yet Islam is the religion of more than 500 million people—the third largest in the world.

For over a thousand years, Islamic mysticism has generally been identified with *Sūfism,* or, as it is known traditionally in Arabic, *tasawwuf.* But far from being a severe, militant and hate-mongering band of fanatics, the Sūfīs have extolled and exemplified love, service and peacefulness. (Murderous sects have appeared in Islam, the heretical *Assassins* of the twelfth century, for instance, who were resolutely opposed by the greatest of the Sūfī theologians, al-Ghāzali.) In historical perspective, the Ayatollah Khomeini would appear more the antithesis of Islamic mysticism than its fullfillment, although he is not entirely an anomaly.

Richard Woods

EARLY ARABIA: THE EMERGENCE OF ALLAH

A Semitic language group such as the Jews, Arameans and Carthaginians, the Arab peoples are, according to tradition, descended from Ishmael, Abraham's elder son by Hagar. The name first appears on an inscription of the Assyrian King, Shalmanezer III in the eighth century B.C. The Bible mentions the Arabs initially in II Chron. 17:11, referring to desert nomads from the east bank of the Jordan, at approximately the same time.

The Arabs' largely nomadic life prevented the development of urban culture, except in a few trading centers such as Yathrib, renamed Medina in the time of Muhammad. Arab religion was also that of a nomadic people, having animistic and totemistic elements in its primitive expressions, as well as idol worship. But a higher form of religious consciousness was not lacking. Peter Mansfield writes: "By the fourth century A.D., the people of southern Arabia abandoned polytheism to adopt their own form of monotheism—a belief in a supreme god known as al-Rahman, 'the Merciful'" (*The Arabs,* p. 16).

It was thus into a somewhat advanced religious culture, if also a warlike one, but one in which poetry, song and a highly developed ethical sensitivity flourished, that a child destined to be one of the world's greatest religious geniuses was born at Mecca in 571 A.D.—the son of Abdullah and Āmina of the Hashimite clan of the Quraysh tribe. Named Muhammad, he would be remembered forever as "the Prophet."

MUHAMMAD: PROPHET OF GOD

At that time, Mecca was a cult-center, possessing a small shrine called the Ka'ba, which was particularly sacred to Allah (or El), the Creator and supreme God, also known as al-Rahman, the Father of the gods.

Muhammad's father died before the child was born, and his mother died when he was six. His grandfather died two years later, and Muhammad grew to maturity under the care of his uncle, Abū Tālib. At 25, he married a wealthy widow for whom he had worked as a merchant, Khadīja. Although fifteen years his senior, Muhammad deeply loved Khadīja, his only wife as long as she lived. She bore him several children, but only one son, who died in infancy.

A religious man, Muhammad pondered and prayed constantly. Each year, he spent a month in seclusion and fasting, after which he visited the Ka'ba, making the circuit seven times, as Muslim pilgrims do to this day. One night in the year 611, as he slept in the cave of Hira during his fast, it is told that an angel appeared to him holding a piece of brocade on which there was writing. "Recite!" the angel ordered.

"What shall I write?" Muhammad asked. Again the angel ordered him to recite, and again Muhammad questioned him. A third time the angel said, "Recite in the name of your Lord, who created all things, who created man of clotted blood. Recite by your most beneficent Lord, who taught the use of the pen, who teaches man that which he knows not" (The Koran, *Sūra* 96:1-5).

When Muhammad repeated these words, which remained indelibly in his memory, the angel departed. Confused, Muhammad considered throwing himself from the mountain, for "none of God's creatures was more hateful to me than a poet or a possessed man; I could not even bear to look at them." Suddenly, a voice from heaven cried out, "Muhammad! You are the Apostle of God, and I am Gabriel!" Looking up, Muhammad saw the angel "in the form of a man with his feet astride the horizon. . . ."

There he was found by Khadīja's messengers. Returning to her, he related the dream and the vision and told her to wrap him in a mantle—perhaps a symbolic gesture. Again he heard the insistent voice, "Arise you who are wrapped up and preach, and magnify your Lord!" (Sūra 74:1-3).

At this, Khadīja set off to her cousin, Waraqa, a Christian holy man. When told of the visions, he cried, "Holy! Holy! By Him in whose hand is Waraqa's soul, . . . he will be the prophet of this people. Bid him to be of good heart." Later, Waraqa also predicted accurately that Muhammad would "be called a liar, and they will use you despitefully and cast you out and fight against you."

Arberry sums up this aspect of Muhammad's life simply: "Thereafter, and during the remainder of his earthly life which closed in A.D. 632, Muhammad heard the voice—identified as the angel Gabriel—at regular intervals. Whatever he heard he repeated to his kinsmen and followers: in course of time the series of revelations was gathered together into a book and called the Koran—a word which means 'recitation' and is derived from the same root as the first word he ever heard descending out of heaven" (*Sufism,* p. 16).

Khadīja became the first disciple of the new Prophet, called in Islam, "the Seal of the Prophets." 'Ali, the son of his uncle Abū Tālib, became Muhammad's first male follower although only a boy of 10. 'Ali was followed in turn by Muhammad's freed slave, the Persian Zayd.

Soon, a party of the Quraysh developed around Muhammad, gaining thereby the suspicison and then hostility of Mecca's leaders. Eventually the small band had to flee to Yathrib. Muhammad's flight, the *Hijra* (Hegira) on July 16th, 622, marks the beginning of the Islamic calendar, the final era of God's revelation to humankind.

The community *(umma)* of the Prophet quickly gained control of the city, which was renamed *Medinat al-Nabi,* "City of the Prophet," shortened to Medina. Hostilities with Mecca turned to war, which ended with victory for the *umma.* The Ka'ba was cleansed of its idols and rededicated, becoming the center of all devotion. To it, Muslims still bow to pray.

Rapidly, paganism began to fade as the Way *(sunna)* of the Prophet spread over Arabia. Muhammad himself remained at Medina, leading a remarkably simple life while organizing the faith of Islam. Arab unity was achieved on a scale never before experienced. Peace prevailed, and an elevated moral code supplanted the previous chaos. In particular, the lot of women was improved. As the Koran was committed to writing, other sayings of the Prophet *(hadīth)* were preserved in memory, collections of which would one day number in the thousands and occasion bitter controversy among various factions, not least among them the Sūfīs.

SUCCESSION AND CONQUEST: THE JIHAD

Muhammad died in 632. He left no sons despite several marriages after Khadīja's death in 619, "the year of tears" in which Abū Tālib also died. The Prophet's daughter Fatima had married 'Ali, his cousin, and had borne him two sons, still infants—Hasan and Hussein, 'Ali himself was still a comparatively young man. Eventually, supported by Aisha, Muhammad's favorite wife, his father-in-law, Abū Bakr, was chosen as *Khalīfat rasul Allah*—"Successor to the Apostle of God."

The *umma* achieved a shaky unity by turning inner disquiet into outer conquest. Quickly, the war-wearied empires of Persia and Byzantium either fell or faltered. Most of Syria was joined to Islam within the year. But Abū Bakr died in 634. He was succeeded by 'Umar, one of the Prophet's early companions, as Caliph and Commander of the Faithful, who continued the *jihad* or Holy War.

Damascus fell in 636, followed by Jerusalem in 638, Ascalon in 644, Tripoli in 645. All of Egypt was won to Islam by 641 and Iraq by 651. 'Umar, however, was assassinated by a Persian slave in 644, beginning a struggle for power which would cause an unbreachable split within the *umma*.

Othman, a member of the powerful Umayyad family of Mecca, was chosen by council to succeed 'Umar. Aged and weak, he was unable to maintain control of the rapidly expanding empire. In 656; he, too, was assassinated while at prayer in his house.

'Ali, Muhammad's son-in-law, became Caliph by dint of a bitter struggle between the Umayyads, whose leader, Muawiya, the nephew of Othman, was supported by Aisha. 'Ali moved the capital from Medina to Kufa in Iraq, where he was stronger, but his triumph ended disastrously. Muawiya soon rebelled and war ensued. In one indecisive battle, a large group of 'Ali's supporters deserted, becoming known as the Kharijites, "Secessionists." The empire was split, and 'Ali was assassinated by a Kharajite in 661.

Muawiya was proclaimed Caliph in Jerusalem, inaugurating the Umayyad dynasty which would rule the Islamic world from Damascus until 750. In Iraq, however, 'Ali's son Hussein rebelled and proclaimed himself rightful Caliph. He was persuaded to abdicate, but his followers, the *Shia 'Ali,* "Partisans of 'Ali," continued to support him as the true Caliph. (The majority of Muslims still distinguish themselves from the Shi'ites by referring to themselves as Sunnites, followers of the Prophet's "Way.")

On Muawiya's death in 680, Hussein again rebelled and was overtaken and executed with his family at Kerbala in 681. To this time, the Muslim world is still divided between the Shi'ites, who regard Hussein as a martyr, and the Sunnites, who represent over 90 percent of the religious population. Shi'ites constitute the majority, however, in Iran, Iraq and Lebanon, where they continue a 1300 year feud and piously cultivate martyrdom in emulation of their saint.

EMPIRE, CRUSADE AND DECLINE

Under the Umayyads, the Empire spread laterally to the Pyrenees, Samarkand, Afghanistan, and the Punjab, as well as northward into Anatolia (Turkey) and Byzantium. Virtually all of Spain and Portugal fell to Muslim rule, which, under the "Moors" from Abdul Rahman I (c. 755) to Abdul Rahman III (d. 961), reached heights of civilization unparalleled in the West.

Damascus remained the seat of the Empire until 750. At that time, descendants of Muhammad's uncle, Abbas, revolted in eastern Persia and established the Abbasid Caliphate with its capital in Baghdad, "the City of Peace." Thus began the golden age of Islamic culture, an era of philosophical, theological, artistic and legal brilliance unmatched before or since. During this time, the Sufi movement also came to prominence. And although slowly eroded by political intrigue and internal dissension, the Abbasid dynasty survived until the Mongol conquest under Hulagu Khan in 1238.

Pressed by the Mongol invasions under Genghis Khan, Hulagu Khan and Timur Leng (Tamerlane), the Islamic Empire gradually turned west. Mercenary Turkish military commanders, the Mamlukes, converted to Islam and slowly began acquiring influence and then power, eventually assuming control of the Empire itself. Egypt at this time had become the domain of the Fatamid rulers, who were overcome by the Kurd, Saladdin, in 1171.

European leaders, awakened to the growing presence of the "Infidel" on their borders, and needing an outlet for developing mercantile and military energies, inaugurated a series of "pre-emptive" religious wars, Christendom's *"jihad,"* the Crusades.

Initially successful, the Crusades progressively deteriorated into factionalism and petty nationalistic conflicts. Besides earning the enduring contempt of Moslems for Christians they once tolerated and respected, the disastrous adventure ended with the Holy Places more securely than before in Muslim control, Europe impoverished and Constantinople in flames. In Spain, however, the expulsion of the Moors, despite their magnificent contributions to science, philosophy and the arts, especially architecture, was completed at the hands of Ferdinand and Isabella by 1492.

The Ottoman Empire, meantime, named for Othman, a thirteenth century Turkish leader, consolidated its dominion by conquest and was essentially complete by 1517. With the fall of Constantinople to the troops of Muhammad II in 1453, Byzantium came to an inglorious end. The seat of a new empire was moved there, however. Under Sulaiman "The Magnificent" (1520-66), Turkish power reached its zenith, then began a pathetic centuries' long decline, culiminating in collapse after the First World War.

The revolt of the Arabs in the twenties, the further fragmentation of the Islamic world and the outstripping industrialization of the West did not doom Islam as a political force or, especially, a religious one in the modern world, however. The glory of Islam may again illluminate the eastern world with triumphs of spiritual and artistic genius, or, fired by new-found wealth and imperial ambitions, it may plunge deeper into chasms of political and economic misery. Much will depend on the destiny of the inner spirit of Islam, which over the centuries has been largely identified with the movement called *tasawwuf*—Sūfism.

MUHAMMAD A MYSTIC?

Despite the opinion of many scholars, including the severe historian of religions, R. C. Zaehner, that Muhammad was anti-mystical, or, as was long held by Christian accounts, a madman, imposter or epileptic, it is difficult to review his life and experiences without concluding that, as a man who knew God in the immediacy of his experience, Muhammad was indeed a mystic. He is, of course, considered to be the fountainhead of Sūfī mysticism in all its traditions.

But even in his own lifetime and in his account of God's revelation to him, the Koran, there can be found reason to include Muhammad in the ranks of the supreme mystics of humankind. Official and unofficial sayings *(hadīth)* attributed to the Prophet corroborate such a judgment.

His experience in the cave of Hira, his encounter with the angel on the mountain, his continuing experience of revelation throughout the remaining years of his life characterize Muhammad as a mystic, much as did similar experiences with regard to Moses. His paramount mystical experience, the "Night Journey and Ascension of the Prophet," is only alluded to in the Koran

(Sūra 17:1), but it is well attested to in many *hadīth* and all early accounts of his life.

According to the account as compiled by Ibn Ishāq, Muhammad was awakened one night by Gabriel and taken to mount a white winged animal, half-mule, half-donkey, whose name was Burāq. He was brought thus to the Temple in Jerusalem, where he encountered Abraham, Moses and Jesus. Then, by means of a fabulous ladder, Gabriel assisted the Prophet to mount heaven itself. There he was granted a vision of hell—accounts of which greatly influenced Dante's *Inferno*. In the higher heavens, Muhammad again encountered Jesus, along with John the Baptist, Joseph and Abraham.

Before the throne of God, according to the version of al-Qushairi (d. 1074), Muhammad exclaimed, "O God, I do not know how to speak your praise." The answer returned, "O Muhammad, if you speak not, I will speak; if you deem yourself unworthy to praise Me, I will make the universe your deputy, that all its atoms may praise Me in your name" (Hujwīrī, *Kashf al-mahjub,* p. 283, cited by Arberry, p. 29).

Later, Muhammad said of his experience, "I am not as one of you; truly, I pass the night with my Lord, and he gives me food and drink." Again, he remarked, "I am with God in a state in which none of the Cherubim nor any Prophet is capable of being contained with me" (Cf. Arberry, p. 29). It is also said of him that henceforth, "every time of prayer was an Ascension and a new nearness to God" (Arberry, p. 30).

In the Koran itself, there is adequate reason to find the origins of Sūfism in teachings about God's nearness and love. Although the all-surpassing transcendence of Allah and his vengeful fury against sinners is calculated to inspire the fear of God in the hearts of the faithful, there are also passages of great tenderness and compassion. A favorite title of Allah is "the Compassionate, the Merciful," in whose name every chapter but one of the Koran begins.

The immanence of God is conveyed in a famous passage

which goes beyond anything in the New Testament: "We have created man and we know what his soul whispers within him, for we are nearer to him than his jugular vein" (Sūra 50:16). Again, "If my servants enquire of you concerning me," God says, "see, I am near" (Sūra 2:186).

Having been a merchant, religious innovator, soldier and diplomat, Muhammad spent his last years in peace and prayer, working and walking in the presence of God. As to the extent of his mysticism, one must judge for oneself, ultimately. In final witness, however, is this eloquent tribute to Muhammad's belief, mystic or not, that God's presence is *everywhere*: "To God belong the East and West; whichever way you turn, the Face of God is there" (Sūra 2:115).

SŪFĪ ORIGINS

"Sūfism" is derived from the word for wool, *sūf,* probably because of the practice of the early ascetics who wore a plain woolen robe, perhaps in imitation of Christian anchorites in the region. According to one recent authority, a Sūfī is "anyone who believes that it is possible to have direct experience of God and who is prepared to go out of his way to put himself in a state whereby he may be enabled to do this" (J. S. Trimingham, *The Sūfī Orders,* p. 1).

Many external influences undoubtedly shaped the early history of Sūfism—Jewish, Christian, Zoroastrian, Gnostic, Hindu and Buddhist among them. But it is more accurate to see it as an internal development of Muslim spirituality which drew on outer resources as it grew.

In Islam, three fundamental attitudes have been considered fundamental from the earliest times: *islām*—total and absolute surrender to the will of God, especially as revealed in the Koran; *īmān*—faith, or the interior aspect of devotion to God; and *ihsān*—conducting onself in constant awareness of the presence of God (see Schimmel, p. 29).

It was out of the interior aspect of Islamic religion that Sūfism developed as an ascetical reaction against the wealth and worldliness of the Umayyad dynasty and early imperial ambitions. The "patriarch" of this mystical movement was Hasan al-Basrī (d. 728). Because of their reactionary attitude to the dominant power, the ascetics were associated with the *Shia 'Ali;* both flourished in the East, both were conservative and austere.

The early ascetics were chiefly concerned with devotion and practical religion rather than theological speculation. A more idealistic tradition developed at Kufa, however, under Abū Hāshim as-Sūfī—the first to be so-called. In the traditions of both Basra and Kufa, renunciation *(zuhd),* the dominant factor for many years and the glory of the Sufis, was their poverty and simplicity. Recollection or remembrance of God *(dhikr)* was especially fostered, becoming over the years one of the central practices of the Sūfī way.

The severity and austerity of the ascetics was carried to various parts of the empire by missionaries, merchants and disciples, but fear of God and renunciation could not sustain the fiery spirit of the Islamic soul. Gradually, asceticism acquired a dimension of service in honor of God, and eventually blossomed into the love-mysticism which has been its primary quality ever since.

THE TRANSFORMATION: RĀBI'A

A great woman saint of Basra has been credited with accomplishing the transition from asceticism to explicit mysticism by her life-long teaching and practice of selfless love. Rābi'a al-'Adawīyya (d. 801) was an emancipated slave, celebrated by her biographer as "one set apart in the seclusion of holiness, that woman veiled with the veil of sincerity, that one enflamed by love and longing . . . , lost in union with God, that one accepted by men as a second spotless Mary . . ." ('Attār, *Tadhkirat al-auliyā',* quoted in Schimmel, p. 38).

Rābi'a never married, dedicating herself totally to the love of God, which she celebrated in mystical verse. She is also credited with introducing the theme of God's jealousy into Islamic mysticism. Her prayers have inspired many commentators in both East and West.

The golden age of Sūfism coincided with the great era of the Abbasid Caliphate. Many outstanding saints appeared and established schools of disciples, some of which would evolve into the Sūfī Orders in later centuries.

Dhū'n-Nūn the Egyptian (Thauban ibn Ibrāhīm) (d. 861) was one such leader who is held to have developed the notion of gnosis *(ma'rifa)*—an intuitive knowledge of the heart directly instilled by God. He, like Rābi'a, nevertheless used the language of passionate love to describe the longing of the soul for God:

> I die, and yet not dies in me
> The ardor of my love for Thee,
> Nor hath Thy love, my only goal,
> Assuaged the fervor of my soul.
> (Arberry, p. 53)

One of the greatest Sūfī masters was Abū Yazid (Bāyazīd) of Bistam (d. 875), who originated one of the two chief "tendencies" in Islamic mysticism, "intoxication" *(sukr)*—ecstatic expression of the soul aflame with the love of God. His favorite theme was, not surprisingly, the heavenly journey *(miraj)* of the Prophet. Abū'l Qāsim al-Junayd, "the Shaikh of the Order" (d. 910), represents the other chief tendency, that of "sobriety" *(sahw)*, considered to be the safer of the two. Junayd stressed the "continuation" *(baqā)* of life in God as superior to and indeed the eventuation of ecstatic "annihilation" or "passing-away" *(fanā)* which precedes it. But Junayd, one of the greatest of the Sūfīs, was no rationalist; he, too, based his entire hope on the surpassing love of God.

Three later Sūfīs achieved sufficient fame even outside of Islam to warrant consideration here—al-Hallāj, al-Ghazālī and Rūmī, the poet.

AL-HALLĀJ: SŪFĪ PROTOMARTYR

Al-Hussein ibn Mansūr al-Hallāj remains an enigmatic and controversial figure, having been considered by various writers a pantheist, a secret Christian, a pure Sūfī saint, an imposter and a magician. A disciple of al-Junayd, Hallāj ("the cotton-carder") scandalized orthodox Muslims and even Sūfīs with his extravagant, ecstatic claims of union with God: *ana'l-Haqq*—"I am the Absolute Reality," meaning, literally, "I am God." But it is doubtful that Hallāj was claiming divinity.

Within the confines of Sūfī ecstatic identification with God, Hallāj's outrageous claim can be interpreted safely, and other Sūfīs were known—and sometimes persecuted—for uttering similar statements while entranced. But for political as well as religious reasons, Hallāj was eventually imprisoned and finally executed in 922. Not least among his "eccentricities" was his emulation of Jesus, rather than Muhammad, as the exemplar of the Holy Man in whom God was incarnate.

AL-GHAZĀLĪ: THE SUFI THEOLOGIAN

By contrast, Abū Hāmid Muhammad ibn Muhammad al-Ghazālī (1058-1111) was a Persian canon lawyer and Sunni theologian at the college of Baghdad. In 1095, however, he found himself unable to speak or lecture. After a tortuous self-examination, he gave up his career and became a Sūfī. Rather than retiring into obscurity, however, al-Ghazālī turned his mind and pen to the refutation of rationalism in theology and a strong defense of mysticism. The importance of the conversion of this *Hujjat al-Islām* ("Proof of Islam") has been compared to that of Augustine in Christianity.

As the greatest medieval Islamic theologian, al-Ghazāli's

conversion and writings, especially his four-volume *Revival of the Religious Sciences,* had the reciprocal effect of grounding mysticism more securely theologically, and requiring orthodox theologians to take Sufism more seriously.

RŪMĪ: THE SŪFĪ POET

Jalāludīn Rūmī (1207-73), poet and founder of the Mevleviyya Order, known far and long as the "Whirling Dervishes," for whom song, dance and music are favorite devices to induce an ecstatic state in which one may come into the presence of God, is one of the most engaging of all the great poets of Islam. His *Masnavī (Couplets),* forty-three years in preparation, is probably the greatest mystical poem in any language.

Many other Sūfī saints, shaikhs and scholars should be included here, but spatial limitations permit only a passing mention: al-Hārith b. Asad al-Muhāsibī (781-857); Abū Bakr al-Kharraz (d. 899); Farīd al-Din 'Attār of Mishapur (d. 1220), Sūfī biographer and Persian poet, author of the exquisite *Dialogue of the Birds;* 'Abdu'l-Qāhir Abū Najīb as-Suhrawardī (d. 1168), the founder of the Suhrawardi Order, and his brother Shihābuddīn Abū Hafs (1145-1234), who achieved even more fame as teacher, leader and writer; Mahyi al-Dīn ibn 'Arabī (1165-1240), the great mystical genius and consummate Arab poet; and Hakim Jāmī (d. 1494), perhaps the last great Sūfī poet.

SŪFĪ ORDERS

The formation of orders was perhaps inevitable, as disciples sought to perpetuate the teachings and practices of their venerable founders. In the eleventh century, the Persian historian of the Sūfī movement, Hujwīrī, enumerated twelve sects or fraternities, although many more have existed before and since. Centers were founded and endowed, novices were received, and traditions developed, some of which exist to this day.

Four great orders were founded in the twelfth century—the Quadiri, Suhrawardi, Shādilīya and Maulawiya (or, in its more familiar Turkish form, Mevleviyya). Hundreds of orders have existed since, enumerating millions of adherents. Each is presided over by a "successor" (*khalīfa,* "caliph") and lesser heads, *shaikhs* or *pirs.* The lodges of the orders house the professional members, whom the lay members outnumber by far. The laity follow the teachings in their everyday lives and attend certain rituals.

Each order has its distinctive ritual, and dress and teaching—its *tarīqa,* "path." Women are admitted to many of them. Gradually, as the orders spread, filling the devotional gap left by the recession of the *Shia,* the *shaikh* or *pir* acquired increasing authority over the lives of professed and lay members. Unfortunately, as leadership tended to become a hereditary office, those who wielded such power were often intellectually and even spiritually incapable of doing so wisely.

DECLINE

Thus, as Islam itself entered the long decline of the Ottoman Empire, so did the Sūfī orders. Charlatanism and chicanery began to replace the intense devotion and religious sincerity of the early Sūfīs; wealth accompanied power. The Arabic word *faqīr,* which means "poor," as *darvish* means "mendicant" in Turkish, had originally been a title of honor, but now became synonymous with trickery and deceit, as is "faker" in English and German to this day. In Turkey, the orders were abolished in 1925, although the traditions of the dervishes have not disappeared entirely.

SŪFĪ TEACHINGS

To adequately summarize the great variety of practical and speculative teachings of the Sūfīs would take many volumes. But as true Muslims, they share certain fundamental attitudes.

Perhaps the most basic element is *tawhīd*—divine unity—both in the sense of the absence of all duality in God, and of union with God as the goal of the Sūfī *tarīqa.* It is the belief in the possibility of such union that in fact connects the mystical tradition of Islam, however tenuously, with that of Christianity and other religious traditions, and yet which also distances it from orthodox Islam, with its age-old horror of "incarnationism" *(hulūl).*

It is not difficult to place love in the center of Sūfism. In a religious tradition in which the majesty and transcendence of God are greatly extolled, immanence, tenderness and love are not wanting, but are more implicit than manifest. It was these elements that were explicitated in Sūfism, extending the love of God to heights of devotion equal to that of any other religious tradition.

Similarly, reconciliation is a pervasive attitude in Sūfism, whether in the form of bringing unity out of the diversity of divine and human wills, the use of paradox, or the practical art of forgiveness and peacemaking.

Living in the presence of God by means of continual recollection *(dhikr),* relying on complete trust in God *(tawakkul),* practicing personal renunciation *(zuhd)* in the form of poverty, abstinence and submission, achieving certainty of the inner light *(yaqīn),* and finally, arriving at union with God *(haqīqa)*—all clearly relate Islamic mysticism to the classical "Three Ages" of Christian spirituality, as noted by Annemarie Schimmel (p. 98).

Meditation *(murāqaba)* and contemplation *(mushāhada)* are important aspects of the spiritual life, similarly, being ranked among the ten mystical states *(ahwāl)* described by most of the great masters as representing the various degrees of mystical development leading to final bliss and contentment *(ridā).* The identification and explanation of these states and the various "stages" *(maqāmāt)* of the Sūfī path (such as abstinence, poverty, patience, etc.) have been extended to lengths that even Christian mystical theologians would find exhaustive.

CONCLUSION

More is known today in the Christian West about the traditions of the Sūfīs than at any previous time, owing in some measure to the popular writings of Idries Shah. Such accounts, however, barely introduce the subject, and render it easy to form a superficial impression of the depth and majesty of this ancient tradition of traditions. "Sūfism Reoriented" and other hybrid versions abound, as well as pseudo-Sūfī notions redolent of the unfortunate decline of a great spirituality into magical manipulations.

But the emergence of an aggressive Shi'ite movement in Iran and Iraq should not be underestimated, nor its spiritual potential for rejuvenating Islam. Apart even from the political issues and internal factions within Islam, the development of a strong and vital sense of destiny itself indicates a confrontation between the remnants of ancient Christendom and Islam. Such an encounter may, with the help of God and the collaboration of serious mystical representatives of both traditions, bring a new era of friendship to the mid-world, much like that of the first days of the great *umma.*

SUGGESTIONS FOR FURTHER READING

A. J. Arberry, *Sufism: An Account of the Mystics of Islam,* London: Allen and Unwin, 1950.

Peter Mansfield, *The Arabs,* New York: Penguin Books, 1978 ed.

Reynold Nicholson, *The Mystics of Islam,* Boston: Routledge and Kegan Paul, 1975.

Annemarie Schimmel, *Mystical Dimensions of Islam,* Chapel Hill: University of North Carolina Press, 1975.

J. Spencer Trimingham, *The Sufi Orders in Islam,* New York: Oxford University Press, 1973.

John Alden Williams, ed., *Islam,* New York: George Braziler, 1962.

Chapter 18

MODERN MYSTICISM

Love him simply as the One, the pure and absolute Unity in which there is no trace of duality. And into this One we must let ourselves fall continuously from being into non-being.

Dag Hammarskjöld

At the beginning of the last century of the second millenium of the Christian era, the world was poised on the edge of political cataclysm and technological change that would exceed anything before experienced on this planet. As if in deliberate imitation of the events of the 14th century, mystical spirituality grew and even flourished during the turbulent 20th, an age born to woe if ever one was. Two major trends emerged fairly early in this century, in keeping with the tenor of the times, one religious, the other secular—a mysticism without God, church or sacrament in any conventional sense of those words. We shall explore these dimensions of contemporary mysticism separately, beginning with the religious expression.

The sources of both currents lie not in the present century, however, but in the remoter depths of the previous one. To understand something of the direction of modern mysticism, then, we shall first have to backtrack briefly.

THE AWAKENING

The end of the revolutionary period in 1848 found Europe in the grip of secularism—the separation of Church and State, rationalism, new forms of critical scholarship, widespread defection of the masses owing to industrialization on one hand and the development of a "modern" mentality on the other by Darwin, Marx, Freud and other pioneers of human thought.

But improved conditions were also on hand in relief and emancipation acts in England, the restoration of the church in France, and the auspicious beginning of the pontificate of the (initially) liberal Pius IX. In Germany, before Bismarck's *Kulturkampf* clouded the religious sky with real and threatened oppression, the mystical element of Christianity received an injection of scholarly enthusiasm from the pens of Friederich Schleiermacher (1768-1834), a Protestant, and Johann J. von Görres (1776-1848), a Catholic.

Mysticism had lingered timidly in the shadows of official displeasure for two hundred years following the excesses of Quietism and Jansenism. By itself, however, theological interest was not enough to restore mysticism to favor. In fact, strenuous opposition to both Schleiermacher and von Görres quickly developed and held the field until the turn of the century.

That did not prevent a real awakening of mystical enthusiasm among the people of God, however, and the 19th century boasts many eminent mystic saints among its children. Further, their influence has continued to grow in the 20th century.

Among these new pillars of the coming mystical revolution were, in England, John Henry Newman (1801-1890), whose spirituality ran even deeper than his theological apologetics; Gerard Manley Hopkins (1844-1889), the brilliant Jesuit poet and man of letters; Francis Thompson (1859-1907), the troubled, ecstatic poet of the "Hound of Heaven"; and the engaging lay theologian and spiritual writer, Baron Friedrich von Hügel (1852-1925), whose study of St. Catherine of Genoa, *The Mystical Element of Religion* (1908), remains one of the classics of mystical theology.

In France, there was, first, St. John Vianney, the Curé d'Ars (1786-1858), whose remarkable charisms were excelled by his simple and self-effacing pastoral spirit. Similarly, humility was the spiritual heart of St. Therese of Lisieux (1873-1897)—the young Carmelite nun who lived and died unknown to her own time but became a light for 20th century God-seekers. Charles de

Foucauld (1858-1916) also lived and died in obscurity, martyred by the Tuaregs he desired to win for Christ and among whom he had ceaselessly and apparently profitlessly labored in the Sahara.

In Spain was found St. Anthony Claret (1807-1870). Italy produced an abundant harvest of saints in the immortal Don John Bosco (1815-1888), St. Gemma Galgani (1878-1903), the stigmatic, and many others. The German nun, Anne Catherine Emmerich (1774-1824), was also endowed with the marks of Christ's passion—such manifestations perhaps being a more eloquent rebuttal to the prevalent materialism and rationalism of the period than any learned refutation.

In America, the continent was engulfed in a great revival period shortly before the Civil War, the Second "Great Awakening." Spiritualism erupted on the same ground in 1848, inaugurating a continuing battle between believers and the incredulous. Contemporaneous with the unchurched mysticism of Thoreau, Whitman and the New England Transcendentalists we find the Shakers and the Utopian movements—all brief flashes in the growing night of skepticism. At this time lived the fascinating Isaac Thomas Hecker (1819-1888), founder of the Paulists and champion of the Catholic Press. The Italian immigrant, Mother Frances Xavier Cabrini (1850-1917), spent herself in the service of the poor, founding schools, hospitals and orphanages.

Not all saints are mystics, of course—at least in the narrower sense of that word as evolved in the "desert" period of mystical theology from the 17th century to the end of the 19th. And the 19th century had many other saints. But a cloud of mystical witnesses was growing steadily over the heads of the academics.

The lightning strokes of recognition that came with the writings of Dean William Inge, the French alienists De Montmorand and Delacroix, William James, von Hügel, Evelyn Underhill, William Ernest Hocking and Rufus Jones could not be ignored. Anglo- and Roman Catholic theologians began to rethink the unfortunate division of the Christian spiritual life into dual tracks, the ascetical and mystical. The vision of the early Greek theologians of Alexandria was retrieved—the *whole* Christian life is in fact mystical when lived with true fervor and loving service.

RECOVERY

Historically, credit would undoubtedly be given the Abbé Auguste Sandreau for inaugurating the revived mystical theology of Christian tradition in his 1896 volume *The Degrees of the Spiritual Life*, in which he claimed that all are called to the fullness of the contemplative life of union with God. He was opposed in his democratic spirituality by Auguste Poulain, S.J., and soon two camps were debating heatedly. Both sides were in fundamental agreement, however, that the authentic mystical spirituality of the Christian life must be recovered in its integrity.

The new spirituality, as it developed in the new century, in fact regained its roots in scripture, sacrament and prayer, owing largely to the progress being made in the areas of biblical scholarship, the study of the Greek Fathers and the liturgical renewal begun in the 19th century by Dom Guéranger and brought into the 20th by Pope St. Pius X. The emergence of Catholic Action as an indispensable dimension of Christian spirituality provided the necessary impetus to retrieve the final link between contemplation and action. The fruit of these confluent developments was perhaps principally felt in the deliberations of the Second Vatican Council.

The spiritual revival was not limited to the Roman church. The Anglican Communion had deepened the spiritual life of many of its members following the Tractarian and Oxford Movements, and the rediscovery of mysticism owes much to the work of English scholars. The Protestant churches, especially in America, underwent a great baptism of fire in the sudden awakening of the Pentecostal movement in 1906—originally a phenomenon in the black churches of the ghetto.

Pentecostalism caused many divisions and conflicts, but it has continued to enliven the American church and has spread throughout the world, influencing the Roman Catholic, Anglican, Orthodox and other even less enthusiastic traditions. Insofar as great stress is laid upon the activation of the presence of the Holy Spirit in the hearts and lives of believers, pentecostalism must be seen as one form of mystical Christianity.

THE PENTECOSTAL EXPERIENCE

Perhaps the most characteristic and fundamental claim of all Pentecostalism is the experience of the active presence of the Holy Spirit, bringing in its wake the charismatic signs of God-possession: speaking in "tongues," miraculous healings, prophecy, inspired teaching, discernment of spirits and casting out "demons"—the "ministry of deliverance."

In the late sixties, in the ecumenical wake of the Vatican Council, "the new Pentecost" dreamed of by Pope John XXIII was seemingly realized for many by the introduction of Pentecostalism in the Roman Catholic church—to the manifest surprise of ardent Protestants both friendly and unfriendly to Pentecostalism. The resulting movement is known in Catholic circles as "the charismatic renewal," and its counterpart in other denominations generally as "neo-Pentecostalism." While still a minority phenomenon, the new Pentecostalism has grown rapidly, especially among Catholics, of whom perhaps as many as 60,000 or more are members.

The mystical character of charismatic Christianity is subject to widespread disagreement. Some experts, such as Frs. William Johnston, Donald Gelpi and George Maloney, all Jesuits, and Dr. Josephine Massyngberde Ford, have affirmed the truly mystical element present in the baptism of the Spirit and charismatic prayer. Other equally adept witnesses are reluctant to concede that a mass movement with intense emotionalism, highly structured authoritarian leadership and social control mechanisms, can be mystical in an authentic Christian sense.

While such a debate cannot be decided abstractly, it seems that the truth lies practically in the middle. Many aspiring Christian mystics should be able to find support and encouragement among their pentecostal brothers and sisters, provided that such groups are not unduly authoritarian, allow full personal freedom to encounter and express the experience of God's presence, and promote holistic spiritual development. On the other hand, an exaggerated emphasis on extraordinary manifestations such as speaking in tongues, and especially exorcism, probably evinces an unhealthy atmosphere for the growth of a true mystical spirituality founded on unity, love and reconciliation. No one has a monopoly on God's grace and self-communication, and his gifts are diverse.

ORTHODOXY

The ordeal of the Bolshevik revolution in 1917 and the ensuing years of communist oppression, as well as the incessant conflicts in the Balkan States in the early 20th century, seriously hindered but did not halt the mystical renaissance of Orthodox Christianity begun in the late nineteenth century. Dispersed like the Jews of old, emigrant writers of brilliant spiritual insight such as Dostoyevsky's friend, Vladimir Solovieff (1853-1900), Sergius Bulgakov (1871-1944) and Nicholas Berdyaev (1874-1948) introduced aspects of Byzantine spirituality into the West, particularly the doctrine of "Holy Wisdom."

In France and England, centers of study, prayer and ecumenical exchange were established, such as the Fellowship of Ss. Alban and Sergius. In the United States, while ecumenical progress was slower, the "Jesus prayer" received sudden attention with the publication of French's translations of *The Way of a Pilgrim* and *The Pilgrim Continues His Way* in the late fifties.

Among spiritual writers today, few can claim so large an ecumenical following as Metropolitan Anthony Bloom of England, or the Oxford theologian, Rev. Kallistos T. Ware, whose works on prayer can be highly recommended to anyone alert to the rich heritage of the Christian East as it still flourishes today.

MODERN MYSTICS: CASE STUDIES

Like sanctity, "mysticism" is often considered an inappropriate designation for a living person, except in a vague sense of idle dreaminess or just pejoratively. But since "sanctity" means *wholeness* in fact as well as in origin, we are all saints at least by calling—and should be in intent. The same holds for the mystical life, which fundamentally means the practical quest for a clearer awareness and felt sense of God's presence in the events of ordinary life. Thus the names of certain living persons or those recently deceased are here included, not to settle matters of dispute nor to claim privileged insight, but to illustrate the quest for God today.

Of the many women and men whose lives provide evidence of an authentic mystical attitude, I have selected only six—three men and three women of different traditions. My chief reluctance in bringing them forward in witness is that they are not "typical." Each is distinctly unique, as we all are. But as the world notes the extraordinary and original as more newsworthy than the ordinary, we have here the geniuses, the rarities, the exceptions, "famous" people.

Perhaps the most "usual" among them is Simone Weil, who suffered so incredibly from sinus headaches and clumsiness. It may be that what we need in order to balance the ledger is the unknown housewife, the barber, the street peddler. But because they *are* unknown, we must settle for the known and exceptional. We should remember, however, that at the beginning of their quest, each of the following mystics was only a promise of exception. And in each of them, at least in some of them, we will discover some echo of ourselves.

Richard Woods

PIERRE TEILHARD DE CHARDIN: SCIENTIST-MYSTIC (1881-1955)

Outside the professional world of geology and paleontology, the intersecting circles of the Jesuit order, and a small group of friends scattered over the world, Teilhard and his writings were unknown until after his death in New York on Easter Sunday, 1955. Yet, in the past twenty-five years, he has become one of the outstanding figures of recent Christian thought and even the center of a devotional cult. In Teilhard, matter and spirit, the fact of evolution and the reality of faith, science and mysticism, were reconciled in a vast synthesis that was suppressed by his religious superiors while he lived.

From his early childhood, Teilhard was keenly aware of the presence of the Creator within his creation. Born near Clermont in the Auvergne, he was fascinated as a child with stones, metal and permanent things in nature. In them, he perceived more than matter and found himself rapt in adoration before a piece of iron. His interest in science was supported and developed when he entered the Society of Jesus in 1899.

His first "mystical experience" seems to have occurred during his studies for the priesthood in Sussex, when he suddenly perceived the universe as surcharged with the energy of a personal *presence.* Called to service during World War I, he became a stretcher-bearer at the front, where his heroism and courage were noted, and he faced the grim reality of suffering, death and the presence of evil. At that time, he had another experience, this associated with a picture of Christ. It was "as though the surface that separated Christ from the world about him was changing into a film of vibration in which all limits were confounded." He sensed streams of light flowing to the nether reaches of the material universe, the entire cosmos reverberating as a single organism.

Teilhard's scientific mysticism remained Christological to the end. He envisioned the universe en route to a final apotheosis, the Omega Point, in which consciousness would transcend itself and humankind would indeed become truly one in Christ, *divinized.* Evolution, the natural history of the cosmos, is thus the unfolding of the divine presence in creation, focused and realized in Christ.

Although sometimes accused of pantheism or panpsychism, Teilhard was more of a panentheist, believing in and sometimes aware of the presence of God as All in all. His interpretation of that fact, once considered so daring as to warrant suppression, is now considered by many to be naively optimistic and unscientific. But his example as a pioneer of religious and scientific integrity, now no longer split into warring camps, but reconciled in an encompassing vision of reality based on cosmic love at the heart of things, will long serve as a model for Christians of the future.

MARTIN BUBER: HASIDIC PROPHET (1878-1965)

As a boy, Buber, a native of Vienna, spent summers on his father's estate in northern Rumania, near where a group of Hasidic Jews lived and worshipped. At the university, however, his interest was at first dormant, as he became an active member of the Zionist movement, which he joined in 1898. But his religious studies eventually led him back into a real and lasting involvement with Hasidism.

Buber merged his political and mystical concerns into a vision of life which he expressed in eloquent books such as the gnomic masterpiece *I and Thou* (1923), espousing a philosophical stance remarkably similar to that of his contemporary in America, William Ernest Hocking.

As an influential editor, professor and ecumenist, Buber became a target for Nazi persecution. He was deprived of his chair of theology and ethics at Frankfurt University in 1933. Five years later he was called to become professor of sociology at the

Hebrew University of Jerusalem, where he remained for the rest of his life.

Buber's Hasidism departs in respects from the classical form—he puts no emphasis on practices of traditional piety or even on Talmudic teachings. His approach is primarily ethical and social in that his underlying philosophy is built on relation, particularly the qualitatively distinct character of I-Thou and I-It relationships (the latter including all "indicative" personal relations as well—to "him," "her," and "them"). God becomes consciously present in our experience of things, as well as in personal relationships, when the "Thou" contained within them and grounding them is allowed to appear.

Buber's political emphasis is based on his belief that a universal kingdom of God can only come about in the concrete realization of justice and peace in the whole of a nation's existence. In this, Buber continues the prophetic traditions of the ancient Hebrews as much as the messianic aspirations of 17th and 20th century Hasidism. Significantly, his influence has been even more pronounced on German and English-speaking theologians than among his Jewish contemporaries.

MEHER BABA: SUFISM REORIENTED (1894-1969)

Although Meher Baba was widely celebrated on his visit to California in the thirties, he is now remembered by relatively few outside the circle of his followers. Born of Persian parents in Poona, India, Merwan Sheriar Irani came to be known as "Meher Baba" (which can mean "Compassionate Father" or "Spiritual Master") after his unusual enlightenment experience at the hands of an old Sūfī woman named Hazrat Babajan and a Hindu guru called Upashni.

One evening when he was 18, Hazrat Babajan called Merwan to her, clasped his hands and kissed his forehead between the brows. Her kiss transformed his life. Later, she made him realize "in a flash" the infinite ecstasy of God-consciousness. For months, he wandered in a daze. He often pounded his head against walls to alleviate the spiritual anguish of his own self-consciousness mingled with that of his consciousness of divinity.

He visited several Hindu masters seeking help, one of whom sent him to a famous guru, Upashni. The guru's response after one look was to hurl a stone at the youth, striking him squarely where he had been kissed by Babajan, thus bringing him to a more normal state of consciousness. But his God-consciousness never left him. Indeed, if not too unusual in Hinduism and certain Sūfī traditions, Meher Baba claimed to *be* God, the supreme realization of divinity, the final *avatar.*

In 1925, Baba announced that for a year, he would not speak. In fact, he was silent until his death, 44 years later. At first, he wrote, then abandoned writing for an alphabet board and finally a set of hand gestures by which he communicated to his disciples. The great revelation promised when he broke his silence has yet to come.

Within the Hindu-Sūfī framework of his claim to divinity, Meher Baba's doctrine centered on unqualified love and service. His devotees are still called "Baba-lovers." The quality he radiated to all, despite his very real human imperfections, was in fact a total, demanding but all-forgiving love. And he expected uncompromising love in return, being fully aware of the manifest limitations of all human devotion.

Meher Baba exemplified love in action reaching out to the most unloved members of Hindu society—the insane. He actively searched for them, especially the God-intoxicated *masts*, whose mystical awareness had deprived them of at least part of their sanity, if not all of it. He personally tended to the needs of the most wretched of them—bathing, clothing and feeding them, daily scrubbing the common latrines before sitting with them in a silent colloquy of love.

Madman, genius, saint or imposter, Meher Baba left a profound impression upon everyone who met him. His disciples still number in the thousands. Photographs—of which there are many, curiously—reveal a man of tremendous compassion and benevolence. And with his teaching that intellectual understanding and self-love cannot bring us closer to God, but only love expressed in service can bring true union, he surely takes his place among the classic mystics of humankind.

SRI ANANDAMAYI MA: MOTHER OF THE UNIVERSE (b. 1896)

Born in eastern Bengal, Nirmala Devi was the daughter of traditional, even pious Hindu parents. Unlike her six brothers and sisters, from an early age she showed awareness of invisible presences and spoke to trees and plants as if they were human. Although bright, she failed to learn to read or write, despite efforts of her teachers.

Married at the age of 12 to Ramani Chukravati, the son of a devout Brahmin family, Ma (or Mataji, Beloved Mother, as she is called) spent only six months at his house, and their marriage was never consummated. As a teenager, she began to manifest signs of spiritual powers. At 25, she became dumb and remained so for three years. Eventually, she was recognized as a spiritual teacher of a very high order.

After 1924, Mataji ended her silence, unlike Meher Baba, and demonstrated in various ways her identification with Kali, the Mother Goddess, protector of life and death. Indian theologians disputed whether she was an incarnation of Kali, an *avatara* or "merely" a devotee who had achieved permanent union with the female personification of God. Whatever her status, Mataji is still treated as if she were indeed Kali by her adoring disciples, for whom the motherhood of God seems to have reached perfect visible expression.

As mother, keenly moved by suffering, Mataji is known to have wrought cures. She remains mysteriously youthful, although now quite elderly. Arthur Koestler, visiting her when she was 63, found her to resemble "a gypsy beauty in her forties."

Although enlightened without being instructed by a guru, Ma's teachings reflect the lofty monistic theology of classical Brahmanism: "Man's true nature, call it by any name, is the Supreme, I myself" (*Amara Vanino*, III, 3, p. 209, cited in Fremantle, p. 218). She is said to have been visited by Gandhi several times, although her interests seem to be completely non-political. Other Indian leaders have expressed special homage to her as India's outstanding woman saint.

SIMONE WEIL: THE CLUMSY REVOLUTIONARY (1909-1943)

A Jewess by ancestry but reared an agnostic, Simone Weil was a precocious, beautiful child destined for a life of labor, suffering and misunderstanding during an era in which the world went mad. An ardent pacifist, anarchist and champion of the oppressed poor and workers, she held and lost teaching positions repeatedly despite her brilliance and generosity of spirit. She had in fact won first place on the entrance exams for the École Normale Supérieure ahead of thirty men and Simone de Beauvoir, who scored second. She graduated near the top of the list, out of 107 candidates.

In her early childhood, after a period of depression, she had suddenly acquired a conviction of the reality of the "transcendent kingdom" which any person could enter "if only he longs for truth and perpetually concentrates all his attention upon its attainment." Although never baptized a Christian, nevertheless "I was born, I grew up, and I always remained within the Christian inspiration" (*Waiting for God*, New York: Capricorn, p. 62).

Her mystical identification with both the working class and Christ developed virtually simultaneously as she worked in factories, taught, did farm work, marched and attempted to fight in the Spanish Civil War. Clumsy, almost clownlike, Simone was inept with firearms and a menace with cooking pots. She was returned to France, disillusioned and exhausted.

Drawn closer to Christ during the Holy Week services at Solesmes in 1938, Simone was introduced to the English mystical poets shortly afterwards. While reciting George Herbert's "Love Bade Me Welcome," one day, "Christ himself came down and took possession of me. . . .". Having never considered the possiblity of real, personal contact between a human being and God, nevertheless, "in this sudden possession of me by Christ, neither my sense nor my imagination had any part: I only felt in the midst of my suffering the presence of a love" (Ibid., p. 69).

After a period of intense mystical absorption, Simone returned to the world, but too ill yet to resume teaching. She began studying Sanskrit and the origins of Nazism. When war broke out, she volunteered to be a front-line nurse, but was again refused. With her parents, she migrated to Marseilles, eventually becoming a refugee to Morocco, the United States and, finally, England. She offered herself as a volunteer to return to France, but was refused by DeGaulle's government-in-exile as being too hopelessly clumsy and "obviously Semitic." She continued to write and work, but exhausted by ill-health and self-neglect, she died in August of 1943.

Poet of labor, apostle of anonymous suffering, political analyst, God-lover, consumed with the passion of Christ, Simone Weil has been considered a saint for an alienated age, an ecumenist of the spirit, an "unbaptized" Christian mystic. "The extreme greatness of Christianity," she wrote, "lies in that it does not seek a supernatural remedy for suffering, but a supernatural use of suffering."

MOTHER TERESA OF CALCUTTA: SERVANT OF THE DESTITUTE (b. 1910)

This small sister typifies to many of the world's people the modern mystic in action. Recipient of the Nobel Prize, she remains a hard-working, "simple" religious woman, poor in name and in fact, having no message but the gospel incarnate in her life. Agnes Gonxha Bojaxhius was born in 1910 in Yugoslavia, the daughter of an Albanian grocer. Her early life was relatively carefree. Yet even as a child, Agnes experienced an awareness of God's nearness, calling her to a life of service to the poor. Eventually, she decided to join the Missionary Sisters of Loretto, who worked in India.

A somewhat "delayed" vocation, Sr. Teresa professed her first vows in 1931, having been sent to Darjeeling. For 20 years, she taught geography in a high school in Calcutta, eventually becoming headmistress. But her heart was responding to a deeper call to work more directly with the most unwanted and destitute.

One day, while returning to Darjeeling by train, she became aware of a distinct call from Jesus to leave her community and go into the slums. Receiving permission to do so from Pope Pius XII himself, she undertook four months of intensive nurse's training, then began her real life.

In December 1948, Mother Teresa returned to Calcutta alone and with only five rupees in her pocket. Undaunted, she began to work. Soon she was joined by others. In 1950, her community of helpers, the Missionaries of Charity, was recognized by the Catholic church. Two years later the first home for the destitute dying was opened. Thousands of abandoned men, women and children, many prematurely born, have been rescued from the streets since then, and half of these have survived what would have been inevitable death. In 1963, the Missionary Brothers of Charity were formed. Both male and female groups were made Pontifical Congregations in 1965. These religious volunteers are now at work in Belfast, London, Naples, Palermo, Rome and New York, as well as in Papua, Ethiopia, Tanzania, Cambodia, the Yemen, Jordan, Israel, Peru and Venezuela.

Besides the Nobel Prize, Mother Teresa has received the

Magsaysay Foundation award, the Pope John XXIII Peace Prize, the Kennedy International Humanitarian award, and the Templeton Prize for Progress in Religion. Funds from these awards have gone to increase the effectiveness of the hundreds of missionary helpers Mother Teresa has inspired to "comfort Christ," as Caryll Houselander would have said. But the fundamental vision remains unaffected by money; neither Mother Teresa nor her sisters and brothers may receive payment of any kind for their services. As she herself has said so many times, the only real service is for love alone, the love of God found in the ghettoes and gutters of the world's teeming slums.

* * *

To this scant number of representatives, dozens of other cases could be added, if space allowed. In this respect, our century may well rival the 14th not only as one born to woe, but also destined for a mystical greatness that will, as then, outshine the apocalyptic shadows of war, strife, plague and famine. That former time can still teach us something. But our mystics—with their hope and vision of unity, knowledge-surpassing love and universal reconciliation—could be no less understood by their precursors, for the Truth they have all sought and served, while never static, remains eternal.

SUGGESTIONS FOR FURTHER READING

Anne Bancroft, *Modern Mystics and Sages,* London: Paladin Books, 1978.

Anne Fremantle, *Woman's Way to God,* New York: St Martin's Press, 1977.

Hilda Graef, *Mystics of Our Times,* Glen Rock, N.J.: Paulist Press, 1963.

Arthur Koestler, *The Lotus and the Robot,* New York: Harper and Row, 1966.

George Maloney, S. J. *Invaded by God,* Denville, N.J.: Dimension Books, 1979.

Jacob Needleman, *The New Religions,* New York: Pocket Books, 1972 ed.
Lancelot Shepherd, *Spiritual Writers in Modern Times,* New York: Hawthorn Books, 1967.

Chapter 19

SECULAR MYSTICISM

> *Any form of promiscuous psychic and supernormal dabbling is definitely undesirable, in my opinion, and unfits the person who indulges in it for serious work.*
>
> Dion Fortune

Concurrent with the resurgence of religious mysticism in the past few decades, a new development has occurred—the appearance of non-religious spiritualities. Part of the pervasive secularization of the Western (and now Eastern) world, such styles of life offer many contemporary women and men an attractive and constructive alternative to religious spirituality, with its links to what they consider untenable traditional ideologies and practices.

Secularization refers basically to a "this-worldly" *(hoc saeculum)* approach to life, as preferable but not necessarily hostile to a religious interpretation of reality. Natural phenomena are seen in this view to be wholly explainable and manageable in terms of physical and psychological causes. There is no need for "the hypothesis of God" to account for events in the world, nor is there any compelling reason to rely upon supernatural assistance in order to meet them.

As a dominant historical trend, secularism followed upon the scientific revolution of the sixteenth and seventeenth centuries which, in the face of increasingly undeniable empirical evidence, replaced supernatural influences previously held to determine natural events with natural forces. One by one the angelic spheres were shattered or deflated by the use of instruments for scientific discovery and research such as the telescope and the microscope, and not least by the development of the seemingly infallible "scientific method."

The theological interpretations canonized by religious tradition were thus replaced by the empirical explanations of Galileo, Bruno, Copernicus, Kepler, Bacon, Harvey, Newton and others—all of them believing Christians. But the inevitable consequence of their pioneering was, as church authorities accurately foretold but vainly protested, a progressive distancing of God from the natural world.

The scientific agnosticism and philosophical atheism of the eighteenth century was muted in the nineteenth, but the process of secularization was extended into the social realm by Auguste Comte, Karl Marx, Louis Pasteur, Charles Darwin, T. H. Huxley, Sigmund Freud, Emile Durkheim and others, many of whom were, again, believers. Creationism became synonymous with credulity.

The present century has witnessed a reappearance of theism among scientists, notably in the works of Einstein, Teilhard de Chardin, LeComte de Noüy, William James, Alfred North Whitehead, Sir Alister Hardy, Dag Hammarskjöld, Peter Berger, Mary Douglas and many more. But the reductionism of the scientific mentality has hardly abated, resulting in the emergence of hybrid forms of scientific, philosophical and theological speculation as well as religious developments such as the "religionless Christianity" of Dietrich Bonhoeffer, Rudolf Bultmann's "demythologization," the secularistic theology of Paul Tillich, and the short-lived but significant appearance of "Christian Atheism" or "the death of God" movement.

The religious and scientific future may well differ from the present with respect to conflicting interpretations of reality, but for now we are faced with real and important "secular spiritualities" including mystical forms, which merit attention. Some of these are plainly scientific in inspiration and outlook. Others are themselves spun off from religious traditions Eastern and Western. Still others are connected with the technological world, whether "positively"—such as the drug movement, or "negatively"—such as occultism, which proposes a return to a pre-scientific approach to life.

The fundamental characteristics of secularistic mystical spiritualities are (1) a tendency to accept scientifically demonstrable fact as the ultimate criterion of truth, (2) a proportionate tendency to diminish the normative function of formal religious doctrines and practice, and (3) a pervasive humanism, that is, a widespread concern for human welfare, health and integrity, as well as a pronounced inclination to assert that "man is the measure of all things," anthropocentrism. Insofar as God enters these systems of theory and behavior, it is primarily to provide an impetus toward full human development. There is little room here for God as judge, law-giver, or even goal of mystical striving as lover, friend and partner.

SCIENTIFIC SPIRITUALITIES

From the sixteenth century onwards, "modern" science was the cradle of practical anti-religious sentiment, the cutting edge of the secular spirit. In more recent times, the spiritual, if humanistic, side of science has produced noteworthy examples of practical wisdom. In biology, Sir Julian Huxley's *Religion without Revelation* was a signal attempt to create an evolutionary, ethical spirituality without God. Arthur Koestler, a scientific analyst and writer, has similarly advanced a responsible humanism beyond the pale of religion in his many brilliant works such as *The Sleepwalkers, Darkness at Noon, The Invisible Writing* and *The Act of Creation.* Mathematics and physics have provided secular gurus as well, including Lord Bertrand Russell. Psychology, however, has perhaps achieved the greatest representation in humanistic mysticism.

Unlike traditional therapies, newer approaches to integration are in fact closer in spirit to Freud, who envisioned psychoanalysis as a kind of secularized, rational spirituality by means of which a person could harmonize conflicting aspects of personality and resume an arrested development toward full humanness, manifest particularly in the realms of love and work. Thus seen, the psychiatrist or analyst is neither a "shrink" nor a "repairman," but a healer and spiritual guide—one freed from the constrictions of an archaic God-figure and the trammelings of religious ideologies. Freud himself was a secular mystic, well-versed in the Jewish mystical tradition, although a rationalistic form of it.

Behavioralism, the "first force" in contemporary psychology, has fewer mystical overtones than other forms, but the writings of B. F. Skinner and certain applications of behavioral modification are not without some resemblances to the more stringent aspects of Zen and Sufi teaching.

"Third and fourth force" psychologies display the greatest mystical tendencies within a recognizably secularistic frame—although God and religion itself are by no means ruled out of court. Among the dominant schools of this persuasion are "transpersonal psychology," easily associated with the work of the late Abraham Maslow, but now a far-reaching and eclectic "tradition." Roberto Assagioli's *psychosynthesis,* Viktor Frankl's *logotherapy,* Gestalt therapies and processes identified with Fritz Perls, the teachings of that troubled and tragic genius Wilhelm Reich, the Human Potential Movement, the journal method of inner integration advocated and taught by Ira Progoff and his associates in their famous workshops, the "Arica Training" of Oscar Ichazo, various programs and publications of the Esalen Center, EST, forms of biofeedback training, and aspects of parapsychological research—all should be considered as important contributors toward a truly humanistic psychology. Many other approaches, schools, programs, tendencies, emphases and the like could be added to these instances. What all have in common is a genuine openness to the creative potential of ordinary human development, a resistance to quantification, and a commitment to reasserting the centrality of freedom, love and responsibility in human life.

Outstanding contributions have been made by individuals who

are not easily identified with a special school. Gardner Murphy, R. D. Laing, Carl Rogers, Walter Houston Clark, Rollo May, Erich Fromm, Claudio Naranjo, Robert Ornstein, Charles Tart, Thomas Szasz and Lawrence LeShan deserve particular mention in this regard. Among them, Dr. Arthur Deikman, a psychiatrist, has made singular contributions to the study of mysticism. His article on "deautomatization," mentioned earlier, outlined a valuable conceptual framework for understanding the psychological processes of mystical development. His slender volume *Personal Freedom* (New York: Bantam, 1977) is a superb example of a profound, readable mystical spirituality in the secular mode.

Other forms of semi-scientific spiritualities have flourished over the years, embodying aspects of psychology, parapsychology, biofeedback and occultism as well as religion in varying proportions. Notable among them is José Silva's "mind control" workshops. Different in degree and emphasis, but not in kind, from organizations such as Ron Hubbard's Church of Scientology and dianetics, these groups are probably more religious than scientific. But in any case, since they are devoid of traditional or denominational affiliation, they can be considered largely secular in practice as well as spirit. In some instances, moreover, they can turn out to be blind alleys of what Chogyam Trungpa, the Tibetan spiritual leader, calls "spiritual materialism," offering power, wealth and success as the goals of their training.

THE OCCULT

At the opposite end of the scale from scientific mysticism, both in historical perspective and contemporary practice, the secular spirit is also manifest in a largely humanistic "neo-occultism." Even witchcraft ("neo-paganism") and modern Satanism are spiritualities in that they offer a pattern of life which promises its practitioners physical, mental and social integration. They and other forms of neo-occultism consist of beliefs, values, and ritual behavior which purport to relate their adherents to the Ultimate Reality of the universe, however that is conceived, in a bond of trans-human love which overcomes all dualistic opposition.

In many minds, especially those inclined to follow the severe corridors of fundamentalistic biblical ideologies, there perdures a link between occultism and mysticism that no number of denials or distinctions can wholly eradicate. And perhaps properly so. The occult, and especially neo-occult "arts and sciences," has long been a refuge for mystical drop-outs anxious for a "short course" or otherwise disenchanted with formal, organized religion.

Further, the agnosticism of the mystics, their resolute resistance to reducing mystery—including *the* mystery of God—to lesser if definite categories of thought has a real tie with the fascination of occultists for the unknown. The "true" occultists of the past were, moreover, often real mystics—alchemy, for instance, represented a *spiritual* effort to extend the redemptive, reconciling power of Christ into the material cosmos. This was but a kind of sacrament, however, the "material" aspect being the alchemist himself. The "great work" was the transformation of this "base metal" by a mystical process, reflected in the chemical processes, into the pure "gold" of spiritual integrity. The alchemists' principal laboratory instrument was, thus, the *priedieu*—the kneeler on which they prayed before the cross of Christ.

Over the centuries, like other mystical sciences—astrology and herbology in particular—alchemy degenerated into mere magic, victim to the conquest of the literal mind far more than to the march of science. The authentic mystical aspects, perhaps always in some danger of being overshadowed by the material processes, largely disappeared as these ancient disciplines became more and more "occult."

Modern occultism, while opposed to technological developments and scientific imperialism, has nevertheless achieved a level of sophistication similar to that of other human pursuits in the realm of the spirit. For instance, most real occultists are aware of the power of *symbolic* language and behavior to alter consciousness and thus to transform experience. But most "witches" no more believe in the literal existence of Diana or the "horned god" than Anton LaVey believes in a real devil.

Despite such "remythologization," the differences between occultism and authentic mysticism are greater than their similarities. This is also true of their secularized manifestations. Experts in the knowledge of both mysticism and the occult, such as Evelyn Underhill, William Ernest Hocking and C. G. Jung have taken pains to segregate them, despite their common elements.

Rationalism and even skepticism are as much a part of the occult today, ironically, as they are of science. It could even be argued that occultism has always been rationalistic, as it has been materialistic, for it seeks to *know* the ultimate mysteries of the universe primarily in order to *use* them. Thus, neo-occultism should be included as at least a tangential aspect of secular mysticism. It is by no means merely the pursuit of the uneducated, superstitious or spiritually depraved, despite the existence of crassly commercialized forms and inevitable attempts to produce half-religious, half-magical hybrids. In this respect, Rudolf Steiner, founder of Anthroposophy and the famous Waldorf schools, was a true occultist and something of a mystic. Helena Blavatsky and Annie Besant, founders and leaders of the Theosophical Society, which Steiner also joined, should likewise be mentioned, as well as Dion Fortune (Violet M. Firth), author of *Psychic Self-defense,* and that "wickedest man in the world," Aleister Crowley, who died in 1947.

THE ROSICRUCIANS

Rosicrucianism, a modern "mystical" brotherhood, claims descent from an alchemical, spiritually enlightened fellowship founded, according to legend, by Christian Rosenkreutz in the fifteenth century. While a Rosenkreutz may have lived, which is doubtful, fraternities called Rosicrucian and sporting the insignia of the rose and the cross have appeared at varying intervals and in different forms in subsequent centuries. Commonly aristocratic societies devoted to Masonry and ritual magic, these associations had progressively fewer connections with the original legend.

Contemporary Rosicrucian organizations, specializing in teaching the secrets of the universe by correspondence courses, have no recognizable links at all. Nevertheless, they continue to attract adherents searching for some sense of meaning and power in their lives, especially in the privacy of their own living rooms. Such "mail order mysticism," complete with arcane initiation rituals and esoteric teachings, is not only a pale and even comic imitation of an ancient mystery cult. Ironically, it is also named in honor of someone who in all likelihood was a literary hoax invented by a young Lutheran scholar, Johann Valentin Andreae (1586-1654) to satirize the alchemical pretenders of his day. Modern "Rosicrucians" are secular primarily in their antiquated antagonisms toward organized religion and the unscientific rationalism underlying their supposed esotericism.

DRUGS AND SPIRITUALITY

Practitioners and theorists have hotly disputed the role and value of drug use and spirituality. Christmas Humphreys, the English Zen authority, notes with acid brevity, "All that has been written about the use of drugs for the attainment of enlightenment is evil" (*The Search Within*, New York: Oxford University Press, 1977, p. 4). Similarly, R. C. Zaehner spent much of his *Mysticism Sacred and Profane* attempting to discredit Aldous Huxley's accounts and recommendation of mescaline use in *The Doors of Perception*. Yet, in the past two decades, drug use and mysticism have become synonymous among multitudes of liberated young people. Timothy Leary and Carlos Castaneda have proposed, although differently, that "psychedelic" drugs should have a place of honor in contemporary spirituality as they have had among indigenous peoples in the Americas and the world over.

These wide differences of opinion, not to mention the vehemence of the debate, ought to alert us to the existence of a complex issue. To begin with, opponents of drug use are often blind to the simple fact that drugs are, for better or worse, a part of everyday life for increasing numbers of people East and West, not just as "medicines" such as common tranquilizers, but also in camouflaged form: coffee, tea, wine, beer, cigarettes, sleeping tablets, stimulants, and so forth.

Secondly, many traditional religions have incorporated drugs in one form or another in their services, from the *soma* of the ancient Aryans and the wine used in Jewish and Christian ritual, to the buttons of the peyote cactus used by American Indians. Wine was also used in Greek and Roman religious festivals in the service of Dionysos and Bacchus. Abuses arose in time, but that should not obscure the positive function of "intoxication" as a metaphor for union with God.

Being "drunk in the Lord" is a favorite formula in most mystical traditions, which describes the state of ecstasy, although in Christian mysticism, sexual images seem to be preferred. But in Islam, Hinduism and Judaism—less so in Buddhism—"God-intoxication" is recognized as a state of spiritual consciousness far transcending physical inebriation. On Pentecost, the disciples were accused of being filled with new wine (Acts 2:13-15). And in his letter to the Ephesians, Paul wrote, "Do not be drunk with wine, for that is debauchery; but be filled with the Spirit . . ." (5:18). For William James, alcohol was the mysticism of the poor.

Without actual alcoholic consumption, the metaphor becomes pointless, of course, just as images of sexual love would lose their power if celibacy were an absolute norm. Moreover, human beings are fallible, and abuses occur. But abuses did not result in a ban on wine in the church of Corinth (I Cor. 11:20-34), and apparently real inebriation was at least an occasional problem in other early Christian communities (see Rom. 13:13 and Gal. 5:21).

Contrary to a popular psychedelic misconception, however, even "ordinary" drug use in religious services as well as among religious people, is not itself a mystical function but, at most, a material means, a "way" to attain a state of consciousness more receptive than that of our normal mode. More generally, it is a concrete metaphor for such states—a hint or sample, perhaps, of what could or should be our "normal" condition. Further, drug abuse easily follows upon drug use because of physiological or psychological addictiveness. Moreover, the temptation is strong to make chemical ecstasy a substitute for the achievement of personal openness and ecstasy—especially among those impatient to progress: beginners.

If drugs were mere catalysts accelerating the process of spiritual development, so much the better. Mere difficulty is no indication of moral superiority. But drugs are not harmful because they are an easy way to nirvana. Reliance on drugs is spiritually harmful (ignoring for the moment possible physical damage) because it represents a new and powerful dependency. The source of our well-being is placed outside of us as the function of a "thing" which we must ingest. Freedom is proportionately diminished and with that our ability to grow is hindered.

Authentic spiritual development requires detachment from artificial supports—and many natural ones, especially those which compensate for internal control and capable direction, the actualization of our deepest potential for enlightenment and integrity. For, as Humphreys noted, no drug can produce enlightenment. "Truth serums" do not make us truthful, they merely inhibit our ability to lie while we are under their influence. A possible function of drugs in the spiritual life could be, similarly, to remove certain impediments to enlightenment by providing a glimpse of the territory beyond the doors of perception we habitually keep shuttered and guarded. But they cannot lead us there.

MYSTERION

True illumination is part of a holistic developmental process which involves moral growth as well as psychological maturation. Drugs by themselves can produce neither, but, unwisely used, can in fact block their progress. At this stage of our spiritual evolution, I think it can safely be concluded that while the "ordinary" drugs of everyday life—especially those sanctioned for religious use, such as sacramental wine—provide an appropriate background for understanding and perhaps achieving mystical states of awareness, further use by those culturally and spiritually unprepared can be disastrous.

Mexican Yaquis and members of the Native American Church perhaps know how to employ peyote in their services, but they and other indigenous peoples have been unable to assimilate alcohol in their lives. The concatenation of caffeine, nicotine and alcohol to produce voodoo trances frequently results in severe toxification. Conversely, Europeans seem unable to handle psychedelics and opiates, and in some instances, even alcohol—as among the Celts, for example.

Mind-altering substances, "drugs," are not immoral. They can be life-serving in medical and psychiatric applications. They are dangerous toys, however. And while there have been spiritual applications, Thomas Merton seems to have put the matter into a realistic framework when he wrote, "The only trouble with drugs is that they superficially and transiently mimic the integration of love without producing it" (*Contemplation in a World of Action*, p. 176).

RELIGIOUS SECULARISM

If the development and distribution of mind-altering chemicals has secularized "God-intoxication," the incursion of scientific method into religious studies during the eighteenth and nineteenth centuries as well as the inauguration of the scientific study of religion itself, produced a secular harvest in the churches. "Modernism" was promoted and condemned by warring groups of both Catholics and Protestants. Judaism, too, was "liberalized," producing a fragmentation similar to denominational differences among Christians.

In many instances, the practical application of modern religious "science" produced spiritualities as noble as they have been controversial, as noted with respect to Bultmann, Bonhoeffer and Tillich. In response, neo-orthodoxy was the theological equivalent of the resurgence in practice of evangelical and fundamentalistic Christianity, including Pentecostalism.

Perhaps Karl Barth's opposition to liberal theology stemmed from his awareness of the *mystical* dimension of the new agnosticism entailed in it, for he was strenuously opposed to mysticism in all forms. And the Heideggerian conceptual uneasiness of many radical theologians has a distinctive mystical ring to it. (But, for that matter, so does Barth's extreme transcendentalism—his emphasis on God as the unknowable "Wholly Other." It is the absence of a balancing awareness of God's nearness, his immanence, that prevents the mystical element in Barth's thought from being more than half-developed.)

In Catholicism, secularity re-entered with the "new theologies" concurrent with the pastoral emphasis of the Second Vatican Council, raising again for many traditionalists the spectre of modernism. With a this-worldly concern came a new sobriety concerning God-language and concepts, such as reflected in Mary Daly's perceptive attack on the sexist implications of a too-literal adherence to God as "father," as well as in the liberation theologies of Latin America.

The mystical significance of such efforts at conceptual reformation is easily obscured, however, by the animosity expressed by the new theologians to the established mystical theologians of the pre-Vatican II era, whose doctrinal stance was anything but radical.

If Western Christianity underwent a partially successful secular revolution in coming to grips with the modern world, Eastern religions were no less "successful" on their importation to the West during the fifties and sixties. Although rooted in Hindu, Buddhist, Sufi and other traditions, these Westernized forms of meditation, martial arts, personality theories and therapies are now largely devoid of religious trappings—yoga, Transcendental Meditation, karate, Kung Fu, Tai Chi, Nichiren Shoshu, etc. The mystical goals of harmony, integration and tranquillity are stressed to the neglect of their doctrinal foundation and implications.

Tossed into the melting pot of contemporary "ecumenical" openness, these secularized oriental arts have in fact found themselves linked with other disciplines, political movements, occult pursuits, even religious traditions of vastly different origin in a kind of "chemical stew" of indiscriminately bonding particles. Consequently, few of these ancient arts have much resemblance to their parental forms, as Harvey Cox has observed plaintively.

In sum, such Western and Eastern secular spiritualities thus have in common a recognizable distance from traditional orthodoxy and orthopraxis—belief and conduct. Rather than teaching God-consciousness, their emphasis is on human improvement, both individual and social, but with slight emphasis on moral development. Finally, they manifest a proclivity to form superficial liaisons with various other "mystical" arts and sciences.

CONCLUSION

Secular mysticism has arisen at least in part because of the default of religious mysticism, the failure of the institutional church to provide a credible goal for many modern men and women, including some of the most talented and brilliant of our era. The secularized forms they have created are mystical in the sense that they are founded on a perception of the underlying unity of all things, the radical limitations of conceptual knowledge in achieving personal transcendence, and the need for reconciliation of opposing elements to achieve, ultimately, a true cosmic harmony. Discipline, enlightenment and integrity are recognized as stages along the way to unity with the Ultimate Reality of the universe.

God has not been so much rejected by secular mystics as displaced as the all-consuming goal and center. The mystical process itself, and its penultimate end, human perfection, have become the central focus. Given the actual harm a distorted God-consciousness has wrought in the world (abundantly illustrated in Ronald Knox's *Enthusiasm* and Norman Cohn's *The Pursuit of the Millennium*), secular mysticism may be more constructive in many instances than its religious rival. Its theological agnosticism can in fact be therapeutic as well as corrective in the wake of religious extremism.

But I doubt that mystical process can long sustain itself divorced from the inward content of God-consciousness and the supportive context of the religious traditions out of which most secular varieties have arisen. For demoting the divine objective of the process undermines the process itself, which, turned upon itself, will eventually consume its own potential. The process cannot *be* the goal.

As the objective (but not object) of the mystical quest, God remains the active power working by attraction *outside* the process, the source thereby of its ongoing capacity to transform human experience in the transcendence of its natural limitations. And because God exists outside the process as well as entering into it, all the God-concepts derived from our experience remain partial, inadequate and, if absolutized, probably misleading. In grasping this paradox, the great mystical traditions have developed an inner corrective, the "negative" or *apophatic* theologies which deny our ability to "know" God clearly in this life.

Lacking such a corrective, secular mysticism will, I believe, take one of two courses in the coming years—down the blind alley of technological rationalism or ahead along the route of a new religious awareness, whether purged of past fundamentalism and open to a future of theistic pioneering, or closed off from the world of scientific and social innovation. Both could conceivably co-exist on the basis of certain shared elements as they have in the past to some degree. But the future of mysticism is another story, one we can only dimly perceive at this point in our journey. To that task we shall devote our concluding remarks.

SUGGESTIONS FOR FURTHER READING

Walter Houston Clark, *Chemical Ecstasy,* New York: Sheed and Ward, 1969.

Harvey Cox, *Turning East,* New York: Simon and Schuster, 1977.

Viktor Frankl, *The Unconscious God,* New York: Simon and Schuster, 1975.

Aldous Huxley, *The Perennial Philosophy,* New York: Harper and Row, 1946.

Julian Huxley, *Religion Without Revelation,* New York: Mentor, 1958.

Alistair Kee, *The Way of Transcendence,* Baltimore: Penguin, 1971.

Thomas Merton, *Contemplation in a World of Action,* Garden City, N.Y.: Doubleday & Co., 1973.

Richard Woods, *The Occult Revolution,* New York: Seabury, 1973.

Chapter 20

THE TEACHINGS OF THE MYSTICS ONE

Historically, the mystics are those who have carried the common art of worship to the degree of virtuosoship; they are those who have preeminent experimental knowledge of the way to God.

William Ernest Hocking

As we have examined it so far, mystical spirituality is manifestly a practical art rather than a theoretical discipline, as has been routinely noted at various points. Mysticism is primarily a way of living, not a collection of facts or, despite the systematic accounts of theologian-mystics such as Sankara and St. John of the Cross, a coherent body of knowledge, much less a secret one. In fact, *as* a life-way, a "practice," Christian mysticism—and most others—emphasizes a non-conceptual attitude toward Reality, a loving openness and outgoingness toward the Whole of Life. Further, this non-conceptual attitude forms the heart of mysticism even as a cognitive aspect of experience, that is, as *theoria, contemplatio, samādhi, satori, fanā:* what the ancient Hindus called *Sat Chit Ananda*—"Being, Awareness, Bliss."

Despite a pragmatic orientation toward holistic consciousness and the ways to achieve it, mysticism nevertheless has a "dogmatic" or theoretical side to it. For every tradition, every mystic who undertakes to understand and communicate something of her vision, proposes or presupposes certain things to be true of experience, if only that everything is an illusion. Thus there is a *content* to mystical teaching beyond instruction, a "what" and even a "why" behind the "how."

Of course, a large part of what the mystics say about Reality is simply taken over from their culture, being commonly accepted notions about "the way things are." While often sound, these ideas are of far less interest than those which the mystics do not derive from their surroundings. For, far from being odd-ball speculations or wishful thinking, these elements of a mystical "worldview" not only resemble those of other mystics in other times and places, they also square rather surprisingly in many instances with the revolutionary findings of contemporary physicists, as well as psychologists and psychiatrists, about the nature of the human and nonhuman world. By means of their strenuous efforts to cleanse the doors of perception through suppression of conceptual thought processes, the mystics may well have seen into the nature of things far more clearly than they realized. If so, they may well have something important to tell us, something perhaps passed over by other thinkers and researchers.

In this and in the following chapter, we shall attempt to take an overview of the mystics' teachings, not as systematically developed by any one of them, but as reflected in their writings as a whole, especially as scrutinized by psychologists, philosophers, and physicists in recent years. To be sure, these analysts, like the mystics themselves, do not always agree as to even the major tenets of a mystical worldview. This is a sign, and probably a healthy one, that we have a long way to go before we can claim anything like competence in the comparative study of mysticism. Still, the areas of agreement are rather noteworthy, and point to the possibility of a unified account, a coherent mystical worldview.

LANGUAGE GAMES

Apparently, most of the world's great religious mystics either wrote themselves or their teachings were later committed to writing by their disciples, as in the case of the Buddha and Jesus. Many have been poets. Some were artists and others musicians;

Michelangelo, Fra Angelico and Beethoven quickly come to mind. The problem of language is very similar in all three cases, though the kind of language varies. For the sake of simplicity, I shall refer primarily to mystical writings.

Encoding and decoding mystical experience presents two fundamental problems. First, the great mystics in particular used language as a tool, not merely to communicate, but to *foster* mystical experience, often by turning language against itself in intentionally bewildering ways. Second, by necessarily employing the common language of their culture, the mystics thereby introduced various social biases, attitudes and even ideas inevitably associated with the very structures of speech and writing.

If the great fourteenth century mystics sometimes had a pronounced effect on the formation of vernacular literature, as did Meister Eckhart, Catherine of Siena and Richard Rolle, it is also true that language has had a pronounced effect on the mystics of all ages. For language concretely structures the ways in which people think and express themselves and predetermines in large measure the limits of communication by its inbuilt character. Eskimos have twenty or more words for "snow," and Arabs as many for "camel." The powerful little word "is" has no equivalent in Chinese, on the other hand.

To begin with, then, in order to avoid (for several reasons) having their descriptions taken too literally, the mystics have resorted to couching their message in metaphors, parables and logical paradoxes and puzzles such as the baffling Zen *koans* and the delightful Sūfi anecdotes. By such devices, the mystics not only remind us that all their descriptions are tentative, they also try to shake us out of our habitual ways of thinking and behaving, the way we regard Reality. "If thy hand sin against thee, cut it off. . . ." "If you meet the Buddha on the road, kill him."

Of course, not all mystics so stretch the capacities of speech and meaning in order to jolt the mind loose from its customary moorings. And even the most outrageous juggler of logic will at times demand to be taken at his word and seriously state: "Amen, Amen, I say to you, inasmuch as you did it to one of these, the least of my brethren, you did it to me."

One way or another, in all traditions, mystical language must be pondered; the mystics are not easy reading. The more deeply they attempt to penetrate the divine *mysterion* they have experienced, the more warnings and booby-traps they set for us in their narratives. To understand the mystics, then, it is first necessary to appreciate their *playfulness* with ordinary language and logic, to recognize the images and metaphors for what they are: challenges to *stop* thinking, to begin to feel and perceive once again.

A basic paradigm of the mystics' method is the joke—an incongruous narrative in which the vital connections are supplied by the audience, who thus open up their own experience for re-examination. Jokes always have existential hooks on them. The flash of insight that occurs when the point sinks in is akin to the mystics' flash of enlightenment—the uproarious response is also often similar. Mystics, as divine jokesters, are arch enemies of the stale, literal imagination, which too often is no imagination at all.

A ZEN *KOAN*

Master: When the light has appeared, where does the darkness go?

Answer: When it becomes light, the lantern is put into the closet and the mattress is folded away upon the shelf.

—From *The Sound of One Hand,* trans. by Yoel Hoffmann, N.Y.: Basic Books, Inc., 1975.

* * * *

SŪFĪ SAYING:

A man once asked a camel whether he preferred going uphill or downhill.

MYSTERION

The camel said: "What is important to me is not the uphill or the downhill—it is the load!"

—From *The Way of the Sufi,* Idries Shah, N.Y.: E. P. Dutton, 1970.

EXPERIENCE AND INTERPRETATION: UNDERSTANDING MYSTICISM

Jokes and mystical reports are both exercises in interpretation—a meaning-giving process of structuring human experience. Interpretation works in two directions: it puts meaning into experience and gets meaning out of experience. But not always accurately.

We are all familiar by now with the famous Sūfi parable about the blind men who sought to describe an elephant on the basis of each one's limited experience of an ear, a leg, the trunk, the tail, etc. "It is very like a fan," said one. "It is like a column," said another, and so on. The descriptions were ridiculous not because the "wise" men were blind or even because they were foolish, but because they allowed their previous experiences to predetermine their interpretation of something really new by filling in the gaps in their perception.

The first interpretations of the blind men were legitimate comparisons. But because their accurate descriptions of various parts were extended inaccurately to the whole, their subsequent interpretation of the elephant was wonderfully misleading. Only a truly wise person can discern when to generalize and when not to. And despite their undeniable volubility, the mystics are even more frequently reticent about their deepest experiences for lack of appropriate ways in which to describe them.

The relationship between experience and interpretation is a notorious problem, especially in studying the mystics. How can we tell that a mystic's teaching is not merely a reiteration of previously-acquired ideas or a reflection of socially-determined values, ideas, patterns of thinking, etc.? The underlying question is even more important: is the experience of the world's mystics fundamentally the same, only the culturally-influenced interpretations being different?

For instance, if a sincere atheist had an experience of the presence of God, would he be able to recognize it at all? And if appearances are deceptive, perhaps many of the experiences reported by theistic mystics are not divine at all, but, like the visions of St. Philip Neri's disciples, demonic illusions or just the delusions of an unbalanced mind, like Don Quixote's windmill-giants. Were the voices of Joan of Arc truly heavenly? Or were they, as was recently suggested, the result of chronic indigestion, like Scrooge's hopeful surmise regarding Jacob Marley's ghost?

Without going into great detail, we can discern several levels of interpretation with regard to the mystics' experience and their reports of it. First-level or direct interpretation is the immediate structuring of the raw data of perception necessary for conscious recognition. To experience a cow, a daisy or a song, I must have some kind of "working concept" of cows, daisies and voices, or at least of animals, flowers and human sounds. At this level of experience and interpretation, cultural biases and presuppositions are minimal, and the reports of such experiences are more likely to reflect the original situation rather than a reconstruction.

Second-level interpretation or "reflection" includes inferences, deductions and conceptualizations of experience now somewhat removed from the here-and-now situation by time or psychological "distance:" "It is very like a fan . . .". It is here, I believe, that we incorporate the patterns of perception, values, ideas and norms we have absorbed from our society into our fundamental experience, often giving it a completely different meaning from that it might have otherwise had. We can even do this *in advance,* "prospectively," by structuring our experience to fit preconceived notions or expectations. If I fear I'll see a ghost in the cemetery at night, I will probably jump with fright if a bush suddenly stirs in the moonlight. Many cows, barns and other hunters have been shot by accident because they "looked like" deer. How many times have we approached an old friend on the street only to find, at embarrassingly close range, a total stranger? Appearances are often deceiving because we tend to see what we want to see.

We can also interpret, or, more accurately, *re-interpret,* experience "retrospectively"—and we can do so indefinitely. "It wasn't a flying saucer you saw, but a reflection in the window of a passing train." This is the way history books are written . . . and re-written. Arm-chair analysts may debate forever about the sources of Joan of Arc's voices. What no one can alter, however, is the *fact* of her experience and the impact she had on Western civilization because of it—whether or not even *she* interpreted them correctly.

We can also distinguish one's own interpretation from that of others—what Ninian Smart called "auto-interpretation" and "hetero-interpretation." In dealing with the mystics, it is a good rule of thumb to let them have the first word in interpreting their experience. Unlike ourselves, they are closer to the immediacy of the event, its "here and now" meaning to them, and can thus speak with greater if not final authority. We should beware of either imposing our own meanings on them or accepting too quickly the learned evaluations of psychologists and philosophers analyzing mystical reports centuries later. Often such commentators intrude their own values and preconceived notions into their "interpretations" while denying the mystics the right to do so.

In general, whether dealing with anticipation or reflection, auto- or hetero-interpretation, we can safely presume that if the meanings assigned to experiences by the mystics themselves or their commentators reflect the common beliefs, customs or values of the times, they can be disengaged as overlaid "superstructures" possibly obscuring the real significance. It is when the mystics' message *contravenes* customary notions and standards that we are likely to be approaching the original vision.

Of course, such claims may be merely idiosyncratic musings as well as prophetic utterances, and here discernment is also required. Comparative analysis can help, especially if the reports can be found to agree with those of other mystics at other times and places with whom there could have been little or no contact. Again, such reports are remarkably strengthened by approximating the findings of contemporary *scientists* with regard to descriptions of the world, time, space, etc., as has recently been demonstrated by Drs. Lawrence LeShan and Fritjof Capra.

THE MYSTICS' SAFEGUARD: GOD THE UNKNOWN

For perhaps the major strand of Eastern and Western mysticism, the problem of interpretation has been greatly helped in at least one critical respect.

Most objects of experience must conform to some kind of perceptual or conceptual pattern in order to be recognized at all. When Sir James Cook arrived at Tierra del Fuego, the natives could not even *see* the large ship in which the explorer had crossed the Atlantic because they had no concept of a man-made object that large. The mystics' case is different.

Just at the point where *some* kind of concept might be invoked to explain or describe ("interpret") the mystics' experience of God, they reject all concepts as inadequate to explain that experience. Only negative statements seem applicable to identify the "object" of the encounter; it is *not* "that" God: in India, "neti, neti," among the Spanish Carmelites, "nada, nada," for the Rhineland mystics, the sheer "nothingness" of the Godhead, the "hid divinity" of the *Cloud of Unknowing*. God is no "thing" among other things. To the mystic, God is All, and there is no concept of All. Thus, the mystical experience is said to be ineffable or indescribable.

Such mystical agnosticism attempts to reduce to the barest minimum the culture-bound, previously sanctioned concepts of God in order to allow the Infinite God room in which to become manifest in human experience once again. It reverses the natural tendency of human reason, guiding it away from concept-formation, holding attention as long and as completely as possible to the immediate Presence of which it is conscious.

The name traditionally given this disciplinary exercise is *meditation*. And when it has become a stable, even effortless quality of consciousness, it is called *contemplation*. And it is the report of contemplative experience, mysticism fully developed and shorn of its cognitive dependence upon social patterns, in which we are interested: How does Reality appear when the doors of perception have been cleansed? As Blake claimed, Infinite?

WHAT THE MYSTICS SAY

For many years, various students have pondered the writings of the mystics from various vantage points and many have attempted to enumerate what they consider to be the essential features or propositions of these teachings. In the *Varieties of Religious Experience*, for instance, William James described four cardinal qualities of the mystical experience: ineffability, noetic quality (i.e., knowledge of some kind), transiency and passivity. In "Mysticism and Logic," Bertrand Russell also listed four main tenets: that there is a better way of knowing than by means of sense experience, that all is one, that time is an illusion and that evil, likewise, is merely apparent. Dr. Lawrence LeShan found three: a difficulty in communicating mystical experience, a problem with "focusing," and the fact that space seems to be no barrier to communication. John White, in *The Highest State of Consciousness*, included four characteristics: ineffability, emotionality, the fusion of intelligence and emotion, and heightened consciousness as the content of the experience.

LeShan cites the central beliefs of the famed medium Mrs. Willett in this respect: the reconciliation of opposites, the dichotomy between appearance and reality, the illusory nature of space and the non-finality of death. Drs. Prince and Savage, in a classic article, found that mysticism was marked by a renunciation of worldly attachments, ineffability, noetic quality, ecstatic feelings and an experience of fusion. Dr. Arthur Deikman in his important article on "deautomatization" mentioned feelings of intense realness, unusual sensations, unity, ineffability and trans-sensate phenomena.

Finally, to curtail this highly condensed overview, Walter T. Stace enumerated eight qualities of mysticism, which he divided into two major categories (probably wrongly), introvertive and extrovertive: All is One, either positively (the Plenum) or negatively (the Void); the One is the inner life of all things/ Being transcends both space and time; a sense of objectivity, reality; a feeling of blessedness, joy, happiness; a feeling that what is experienced is holy, sacred or divine; paradoxicality; and ineffability.

Obviously, most of these notions (James' for instance), refer to the mystics' experience; others, such as Mrs. Willett's, pertain to the nature of Reality as encountered. A few here and there have to do with the mystics' lifestyle. Sorting them out is a rewarding exercise, if only to reveal the wide range of interpretations given the mystics' teaching by their analysts.

Let us dig in by attempting to describe, first, the mystics' experience as they perceive it, then the qualities they attribute to Reality apart from their experience of it and exclusive, for now, of their theological teachings, which we shall consider separately along with their psychology, ethics and cosmology.

THE QUALITIES OF EXPERIENCE

In the relatively short history of comparative mysticism, it has been notoriously difficult to separate psychological accounts of the nature of mystical experience from theological or philosophical statements about the nature of Reality as encountered in that experience. And, as Hocking noted in 1912, even if we segregate the categories, it is only by accumulating characteristics that we are able to differentiate mystical experience adequately from other forms. For, as Hocking observed, in important respects, *all* experience worthy of the name human is immediate, unitary and ineffable. (Mystical experience, he thought, was more so.)

Let us take as characteristics of the psychological aspect of mystical experience, then, the following qualities (in addition to ineffability, unity and immediacy), which are not necessarily properties of Reality as experienced.

It is somehow *"noetic,"* that is, it has a true mental component, intelligibility and meaning; it is *transient*—the moment passes, leaving the mystic perhaps disappointed, as Hocking quipped, but not surprised. It is *passive,* in that the mystic feels more acted upon than active. Yet the experience tends to be psychologically *holistic* or global rather than sharply focused.

The experience is usually accompanied by feelings of transcendent *joy and peace,* an exaltation that can lift the mystic into an ecstatic condition. Yet, as White noted, this emotional state is not devoid of awareness. It is in this a true *feeling* in the original meaning of that word—a total human response. And the entire experience conveys a sense of the most vivid *realness,* about which the mystic remains totally *certain.*

Other features can be added: the *novelty* or creativity the mystic often expresses as a characteristic of perception (Hocking)—seeing customary things as if for the first time. Or, as well, the sense of *sameness,* the realization of continuity despite sudden swells and eddies in the stream of consciousness.

We return ultimately to the features mystical experience shares with other deeply authentic experiences—unity, ineffability and immediacy. *Immediacy* simply means the "here and now" freshness of experience, a sense also conveyed by the word "presence." *Ineffability* refers to the incommunicable quality of the experience itself, which transcends all human ability to adequately describe it. It is this quality of indescribability that has, in fact, given mysticism its name, from the Greek *muein,* to keep "mum."

Unity brings us to the brink of the objective aspect of mystical experience, for it is the prime characteristic of mysticism that it spans the gaps between subject and object, I and Thou, Observer and Observed, Lover and Beloved, Experience and Reality. Almost all students of mysticism thus identify the experience of unity as its principle feature, for instance, Stace in *The Teachings of the Mystics:* "the apprehension of *an ultimate, non-sensuous unity in all things,* a oneness or a One to which neither the senses nor the reason can penetrate" (p. 14-15).

REALITY AS EXPERIENCED

It can be said that, as a whole, mystical experience represents a heightening of ordinary perception, a widening of the field of consciousness, a lowering of the threshold of awareness, so that aspects of reality ordinarily ignored or undetectable become suddenly manifest. In this estimation, the psychologist and the philosopher agree. But William James himself pointed out a crucial element which makes all the difference between "psychedelic" and mystical experience. Central to the heightened consciousness of the mystic (in the ordinary sense of that word) is a "sudden realization of the presence of God" (*The Varieties of Religious Experience,* p. 302).

It should also be noted that in their description of the mystics' psychology there is no allusion to a special "organ" of mystical perception—another clue to the fact that mystical experience is not another *kind* of experience, but an intensification of the essential structure of all experience, a grace-full perfection of *ordinary* human nature. In this, the modern interpretation of human psychology differs significantly from medieval notions.

Given its transcendent unity (to which we shall return), what do the mystics tell us about Reality as they see it with their eyes at last "wide open?" It is possible and, for the sake of brevity at any rate, necessary to gather their observations into categories, such as statements about the physical universe, space and time, human nature and behavior, and, above all, the character of the mystical journey itself, if not its transpersonal and ineffable Goal and Guide.

Prior to these issues, which are secondary in the mystics' scheme of things, there is an overall "teaching" which grounds the rest and forms the nucleus of the mystics' perennial message. It is possible to abbreviate this core of doctrine in the form of several basic beliefs, which are, in fact, conditions for the possibility of mystical experience and mysticism in the first place.

THE ESSENTIALS OF MYSTICISM

As described earlier, in order for the mystics' experience to be valid, three fundamental conditions must be true, and these represent the most basic beliefs of all mysticism.

1. The Ground and Goal: "*God is, and God is One.*" As William Ernest Hocking realized, this is the most telling of all mystical principles. It is the one *fact* on which all the others depend: the central focus of the mystics' vision is not an illusion, no matter how inadequate any and all attempts to represent the Reality of that awareness inevitably must be. The mystics' essential conviction lies in the experience of the living God, and pervading unity is the chief note of that experience. Further, *it is possible to be one with God.* Loving communion with God, beyond mere knowledge *that* God is, demands a certain capacity, a character of the human person. As we shall see, at times this has been described as a special faculty or function. However we interpret the fact, it remains evident that in the mystics' experience a progressive closeness to God leading to true and lasting union is a possibility for all human beings and an actual experience of many.

2. The Path. *The way to union with God is not by knowledge, but by love, accomplished by a union of wills.* The mystics

maintain that neither intelligence nor power, not even "virtue" but only a radical openness of the human heart in love and selfless service can lead to union with God. This is perhaps the most distinctive mystical tenet. The inquisitive mind must be stilled before it can learn to "know," for concepts bar God from consciousness. And the heart must be purified of all that is not God in order to be filled with the God of All.

3. The Journey. *"The path to the One is through a reconciliation of opposites."* From the earliest times, mystical unity has been experienced not as an abolition of differences, but as their total integration. The "Many" form a unity in God, so that all dualities are transformed into complementarity: love and knowledge, female and male, dark and light, left and right, yang and yin. Ultimate mystical integrity achieves the reconciliation of Creator and Creation in a mighty act of God, the *apokatastasis* Teilhard envisioned as the Omega Point of history. Thus, mystical consciousness like the Reality of which it is an aspect, like *God,* is not a simple and undifferentiated unity, but a complex, harmonious *Whole,* a community, while yet One. And the One is a "We."

The rest of the mystics' teachings flow out from and feed into these main streams whether above or below the ground of conscious awareness.

SUGGESTIONS FOR FURTHER READING

Fritjof Capra, *The Tao of Physics,* Boulder: Shambala, 1975.

William Ernest Hocking, "The Meaning of Mysticism as Seen through Its Psychology," *Mind* 21 (1912), pp. 38-61.

William James, *The Varieties of Religious Experience,* New York: Mentor ed., 1958.

Lawrence LeShan, *The Medium, the Mystic and the Physicist,* New York: Ballantine, 1975.

Raymond Prince and Charles Savage, "Mystical States and the Concept of Regression," in John White, ed., *The Highest State* of Consciousness, Garden City, N.Y.: Doubleday, 1972, 114-134.

Bertrand Russell, *Mysticism and Logic,* London: Unwin Books, 1963.

Walter Stace, *Mysticism and Philosophy,* New York: Macmillan, 1960.

________, *The Teachings of the Mystics,* New York: Mentor, 1960.

Chapter 21

THE TEACHINGS OF THE MYSTICS: TWO

> *The fact of the religious vision, and its history of persistent expansion, is our one ground for optimism. Apart from it, human life is a flash of occasional enjoyments lighting up a mass of pain and misery, a bagatelle of transient experience.*
>
> Alfred North Whitehead

Equipped with the more respectable new nets and sieves of contemporary psychologists, biologists, physicists and philosophers, it is possible to venture further into a fascinating realm beyond the psychological parameters of mystical experience itself and its specific theological interpretation, by straining out the mystics' views about the world, space, time, life and the human person. But as there is yet no unified field theory in physics or biophysics, there is none in mysticism—here again a not-too-remarkable parallel.

In this chapter, we will be dealing with *aspects* of a whole, the ultimate form of which remains unknown. We may well be dealing with something unknowable, a true *mysterion.* The Whole may forever transcend our ability to comprehend it. The following observations are, therefore, tendered as suggestions, hints, clues, "leaks," and sometimes fanciful hypotheses.

THE POSTULATES

The teachings of the mystics, as observed in the last chapter, can be conveniently categorized under three major headings:

I. *The Principle of Unity:* Reality is One, a unified Whole; or, in its specifically religious form, God is One, the principle of universal harmony.

II. *The Principle of Love:* It is possible to become one with Reality by a discipline primarily moral rather than cognitive; love is the power that unites all opposites.

III. *The Principle of Complementarity,* or *"Enantiodromia":* the path to the One is through the reconciliation of opposites.

(Here again, it is important to recall that the theological character of mysticism can be more or less explicit. Some genuine mystical experiences may have little or no *evident* religious significance at the time or even subsequently.)

Each of these subject areas or Principles has many corollaries or implications, and each is expressed with different and characteristic emphasis in terms of cosmology, biology, psychology and ethics. Yet I believe that most mystical views can be subsumed under one or more of these major categories.

For instance, under the Principle of Unity, one corollary is that the Whole is present in each of its parts, and therefore *the part stands for the whole.* In cosmic perspective, this provides the principle, "man is the microcosm of the universe (macrocosm)." Further, in astrology, as a concrete example, the human body is related to the universe as a whole, part corresponding to part in terms of the constellations of the zodiac, from Aries (the head) to Pisces (the feet). Symbolically, the human person becomes a replica of the cosmos, experiencing in its term the effects of universal history. The regions of the earth are also so identified, the globe representing the cosmos, so that the various continents and nations are associated with a constellation, planet, etc.

In other traditional or mythological "sciences" such as alchemy and herbology, the correspondence of minerals, metals, plants and animals with the human body and the cosmos constitutes a symbolic theoretical framework. In the history of religions and the study of popular culture, much of this kind of ecological thinking is metaphorical or even magical, but the systematic integrity of the universe and the unique position of each human person within the space-time continuum is as much a contemporary scientific notion as a poetic, mythical or mystical image. The ecological sensitivity behind the recent concern of many scientists about planetary pollution, the depletion of natural resources, wasted energy, etc., is not far removed from the *karma* of the East or Jesus' aphorism: as you sow, so shall you reap. The universe is not only a spatial-temporal, bio-energetic whole, it is also a *moral* whole.

PHYSICISTS AND MYSTICS: TOWARD A COSMIC SYNTHESIS

To the mystic, the world ordinarily looks pretty much the way it does to everyone else, including physicists. But there are differences in perception which emanate from the mystics' deeper awareness, greater sensitivity or whatever, and which find occasional utterance in their writings. We shall attempt to organize these scattered observations, tentatively, under our major axioms or postulates in terms of a vision of the cosmos, a fundamental biology, a working psychology and a systematic ethics.

Physics, or as it was once called, cosmology, deals with the fundamental elements and structures of the universe—matter, energy, space-time, gravitation, motion, etc. On one hand it peers into the infinitesimal depths of the subatomic realm. On the other it scans the farthest reaches of the universe, studying entities as odd to those of us in the "zone of the middle region" ("Middle Earth"?) as are quarks, mesons, gluons and psychons; pulsars, quasars, curved time and weird "holes" in space.

As a rule, mystics are not much concerned with precise observations and measurement of the cosmos—with the exception of those who were also physicists, from Kepler to Einstein. But they do have something to say about reality, space, time and energy which sounds peculiarly akin to the puzzling statements of relativity and quantum physics.

Dr. Lawrence LeShan has collected, analyzed and subjected statements of both mystics and physicists to rigorous testing procedures and found that very few people can distinguish a mystical statement from a scientific one when taken out of their general context.

Compare, for instance, the following:

"Man disposes himself and construes this disposition as the world."

"It is the mind which gives to things their quality, their foundation, and their being."

". . . the reason why our sentient, percipient, and thinking ego is met nowhere in our world picture can easily be indicated in seven words: because it is ITSELF that world picture" (quoted in LeShan, *The Medium, the Mystic and the Physicist,* pp. 258-59.)

The first quotation is from the Zen master, Dogen; the second is from the *Dhammapada;* and the third by the physicist, Schrödinger.

Similarly, Dr. Fritjof Capra has published an extensive account of the congruence of Eastern mystical views of the universe and those of modern physics. Unfortunately, Capra tends to disparage Western mysticism for the very odd reason that it was ostensibly not so well integrated into science and philosophy as was its counterpart in the Orient. However, Capra's knowledge of Western mysticism and its interaction with science and philosophy, for instance in the experience of Kepler and Newton, not to mention Bohr, Heisenberg and Einstein, is inferior to his acquaintance with Eastern mysticism. Some of the great physicists in the West, were in fact mystics, Einstein not least of all.

In all instances, it should be remembered that a comparison is being made among *reports,* not experiences. The physicist is concluding, inferring or reporting events which neither he nor anyone else has ever directly witnessed. Further, physicists work in what we can assume is a state of ordinary consciousness. The mystic, on the other hand, is attempting to relate the quality of a direct experience. And even if she is in her "ordinary" mind when inferring, reporting or describing, she is just as likely to have been in ecstasy or *samādhi* at the time of the experience. Thus, the experimental situation is different for the mystic and the physicist, even if they should happen to be the same person.

Perhaps the chief tenet of the mystics with regard to the physical universe is (not surprisingly) their stress on unity. The physicists' quest for a unified field theory is not far removed from the mystics' experiential assurance that "all is One." The mystics' recourse to paradox and opposition finds an echo in the complementarity and logical puzzles of physics, such as the dual nature of light—at once and impossibly both a wave and particulate.

A further similarity exists in the belief asserting that matter is not the ultimate reality of the universe. For centuries, the speculations of the mystics have been associated with *idealism,* a philosophical approach to the world which posits mind, spirit or consciousness as the ultimate "stuff" of the universe. As old in its formal articulation as Socrates, perhaps, this view is directly opposed to *materialism,* which, contrariwise, finds matter to be the ultimate stuff of reality and mind to be an "epiphenomenon" spun off by material interactions. Possibly even older than Platonic idealism, materialism was proposed by Leucippus and Democritus and represented the dominant philosophical position of modern physical science up to the present century.

The religious temperament has, conversely, been most favorable to some form of idealism. The doctrine of "creation *ex nihilo*" means, simply put, that the material universe is a concretized thought of God's. In this view, the human self or spirit is not just a by-product of molecules in motion, but a "special creation" irreducible to material process. Overall, the vision of the mystic is not far from that of the physicist:

". . . in this [showing] He showed me a little thing, the quantity of an hazel-nut, in the palm of my hand; and it was as round as a ball. I looked thereupon with eye of my understanding, and thought; what may this be? And it was answered generally thus: It is all that is made. I marvelled how it might last, for methought it might suddenly have fallen to naught for littleness. And I was answered in my understanding: It lasteth, and ever shall for that God loveth it. And so All-thing hath the Being by the love of God" (Julian of Norwich, *Revelations of Divine Love,* ch. 5, Warrack trans.).

". . . the stuff of the universe is mind stuff" (Sir Arthur Eddington).

The distance encompasses a factor that physics has no instrument to measure, however; mind alone, the mystics tell us, is not a sufficient appraisal of the universal stuff. For the Mind behind the world is a Mind that loves. Relativity is not alien to the mystics' worldview, but it is a *divine* relativity, a Love that overcomes the limitations of time, space and matter, even mind itself.

Reconciliation and paradox have been noted several times with respect to the mystics' attempt to describe the reality they have encountered, choosing to say "both-and" rather than "either/or." So, too, in modern physics, where the precise elegance of a former century has given way to conundrum and riddle, no less elegant for that: "As far as the laws of mathematics refer to reality, they are not certain, and as far as they are certain, they do not refer to reality" (Einstein).

It seems evident that in a Wonderland where particles apparently travel backwards in time, where something is a particle and a wave simultaneously, where relativity and indeterminacy set the upper and lower limits to observation, the doctrine of reconciliation of opposites would not seem peculiar. The inscription on the Danish physicist Niels Bohr's coat of arms fittingly reads: *Contraria sunt complementa.*

THE BIOLOGY OF GOD

If the revolution in physics altered the scientific conception of the universe at the turn of the century, the theory of evolution published by Darwin and Wallace in 1859 ushered in no less an upheaval in the life sciences. It eventually proved a fatal blow to the fundamentalistic notion of a block universe created by God on an October afternoon in 4004 B.C., as calculated by the 17th century Irish divine, Archbishop Ussher. For a few decades, materialism seemed triumphant. Not only humankind, but *everything* had ostensibly emerged out of simpler, older forms of life, matter and, ultimately, energy. Scientific research since then seems almost daily to confirm the evolutionary hypothesis.

Two remarkable facts should be noted, however, especially with regard to the mystics' view of life. Once the scientific and philosophical world recovered from post-Darwinian shock, it became clear that the evolutionary process did not negate religious belief in creation, but rather liberated it from the prison of the past. Creation, as Meister Eckhart and other mystics had asserted, is *here, now.* Secondly, as Hocking, Bergson, Whitehead and Teilhard de Chardin realized, universal dynamism implies something like "vitalism" or "pan-psychism" or what amounts to the idealistic hypothesis that matter is either a forerunner or an excrescence of life and that therefore in some sense, even the most primitive molecule is relatively "alive" or "conscious." It smacks of *mind.*

Both these views not only mesh well with those of the physicists mentioned earlier, but with the vision of the mystics, for whom, as W. T. Stace recounted, the One is "an inner subjectivity, or life, in all things" *(Mysticism and Philosophy,* p. 141).

Many great biologists of our time, such as Sir Julian Huxley, Jacques Monod, George G. Simpson, and other biologically trained scientists such as the astronomer Carl Sagan, still cling to the materialistic hypothesis, refusing (or failing) to find more in life than an extension of mass-energy. Other scientists, just as brilliant, maintain the opposite, however, backing their conclusions with remarkable data—Sir Charles Sherrington, Sir Alister Hardy and Dr. Lyall Watson among them.

Hardy has been particularly prolific in documenting what he

has happily entitled one of his most recent works, *The Biology of God,* by which he means the biological evidence for the reality of the spiritual world. Here, and elsewhere, significantly, the great mystics can be found roaming the pages of his thoughts.

For the mystic, it is too little to say that all life is sacred. Not only is life the fundamental reality of the universe, it is in essence divine. St. Francis of Assisi was by no means alone among Western mystics in his love of nature; it pours from the pens of Richard Rolle, John of the Cross, of Whitman, Blake and Emily Dickinson. Bergson and Teilhard, both mystics and scientists, are no less in love with life than the poets. For them, as for many process thinkers, the universe itself is in some sense alive. And it is going somewhere.

In the Orient, where life seems so abundant and precarious, love of life and reverence for all that breathes permeates mystical wisdom from the Vedas to Zen. The ancient Hebrews also held that life was God's, shrinking in horror from blood vainly spilled. Even today in orthodox Judaism, every beast slaughtered is a sacrifice to God, the kill supervised by a rabbi, the blood poured upon the earth.

From time immemorial, women and men found God in nature, the more so perhaps that they rendered urban life godless. But nature is no Garden of Delights—we witness the merciless savagery of death in abundance, the apparent wastage of life to an unimaginable extent. Natural selection, we are told, operates by means of reproductive excess; evolution proceeds by the survival of the fittest, those less fit becoming food for the fitter.

But the mystic believes, as does the scientist, that despite the carnage, all is one—*nothing, ultimately, is lost.* Dr. Lyall Watson, director of Biologic of London, wrote in *Supernature:* "Even those that die have not lived in vain, because news of their failure is broadcast and becomes part of the inheritance of Supernature. This communion is possible because life shares a mutual sensitivity to the cosmos, has a common origin, and speaks the same organic language" *(Supernature,* p. 314). For the mystic, it is

God's presence in nature which acts to conserve, preserve and enhance.

Despite the spectacle of nature red in tooth and claw, moreover, this preserving Presence has as its most powerful ancillary, if not its inner heart, the binding force of *care and affection,* what is undeniably a form of love. It burns very dimly in the lower forms of life, but as we ascend the scale of what Teilhard calls "complexity-consciousness" it begins to shine out in the tender care of mother-love, in the devotion of animals such as swans, wolves and dolphins which mate for life, in the remarkable ability of dogs and, to a lesser extent, cats and horses, to "fall in love" quite biologically with their human mistresses and masters.

Sir Alister Hardy has devoted much of his recent study to religious experience. A marine ecologist, Hardy, like other observers of animals in their natural habitat, has found there impressive evidence for something resembling spirituality in human beings. Our awareness of God, it would seem, is not something alien to the world of nature, but an ever-present potentiality which, in the case of human persons, is becoming consciously actual.

Perhaps it is because we have looked too closely that we have failed to perceive "soul" in nature. Hardy has suggested that it is in their *unity* that animals (and, I would hazard, plants) transcend the merely material. Hardy envisages something like an "oversoul," a "group morph," which represents the pooled awareness of animals and which is in some sense conscious, an animal "spirit" in which each individual participates. Here surely is something like biological "field theory."

Finally, and briefly, it is this transcendent aspect of animal life, a dim reflection, perhaps, of the "noosphere" of Teilhard, that suggests the reconciliation of opposites, the resolution of the One and the Many. If the Many constitute a true unity which has operational abilities, from the sponge to the hive, and even if this unit is somehow conscious, each individual element remains itself—wholly unique, unrepeatable and important.

Statistics alone can never truly represent the experience and contribution made by each member of the Kingdom of Life. Somehow, however, in the enduring memory of species, nothing is forever lost. Every sparrow retains some vestige of its reptilian past, though it will never grasp that its feathers once were scales.

Human individuality far transcends even a flock of sparrows, as a famed Teacher once claimed. And here the biological miracle finds its culmination, unless we are indeed poised unknowingly on the brink of another unfathomable evolutionary leap. Sir John Eccles, perhaps the world's outstanding brain physiologist, observed that not even the genetic code, unique though it is, is the sufficient determinant of the uniqueness of the person as an experiencing self. "My coming-to-be is as mysterious as my ceasing-to-be. I believe that there is meaning to be discovered in this personal life of ours. I believe that we have to live life as if it is a great adventure, and I believe that we have to recognize this for all others. Each human being is a person with this mysterious conscious self associated with his brain" *(The Understanding of the Brain* N.Y.: McGraw Hill Book Co., 1973, p. 273).

We are not, however, thereby entitled to regard "lower" animals, who apparently lack a conscious self associated with their brains, as mere "things." They, too, are part of the adventure, and with them, in the remote depths of our history and our experience, we are *spiritually* one. As the late Itzhak Bentov showed, we are involved with all living beings, with the stars and planets, the great cosmic fields that surround us, and with the very earth itself, in a vast network of interaction which truly *vibrates* in an immense symphony, surely the Song of God.

MYSTICAL PSYCHOLOGY

From the pioneering work of William James at the turn of the century to the present, psychologists have increasingly turned to the mystics, whether as specimens of health or sickness. Today, having largely overcome the bias of what James appropriately called "medical materialism," and more at home with the use of symbols and metaphor, "transpersonal" psychology in particular has contributed greatly to our understanding of mysticism. The growing interest in mysticism has also contributed undeniably to the development of transpersonal psychology. This latest branch of a fertile tree not only recognizes but also utilizes the insights of the mystics in order to describe and collaborate with the transcendent dimensions of human experience in order to promote individual health and social development.

Among those who have contributed significantly to this creative interchange are Victor Frankl, Rollo May, Abraham Maslow, James Fadiman, Charles Tart, Robert Ornstein, Lawrence LeShan, Walter H. Clark, Roberto Assagioli, Ira Progoff and many others.

Psychiatry, too, has entered into a more respectful phase of dialogue with the mystics, here following the example of Jung and even Freud, whose roots in Jewish mysticism have been traced by David Bakan. Arthur Deikman, June Singer, Ian Stevenson, Erich Fromm and others have greatly extended our awareness of the therapeutic aspects of authentic mystical experience, however it is designated.

Parapsychology, too, as we have already seen, has both benefited from studying the experiences of the mystics and also contributed to our understanding of some of the unusual by-products of such experience by examining them in non-mystical contexts. Significantly, both James and Freud were members of the original Society for Psychical Research in London.

As we have noted, the mystic maintains that sensory knowledge is not the sole source of information about the nature of Reality. Not necessarily an advocate of innate ideas, the mystic rather *knows* that communication can be direct, spirit to spirit, and Spirit to spirit. Deep within each of us, moreover, lies the Source of what gives meaning to all human experience, and to which (or Whom) we have only to attend to "learn." It is our participation in this universal Field of Reference which gives all persons everywhere the inclusive sense of Oneness. Moreover, this Oneness is a bond of love which overcomes all opposition.

Anthropologically, the mystic's premise is, as Evelyn Underhill noted, the existence of a self capable of communion with God. This, as we have seen, is equivalent to saying that person *means* "spirit"—a radical capacity to receive and transmit the life of God. For the mystics, then, psychology consists almost wholly of expounding practical ways in which the human spirit is thus divinized and their ethics are ways in which human relationships should be reconstructed in order to enable everyone to become "oned" with God.

At one time, it was customary for mystic sages in the West to refer to a special faculty or power of the soul by which human persons came into contact with God. This *synteresis, Fünklein* or *scintilla animae,* the "spark of the soul," or the *apex animae,* "point" of the soul, seems to argue for something like a mystical organ of "divination" (Rudolf Otto), which Descartes eventually took the pineal body to be.

Similarly, in Hindu thought there are held to be seven (or more) *chakras* associated with centers of nervous energy in the body which constitute a mystical ladder which the divine energy, *kundalini,* scales as it ascends from the lower spine to the apex of the spirit. Other mystics speak, however, of the "ground" of the soul, the hidden depths, the lowest point, the "inner desert" or interior cell where the living God awaits in loving silence.

Ultimately, all such talk is a way of characterizing the spiritual nature and development of the human personality, activated in ways never imagined in the waking dream we call life. True mysticism needs no special organ; it is the heritage of all.

The principle of unity, close to the mystics' worldview, found psychological expression most notably in the work of Carl Jung, founder of analytic psychology, in his concept of the "collective unconscious." Jung believed that all human persons were united in the depths of the psyche, sharing the same primordial structures of symbolic meaning which he called "the archetypes." These become manifest in dreams, fantasies and fairy tales the world over.

Furthermore, Jung held that parapsychological phenomena such as telepathy and clairvoyance, which are apparently free from the limitations of space and time, are also manifestations of a deeper psychic linkage among all human beings and perhaps all sentient creatures. Psychokinesis, similarly, reflects a fundamental connection between minds and the material universe, which often finds expression in meaningful coincidences, as we shall shortly see.

If by the will, we mean all the non-cognitive, dynamic processes which direct human experience, then with regard to the second major mystical postulate, Jung espoused the primacy of the voluntary much more than Freud had, and more as did other post-Freudians, such as Adler, Rank, May, Brown and others. Jung's studies of alchemy, astrology and Eastern mysticism showed clearly enough the intent of these works to purify, strengthen and perfect the will. For Jung, as for Einstein, there are ultimately no chance events: God does not play dice with the universe. Fate is somehow willed.

Perhaps the most fascinating and mystical aspect of Jung's speculative work concerned *enantiodromia,* the Hermetic principle of reconciliation. With the assistance of the brilliant physicist, Wolfgang Pauli, Jung elevated this ancient principle to the status of a psycho-physical axiom, the "Principle of Synchronicity." For Jung and Pauli, the *coincidentia oppositorum* manifests itself in human psychology as symbolically meaningful coincidences, a fact noted and briefly pursued by Freud before them but not to the extent to which Jung's devouring curiosity drove him.

Briefly, and therefore inaccurately, stated, the synchronicity principle means that meaningful but not causally related events (coincidences) reflect another level of psychological causation or influence, a third unifying factor or agency which is directly but unconsciously related to the human psyche.

Far more than Freud, but in the same vein, Jung believed that the nether depths of the collective unconscious (or, in Freud's case, the psyche) was *divine*—or, to put it differently, God "dwelled" there and could be found there. In this, surely, Jung is not far from Meister Eckhart or the *Cloud* author. And, like his medieval predecessors, it is never too clear just what he means by "God."

ON ETHICS

In some ways, all mystical teachings are ethical, insofar as they propose certain "truths" about the human condition which imply or demand qualities of relationship and behavior in order to realize full human potential. Mysticism, like ethics, is basically a practical *art,* rather than a body of abstract information. Certain fundamental ethical principles can be discerned, however, which I think structure the more extensive ethics of various traditions.

Perhaps the most striking and powerful of all mystical teachings concerns the "mere" fact of unity, as we have seen in other respects. The "communion of saints" is an *experience* for the mystics, however, not a belief. They feel the oneness of all beyond time and space and all limitation. And what they feel, they understand as a promise, a latent reality despite all the wars and strife that separate individuals and nations. Because they know supreme human unity in the immediacy of experience, they are certain that all people everywhere can also come to know this brotherhood and sisterhood. Human unification in God becomes their goal and to that end, the mystics marshal all their eloquence and example.

The only bond which truly unites is love, and to the mystics we owe the unleashing of the most powerful political force the world has ever known: *agâpe,* unselfish concern for the total welfare of the other, for all others.

The ethical basis of mysticism is related to the primacy of the will in human experience, and this in two related respects. First, the will is the source of action, and mysticism without action is divorced from the world of truly human significance, as Hocking, Bergson and others have insisted. Contemplation is not enough, else old Plotinus would not have needed the corrective of Christianity. Further, knowledge—even practical knowledge—is barren without love.

The will to love is the second cornerstone of the mystics' ethical edifice. The motive and cue for action is love. But love is more—it is even more than the deep heart of the mystics' experience of God. It is the *principle* of unity itself, the "bond of perfection," the Holy Spirit; indeed, *God* himself. With true love as a guide, action leads inevitably to union—as St. Augustine said simply, "Love and do what you will."

For the Christian and the Sūfi mystic, the identity of God and love is the power that reconciles opposites, a belief harkening back to old Empedokles and Herakleitos, but no less the universal witness of the human heart. So, too, in Buddhism, with its ethical eye focused on compassion. In Hindu spirituality, from the eroticism of Konarak and the *Kama Sutra* to the *bhakti* devotion to Krishna and the gentle *ahimsa* or loving non-violence of Gandhi, the power of love is believed to unite all contraries. But love is also seen to spring from the realization that all are one, that there is no enemy, no real (that is, irreconcilable) opposition, if in fact reconciliation is willfully impeded.

CONCLUSION

The resolute refusal of many scientists to consider the evidence for a transcendent dimension of human experience, marshaled into court by scientists themselves, such as James, LeShan, Capra, Hardy, Eccles, Watson and others, has resulted in a backlash of sorts. Once again, a chasm has opened between science and religion—although science is no longer claiming to be "free" from values and humanistic concerns, and religion refusing to test and evaluate. "Anti-establishmentarianism" has appeared in works such as Philip Slater's *The Wayward Gate,* which is a stinging critique of scientific prejudice, summing up the ghost of Charles Fort and his delightfully irreverent *Book of the Damned.*

But bridges still stand over the chasm, solidly buttressed on either side by what are claimed to be the hard rocks of fact. Physicists, philosophers, theologians, sociologists, and, not surprisingly, artists, lovers, madpersons and mystics are guarding these bridges like bands of dedicated, often beleaguered hobbits, dwarves and elves. They are cheered in their task to keep the passages open by an unshakable belief in the truth of their vision and confidence in the Power of truth to sweep doubt, error and bias before it until Time has again had its fill, and full communion is possible.

SUGGESTIONS FOR FURTHER READING

Itzhak Benthov, *Stalking the Wild Pendulum,* N.Y.: E. P. Dutton, 1977.

Fritjof Capra, *The Tao of Physics,* Boulder, Colo.: Shambala, 1975.

Alister Hardy, *The Biology of God,* N.Y.: Taplinger Pub. Co., 1976.

Lawrence LeShan, *The Medium, the Mystic and the Physicist,* N.Y.: Ballantine Books, 1975.

Philip Slater, *The Wayward Gate,* Boston: Beacon Press, 1977.

Lyall Watson, *Supernature,* Garden City, N.Y.: Doubleday, 1973

Chapter 22

THE FUTURE OF MYSTICISM

This hypothesis of a final maturing and ecstasy of Mankind, the logical conclusion of the theory of complexity, may seem even more far-fetched than the idea (of which it is the extension) of the planetization of Life. Yet it holds its ground and grows stronger upon reflection. It is in harmony with the growing importance which leading thinkers of all denominations are beginning to attach to the phenomenon of mysticism.

Pierre Teilhard de Chardin

"The human adventure is just beginning." This line of advertising copy from *Star Trek: The Motion Picture* sums up a good deal of the hope people feel for a future less encumbered than the present by humankind's enduring birth pangs. The film's fun if pretentious poke at "technological mysticism," the union of the human spirit with an absolute mechanical intelligence, also points to two related facets of contemporary spiritual awareness.

One is the persistence of the secular, in this instance the untrammeled evolution of technological "thinking" in the form of self-observant, virtually autonomous computers. "Man" is indeed the Creator in this case. However, the possible emergence of less altruistic cybernetic organisms than *Star Trek* envisages when such "union" is attained has been explored by other, scarier films such as *Alien* and by excellent science fiction writers with a flair for social satire such as Ray Bradbury and Arthur C. Clarke. The "mystical marriage" of a still-unregenerate humanity with its own soulless, technolgical spawn *could* result, they caution us, in some Frankensteinian futures, to be sure.

Given only the sheer cost (and therefore unlikelihood) of producing such bionic hybrids, at least in quantity, the second facet warrants a word: we are probably in for some real surprises in our concurrent exploration of the universe and the psyche. Clarke's *Childhood's End* is still a parable worth pondering in this regard. Films like *Star Trek* and Disney's *The Black Hole* remind us, further, that many of our concepts of God and "his" relations with the cosmos have become blasphemously rigid and are thus due for some spiritual lubrication.

The scandal of technological overdevelopment in the midst of human misery on an unprecedented scale may also shock us into recognizing that our priorities are even more blasphemous than our conceptual idolatries. As a result of such "deautomatization," turning against technology out of compassion for the oppressed on the basis of a mystical sense of human solidarity is a strong probability for many sensitive religious persons.

Thus, two conflicting approaches to the future of mysticism limit the range of alternatives most of us will face if we have not already done so. First, there is a secular development of progressive integration with the forces of technology themselves, a "scientific" mysticism such as John Dewey might have devised or Carl Sagan would find comfortable, one in which "God" functions as the outer limit of human ideals capable of realization. It is significant in this regard that the "scientifically" chosen evidence of human civilization on this planet placed in the Voyager spacecraft apparently contained not a single reference to religion among the hundreds of pictures and sounds selected by Sagan and his committee.

The second alternative represents an anti-technological religious stance as proposed, for instance, in some of C. S. Lewis' science fiction, in which union with God occurs outside the scope of scientific culture and human achievements in general.

Within these limits, neither of which are all that likely to be realized in pure form, there is room for a variety of mystical futures. I tend to think that a plurality of such forms, many of which already exist at least *in ovo,* will in fact enrich tomorrow's spiritual life. However, the middle path, something like the spiritual trajectory envisioned by Teilhard de Chardin, in which traditional religious wisdom and responsible scientific progress will combine in a constructive synthesis, offers the best hope for both advanced and developing nations as well as for individual persons committed to working and loving in the midst of the real world.

In concluding this brief tour of contemporary mystical spirituality, it is appropriate to look ahead toward these possible futures. Sighting a personally significant goal to aim for can provide us with the rudiments of a course to follow, a map of the heart which will keep us on track when the inevitable obstacles of an inevitably surprising future rise up to block our vision. Before surveying tomorrow's mystical journey, it will also help to glance back briefly at the terrain we have so far covered in order to confirm our bearings. It is important to recall, as we do, that sighting the goal and checking the course are not equivalent to being on the way itself.

THE FUNDEDNESS OF THE PAST

From the earliest times and wherever the human spirit has emerged in conscious recognition of the reality of God, the mystical element has appeared in explicit form as the inner heart, the kernel of religious sensitivity. In the major non-Christian religions, as in Christianity, union with God, or, in the case of Buddhism, blissful awareness of the ultimately Real, has figured as the goal of spiritual development. With Bergson and Underhill, I believe that Christianity occupies a unique position among mystical religions, however, for practical as well as theoretical reasons. Historically, Christian mysticism lies along the central axis of development; it holds the middle.

As an outgrowth, at least in large part, of Judaism, in Christian mysticism, the transcendent otherness of God continued to exercise a dominant influence, especially in the "negative" theology of the early Greek Fathers. Divine immanence, closeness, is similarly stressed, but not to the point of identification between God and the human spirit which is found, for instance, in many forms of Hinduism. On the other hand, like Hinduism, but unlike Judaism and Islam, a substantial unity of the divine and human person is possible. In fact, it is the actual cornerstone of Christian theology and the model of Christian spirituality. Unlike Hinduism, Christianity affirms only one, unique Incarnation, once for all.

The mystical anthropology of Christianity thus rests on the belief as well as the experience that all human beings are united in a common nature, so that the assumption and transformation of that nature in the one Instance involves the totality in virtue of human solidarity. But the actual divinization (*theosis*) of humankind is communicated to each person by actual development—the explicitation of that divine potential by deliberate conformation to the primary Instantiation, the Christ, *however he is known.* (See in this regard Panikkar's *The Unknown Christ of Hinduism.*)

In other words, the further divinization of humanity has to be actualized in each instance by a choice for unity made in love and hope. Such a decision, Christians believe, can be made and ratified by the power of God alone, operating "gracefully" in the human spirit, whose co-operation is thus in fact a response of faith.

In many respects, Christianity and Buddhism seem to dwell at the antipodes of the mystical world. Yet there are real connections here, too, as many expert scholars and mystics have shown. Theravāda Buddhism and the "negative" theology of Dionysios the Areopagite, Meister Eckhart and St. John of the Cross have many striking features in common, some of which they share with the non-dualistic *(advaita)* Vedanta of Sankara, for example. Similarly, an emphasis on right action, compassion and non-violence is common to Buddhist, Hindu, and Christian mysticism in their most developed forms.

As we have seen, there are also manifold connections among

the mystical elements of the religions "of the Book"—Judaism, Islam and Christianity, despite important underlying differences. But Christian mysticism is perhaps less well-integrated in the religious life of the majority than in all the other great religions, including Judaism and Islam. However, this is largely an historical accident rather than a theological or experiential necessity.

Mystical spirituality was, as we have seen, originally synonymous with the whole Christian life in its scriptural, sacramental and practical, everyday aspects. Segregating "ascetical" and "mystical" *aspects* of the spiritual life into different "ways" was the tragic result of a schizoid dualism introduced only after the humanism of the Renaissance and the excesses of Quietism had aroused the fears of the theologically faint of heart and timid of mind.

Other mystical traditions have also experienced difficulty in fitting into the orthodox patterns of belief and practice of their dominant religious context. But all have achieved a more or less steady state of peaceful co-existence. I think that today Christianity is well on its way again toward achieving a unified vision and an harmonious interplay between its mystical dimension and its dogmatic, liturgical and moral dimensions.

Still, we should bear in mind for what it's worth that during the centuries of opposition and disintegration, Christianity produced some of the world's greatest mystics: Eckhart, Catherine of Siena, Teresa of Avila, John of the Cross, George Fox and the "Little Flower," Thérèse of Lisieux. There may well be a lesson here to be discerned about the inner dialectic of divine and human intentions.

THE ELEMENTS AND TEACHINGS OF MYSTICISM

Looking further back, "beneath" the surface particularities of concretely historical traditions, we found that mystical spiritualities West and East *tend* at least to display several major similarities in their vision and methods.

Richard Woods

Practically, which means primarily, mysticism is a "way," a path through the events of everyday life. Whether aided by an enlightened teacher, directly or by written instruction, or whether taught by life itself, the mystic's goal on this path is consummate integrity, personal unification on every level of experience.

The "negative" aspect of the path toward union consists largely of renunciation and the discipline of body, mind and spirit—the essential disclosure of and disengagement from social ties, dependencies, customs, habits, beliefs, values, attitudes and inclinations. In more contemporary language, such "deautomatization" is necessary for the attainment, however partial and transient in this fallible world, of individuation (Jung), that is, of personhood, autonomy, maturity, self-hood, responsible independence.

The second, "positive" portion of the path is the process of Enlightenment, insight into the true meaning and value of the human situation, recognition of the cosmic interplay in human destiny on all levels, intuition of God's presence everywhere. The chief "exercise" leading to mystical illumination is *meditation*, the art of attending, which gives way to the effortless beholding of *contemplation*.

The spiritual journey is not complete with the achievement of personal integration and realized union with God. The mystic, having embarked upon her "perilous voyage" into the wilderness of the spirit, must return to the social realm she took leave of. For the truth of her quest must be tested and confirmed at the point from which it was launched. There can be no authentic union with God which does not promote a further union of human persons. Mysticism is a social process.

The mystic who returns to the world that has produced him becomes the prophet in action, attempting to translate the solitary vision of illumined compassion into collective fact. Typically, the mystic resumes the history of the unification of humanity by seeking out the most oppressed and forgotten members of society. Only if there is hope for the wretched of the earth is there hope for all.

The mystics' vision, I think, has been admirably and simply summarized by Hocking, Underhill and others. Wherever we find them, these friends of God—even those to whom "God" is still only a word—see reality in terms of the Whole: all are One in the deep currents of life and being sweeping through time and space. Further, unity with the Real is the achievement of love and surrender as much as—or far more than—it is of knowledge and effort. Third, unity is created out of disparity by means of reconciliation, not amalgamation. The tension of difference remains even in the union of perfect love, the most sublime and fitting human symbol of which is sexual intercourse.

Finally, the component structure of mysticism was disclosed as a systematic or organic interaction grounded in the divine field of experience, which is the condition for all possible communication in the spiritual realm: I, It and Thou—the self, the world of nature and society and the direct "other," the *you* of intersubjective encounter. Every dimension of mystical experience is thus personal, natural and social as well as theistic, whether or not we are aware of it at the moment. God must be found in the city, the forest and the sea as well as in the dark abyss of our inner self-consciousness or it is not yet God whom we have found. And God discovered is God shared.

SOME CHARACTERISTICS OF A FUTURE MYSTICISM

By projecting the trends of the past and present situation ahead, we can identify certain characteristics of mystical spirituality as a future lifestyle. Needless to point out, I trust, such an extrapolation cannot take into consideration the surprise elements that are surely awaiting us. The following descriptions should be taken, then, as a provisional and tentative surmise.

Richard Woods

Above all, the mysticism of tomorrow will be *ordinary*. Our everyday life will continue to be the field and school, the realm of the actual in which alone our latent mystical aptitudes can become realized. Extraordinary states of consciousness and adventures will no doubt occur as they have in the past—but less so if the more insightful theologians such as de Guibert and Garrigou-Lagrange (and Freud!) were correct. For they saw the raptures and paranormal experiences that unfortunately became synonymous with mysticism among the public as no more than by-products, sparks flung off by the adaptation of the psyche and the body to the novel demands upon the deeper capabilities of the spirit. But such epiphenomena are transient in the lives of the saints, and I believe they will similarly pass in the life of humankind as we gain the skill and wisdom of age. True ecstasy will not fade, however—the passing-away (*fanā*) but continuation (*baqā*) of the soul in Love's embrace.

Integrity

The spiritual life of tomorrow's mystic will continue to be integrative, especially as the pressures of life tend toward greater fragmentation. Mystical integration will be personal, social, physical, mental and spiritual. It will also bring the worlds of science and humanism into greater harmony.

Sociality

The previous stress in individualistic, dualistic spirituality on "God-and-me" will continue to be replaced by emphasis on "God-with-us." The possibility of a transformation of humanity by the mystical encounter is a social possibility—both in origin and in consequence. We are more and more involved with the development of the human race as a whole; we travel as a group.

Science and Technology

The world of the future will undoubtedly be affected in greater measure than ever by scientific discovery and technological development. As we have seen, the mystics' vision and the scientists' perspective on the universe have grown progressively closer. The humanitarian capacity of both mysticism and science may well be the only combination that will prevent unfettered technological expansion from mechanizing the last vestiges of nature and culture. Certainly, no future mystic will be able to contribute much to a world of scientific preoccupation if her own stance is anti-scientific.

Humanism

The affirmation of the human person—body, mind and spirit—which has characterized both recent secular and religious mysticism will continue to guide the mystical currents of the future. Technological developments could thus be able to find broader application in eliminating disease, promoting health and eradicating hunger, poverty and ignorance rather than elaborating newer and more terrible weapons. Technology is based on routine as well as capability; mysticism functions by de-routinizing life . . . *routinely.*

Ecology

Having known the wonder of the deep connections of all things, the mystic of the future will strive to preserve the balance of nature and human society, so that the vast but delicate cycles of life will not be decentered nor families of living things doomed to inevitable extinction in order to satisfy the artificial needs of expanding markets.

The natural world is a vital element in the mystical development of persons and of the human race. Deforesting Eden and killing off the unicorns has not advanced our ability to perceive the presence of the Creator in the midst of Creation. Life is the most sacred Fact of the universe. It must be protected and enhanced in *all* its multiple manifestations. If we cannot respect life on earth, whether that of the fetus or the foot soldier, much less whales and thrushes, however will we be able to revere life-forms we may encounter beyond the earth?

A mystical spirituality which is not radically life-affirming has no place in a God-conscious, *humane* future on or off the planet.

Ecumenism

Official inter-faith discussions seem frequently bogged down in attempts to unravel centuries-old theological tangles which have little bearing on the day-to-day life even of the disputants themselves. However, effective ecumenical exchanges have been quietly transpiring on a "grass-roots" level for centuries among the mystics. As Hocking observed, "The true mystic will recognize the true mystic across all boundaries and will learn from him" (*The Coming World Civilization*, p. 190). Tomorrow's mystics will surely continue the concrete dialogue among the great religions and within them, being well-equipped to do so, among other reasons, by their conceptual uneasiness about "definitions" of God and rigid dogmatic categories.

Transformation

The mysticism of the future, in order to be viable in a rapidly changing world, will have to be stable—grounded in the unshakable steadiness of the divine presence, wherein relativity has always made sense: one day is as a thousand years, a thousand years as a day (2 Peter 3:8). It must no less grow, adjust and, when necessary, change. As a life process, mystical spirituality must thus reflect the character of life itself—rootedness and adaptability.

As a practical way of living, authentic mysticism will lead each person toward full transformation (whether they get there in this life or not) through various stages of development according to their individual personal differences. Theoretically, mysticism will not be tied to the past, but related to it, as a command module rises on its engines, deriving its thrust and direction from what is "behind." We do not just stand on the shoulders of giants in our past; we are lifted by them as we grow.

The key notion in this view of mystical process is *transformation*—a perhaps rather pale, secularized word for *theosis*, divinization. The triumphs of an Eric Heiden remind us that *human* beings grow by exceeding their limits, not reaching them. The ever-receding goal of human completeness, drawing us always toward further development as a race as well as particularly, is "God the future of man," as Schillebeeckx so accurately (if chauvinistically) puts it. But, the mystics insist, we must also remember that as promise and power, we *already* possess our treasure in even these earthen vessels.

MAN THE FUTURE OF GOD

Most, if not all mystical traditions have at one time or another run up against the distrust and opposition of orthodox religious systems because of their peculiar attitude toward God and its behavioral implications. Fundamentally, this unnerving mystical discovery is that *God is not religious.*

Religion is a human invention, our attempt to relate ourselves meaningfully to God. If God is a willing captive in the net we have woven to hold divinity, it is because God knows that only by so entering human history is it possible to lead women and men toward their own truest fulfillment. Not surprisingly, that fulfillment is found in the presence and possession of God—not the conceptual ownership that veers so easily toward magic and idolatry, nor the moral proprietorship which produces bigotry and hypocrisy, but the personal commitment of love and self-giving which transforms human experience. And perhaps *God's* "experience" as well, for the links that thus bind God to humanity are real ones. God's involvement with people, consummated in the Incarnation, has changed God's own history, or, perhaps more accurately, "created" it. The meaning of Christ's humanity is that God couldn't get free of us now even if "he" wanted to; *he is one of us.* Humanity is also the "future" of God.

GOD-TALK

The use of quotation marks, such as those setting off the qualities attributed to God above—"experience," "created," "he," and "future"—is only a grammatical short course in negative or *apophatic* theology. Such words only apply to God relatively, from *our* angle of vision. What they mean to God is impossible to say.

Apophasis literally means "off-saying," to *deny*. The mystics' negative theology is thus a way of reminding themselves (and us) that all our concepts of God are human constructions which are at best only approximately accurate and more likely misleading if taken too literally, that is, humanly. Thus God is *not* good in any way we can really understand. Divine goodness is the sunshine revealed by the shadow it casts behind the objects it illuminates. Human goodness is such a shadow; the rays of God's goodness cannot be "seen."

Religion is also such a shadow—definite, perhaps precise, but not God. Religion is the projection of human dependency upon God's covenant with the human race. As such it is a positive phenomenon, but not the "thing itself." Nor is the church God. Morality is not God. Piety and liturgy are not God. Only God is God.

Without a positive anchor-hold in which to sink the flukes of unknowing, however, mystical theology would waft in agnosticism and moral aimlessness. Negative theology, being only one perspective, needs *kataphatic* ("down-saying," affirmative) theology to preserve the integrity of religious commitment as a way toward union with God.

Religion is thus a real help, a hint, a way toward God. But when the journey is completed, the vehicle is no longer needed, except to help bring others along. In heaven there is no "church." When all are safely home, the vehicle disappears.

Hence the mystics' tendency to regard religion suspiciously when its adherents attempt to endow it with the absolute sovereignty that belongs only to God. Creeds, codes and cult are of their nature *relative*, approximate, limited—pointers toward God. Unfortunately, those whose livelihood depends upon promoting religion are prone to convert these helps and norms into values, which protect them from the messy business of discernment and adaptation. We all carry our treasure in earthen vessels. The trouble is, we can see only the vessels most of the time and we understandably tend to mistake them for the treasure.

Mysticism is honest religion, or religious honesty, refusing to take itself with undue seriousness. It recognizes the importance of orthodox teaching, standard practice and moral norms, but it refuses to petrify and worship them. The mystic is primarily concerned with the sun, not the shadows. But the mystic also knows that without shadows, sunshine becomes blinding. Thus, true mystics are paradoxically among the most orthodox of believers and practitioners. If their contemporaries are somewhat reluctant to admit it, subsequent generations are often more generous, recognizing in past suspects, pioneers who made present faith and moral integrity possible. Mysticism is the orthodoxy and orthopraxis of the future.

Perhaps the greatest act of personal detachment, and that most necessary for the completion of the mystical catharsis of the individual and the group, is the abandonment of God-concepts, our thoughts *about* God. This is the midnight hour of the dark night of the soul, as we struggle to break the confining vessels in which we guard and try to possess our treasure. But the darkest hour comes toward dawn, when, having exhausted ourselves even in the effort to dethrone the idols of our minds, the vessels are removed from our hands and shatter of their own accord.

Theologically, our era can be considered to have entered the dark night of the human spirit collectively. In this respect, and especially from a social perspective, the culmination for former mystic saints may well be the starting point for modern men and women. But we must have faith that as we approach the hour of enlightenment, the dawn of the unified spirit, the active presence of the God who cannot be thought or represented will become *felt* again in the nearness of all-encompassing love and renewal.

FINAL REFLECTIONS

Mysticism is not a collection of beliefs about God or the world, nor a body of programmed activities which must be dutifully performed. It is a way of *life*, of being in the world, an approach to existence characterized by a *wide-openedness* to the unfolding mystery of Being, the Becomingness of things. It is a *ready willingness* to co-operate in that process which is realized in *right action* in the present moment. As no situation or event is too small to contain the presence of God, so no achievement is too demanding for human abilities empowered by grace. Mysticism is therefore an attitude of *attentiveness*, a patient expectancy free of predetermination.

Christian mysticism manifests itself in two chief areas of active concern: justice and friendship. That is, rectifying the imbalances that diminish the freedom and dignity of God's children, that prevent their growth to full maturity as God's friends and companions, lovers and fellow-workers in the cosmic harvest. In addition, it promotes the peace and harmony, the goodwill of all human persons and, as well, the family of Creation. Love is the heart of justice.

Thus in Christian tradition, the mystical life has been seen as a double restoration which is at the same time a new achievement—the realization of the promise of Eden, the bountiful harmony of Creation at peace with its Creator. It is also the healing, the "whole-ing" of humankind, the mending of wounds and setting of new goals. The Christ, the anointed one of God, is therefore the Alpha and the Omega, the paradigm of Creation and the goal and focus of re-Creation.

Mystically, the history of humanity is a journey, a process toward the fulfillment of the Promise made and remade from our beginnings. It is a quest involving real progress, not the illusory goal of nineteenth century industrial optimism. The plan, the map of this journey, is called the Will of God—human salvation ("safe-making," fulfillment). Its dynamism is known as Providence, which means not only foresightedness, but *antecedence*, going ahead to chart the course, as well as to forestall opposition wherever possible. Hence, the inevitable development in mystical teachings West and East of what the great Jesuit teacher, Jean-Pierre de Caussade called "abandonment to divine providence." Simone Weil called it "waiting on God." In biblical terms and the ordinary language of men and women everywhere, it is, simply, *trust.*

SUGGESTIONS FOR FURTHER READING

J. M. Cohen and J-F. Phipps, *The Common Experience*, London: Rider and Co., 1979.

Aelred Graham, OSB, *Contemplative Christianity*, London: Mowbrays, 1974.

————————, *The End of Religion*, New York: Harcourt, Brace and Jovanovich, 1971.

Ursula K. LeGuin, "The Field of Vision," in *The Wind's Twelve Quartets*, New York: Bantam Books, 1976.

William McNamara, OCD, *Mystical Passion*, New York: Paulist Press, 1977.

Emma Shackle, *Christian Mysticism*, Butler, Wisconsin: Clergy Book Service, 1978.